TRAVEL WRITING

JAMES FAIR

ROBERT HALE · LONDON

© James Fair 2014
First published in Great Britain 2014

ISBN 978-0-7198-1068-8

Robert Hale Limited
Clerkenwell House
Clerkenwell Green
London EC1R 0HT

www.halebooks.com

A catalogue record for this book is available from the British Library

2 4 6 8 10 9 7 5 3 1

Printed in Great Britain by Berforts Information Press Ltd

CONTENTS

1. DREAMING OF MONTE CARLO:
WHY BE A TRAVEL WRITER?

INTRODUCTION

TAKE A QUICK PEEK at many travel writers' websites or blogs, and one of the great universals is a page with some well-worn travel quotes. Often there will be a whole heap of pithy phrases about how travel opens the mind. Quotable writers range from Henry Miller: 'One's destination is never a place, but a new way of seeing things' to St Augustine: 'The world is a book and those who do not travel read only one page.'

After reading a few too many of these aphorisms, I feel like I've overdosed on sugary sweets, and long for something with a spicier edge, something along these lines by Paul Theroux, for example: 'Tourists don't know where they've been, travelers don't know where they're going.' I like this last one because it not only pokes fun at tourists (for being ignorant) and travellers (for thinking they're above tourists) but also at people who spend their time debating the differences between tourists and travellers.

My favourite quote, however, is specifically about travel writing, and I read it on the *Wanderlust* magazine website. It was uttered by one of the most well-read travel writers of the past twenty years or so – Bill Bryson: 'A basic error with travel writing is assuming everybody's interested. You have to work from exactly the opposite assumption: nobody is interested. Even your wife is not interested. You have to somehow make it so that they become interested.'

This is a brilliant and essential starting point for any travel writer (arguably any writer, but particularly travel writers), because I think travel falls into the same category as dreams with regard to its level of interest for other people (i.e. people are largely only interested in their own experiences!). I happen to enjoy looking at friends' or relatives' holiday snaps, and I like to think that it's because I have a strong desire to learn about other places – even if it's a 'gated' tourist resort in Gambia. But we've all been in that situation where our heart sinks and our eyes glaze over when somebody offers to show us their overexposed and unedited snaps of their trip around the Greek islands. A few years ago, I was showing my mother pictures of lowland gorillas and forest elephants from a recent trip to Gabon when she found something infinitely more important to do concerning the baked potatoes in the oven. I'd just spent a week in some of the richest rainforest habitat on the planet, surrounded by some of our closest living relatives, and all my mother could do was check pointlessly on the supper. But I'd made a crucial error: I'd assumed that she would be fascinated by my globe-trotting exploits and just started scrolling through the images on my laptop. It was the equivalent of starting a piece of writing with, 'I arrived in Nairobi in the morning, and checked into my hotel before going out to buy myself a sunhat.' Bill Bryson had it spot on: you've got to work harder than that to capture the reader's attention.

I'm not sure I agree with Bill Bryson when he says, in the same interview, that you must 'prepare to be loathed' if you want to be a travel writer. I do think you have to prepare for nonchalance though, sometimes to the point of total indifference, from friends, family or work colleagues.

I was once told a story by a wildlife conservationist called Carl Jones. A friend of his had been working out in the Philippines for a year or so, studying monkey-eating eagles and running into trouble with the police at times because they thought that anyone who was running around remote areas of rainforest must be up to no good. He had all sorts of adventures and had enough anecdotes to last half a lifetime, and when he went back to his local pub after returning home, all his friends were still there in the same chairs, talking about the same stuff. 'Where have you been?' they cried. 'I've just come back from the Philippines; I've been studying monkey-eating eagles.' 'Oh yeah – did you hear, United won on Saturday!'

They just weren't interested. Perhaps they were eventually, but local gossip will almost always trump even the most remarkable story from a far-flung part of the world. I think the only exception to this – or the most obvious exception anyway – is near-death experiences. People love those. I certainly do.

I met a Frenchman in a restaurant in Cuzco in Peru many years ago, and he chain-smoked while he told me and a group of assorted 'travellers' from around the world how he'd narrowly cheated death after the small boat taking him and some twenty other people to the Bay Islands (*Islas de la Bahía*) off the north coast of Honduras sank, with virtually no warning, in the middle of the night. There was no lifeboat, and either there was no time to grab any life jackets or (more likely) they simply didn't exist. By chance, the boat had sunk near a large navigation buoy, and some people were able to climb up onto it and right out of the water, though our narrator had to make do with just holding on while remaining in the water. He clung on through the remaining hours of darkness, and discovered as the day dawned that they were out of sight of land and there was no shipping traffic nearby. Eventually – around midday, he said – he and another person decided that, if they were going to die, they might as well die making an effort to be rescued, so they struck off in what they thought would be the direction of the Bay Islands. After about an hour or so, and as they were beginning to wonder how much longer they would last, the pair were seen and picked up, and they were able to direct their rescuers back to the other people clinging to and standing on the buoy.

Listening to the story, I felt like Samuel Taylor Coleridge's wedding guest held rapt by the Ancient Mariner, because it was such an extraordinary and mind-blowing story. What would we have done, we all wondered? Would we have stayed on the buoy or swum off (and in which direction?), believing that almost certain death would be the result, whatever we did? The tale was calmly told, though the chain-smoking suggested the guy was still, unsurprisingly, traumatized by his experience. (Then again, he was French, and this was the 1990s – he probably chain-smoked anyway.)

I've had a near-death experience, too, though it was very different in nature: I fell down a very steep, at some points vertical, hillside in the Apolobamba Mountains of Bolivia and was fortunate not to break my neck. I did these giant cartwheels down a slope ranging from undulating to precipitous, and every time I bonked my head on the rocky ground, I thought, 'There goes one of my neck vertebrae.' In truth – and, of course, travel writing is not always about being truthful (Bruce Chatwin was famously economical with the *actualité*) – I didn't have time to think all that, but I do remember wiggling my toes when I finally came to rest at the bottom, just to make sure that my spinal cord was intact.

The point is that neither of these stories needs to be brilliantly told to have an effect on their audience. I got an article out of my experience and I have retold the story many times. You always get people asking questions about it, such as the standard: 'Did your life flash in front of your eyes?' (Answer: disappointingly, no, not really – my thoughts were mainly what a total idiot I was.) But no one could sustain a travel-writing career based on having a whole series of near-death experiences – I suspect that they would run out of steam eventually. Or die.

So, if you truly want to be a travel writer, the first thing you have to appreciate is that however gob-smackingly amazing a place, person or experience seems to you, other people will have a very different perception of it. Unlike my Frenchman in the Cusqueño restaurant, *you're* going to have to work extremely hard to make where you've been and what you've seen sound interesting. So, how do you do this? Some of the very best travel writers visit well-trodden places and actually do no more than illuminate something that's obvious about a location but which hasn't been said about it until now. I think that comes from combining excellent observational skills (you'll need those in buckets) with a sharp, almost surgical analysis of the things you observe (what does this *say* about that place or its people?).

Others will do stacks of research and reading and attempt to do the opposite – to reveal the 'hidden' side of a destination. How many times have you seen travel articles that are promoted on the cover of a magazine with that catch-all word beloved by editors: 'secret'? 'Secret Cornwall', 'The Secret Canaries', 'Secret Coventry' (well, possibly not the last one). Editors love this word because they believe it sells magazines – it's telling the potential buyer that there's something in this product that they can't get anywhere else.

Of course, some 'secrets' are probably not worth tracking down and revealing. There is, for example, little point in writing about the Crown Green Bowls clubs of Riga – undoubtedly, an overlooked subject – because you will find it extremely hard to track down a commissioning editor who'll buy it. These days, the one person who could get away with this is probably Bill Bryson, but I don't think even he has ever gone down such a blind alley. So, your job as a travel writer is both to reveal the obvious but uncover the secret, too. If it feels like holding two contradictory thoughts in your head at the same time, then I think you've understood it perfectly.

I'll be turning in detail to the technical aspects – the craft – of travel writing in Chapters 5, 6 and 7, so I'm not going to say a great deal about them here. The one thing I will say is that repeating those stories of near-death experiences had another point: they *are* stories, and that's what makes them so compelling. Humans love stories; they are an elemental part of the fabric of our culture, while (sorry to say this) travel writing, by and large, isn't. Most books and other travel writers will say that the primary requirement of great travel writing is 'to take the reader there'. I don't disagree, but I think a lot of extremely competent, even vivid, travel writing is let down by the fact that it does this, but only this. I remember at school being berated on the football pitch for making a great pass and then failing to move into a position where I could get the ball back again – travel writing that delivers lovely, inspirational descriptions of a location but doesn't even attempt to find a story is doing the same thing. The important thing is to find in your experience a series of connected events that you can interlock, giving your piece greater substance. Any travel editor will be delighted to receive a piece of writing that rises above the humdrum and routine, and this is one way of doing that.

CAN YOU MAKE A CAREER OUT OF TRAVEL WRITING ALONE?

THE ANSWER TO THIS is that some people do, but many don't – not in the UK, anyway. A quick look at the maths will give you some insight. Different newspapers, magazines and websites will pay varying amounts of money for articles, and the standard way of paying is a certain amount per 1,000 words – or per word, if you like, but most editors usually express it as £xxx/1,000 words. I certainly do.

At the time of writing, at *BBC Wildlife* magazine, we pay (on average) £275-£300/1,000 words, which is probably better than most publications, if you take the industry as a whole. While bigger newspapers such as the *Daily Mail* can pay considerably more, many pay less. Some magazines, and many websites, pay such a derisory sum that it amounts to a nominal fee. I've seen fees of £20–40 quoted for articles as long as 1,500 words – there's no way that anyone could sustain a career in travel writing on that basis. Some websites don't pay at all, but just offer to put a nice biography about you next to the piece and a link to your own personal website or Twitter feed. There may be some gain for novice writers from the exposure they receive, but I'd be wary about writing for free for such sites on a regular basis – ultimately, it won't earn you any money.

Taking freelance journalism as a whole, I think it would be fair to say that travel writing is firmly in the lower-middle quartile in the way it rewards writers. Take a magazine such as *Wanderlust*, a beautifully produced, thoroughly professional, glossy magazine that's also a great read – every travel writer in the land is fighting to get their words and pictures into this magazine, and yet, at the time of writing, it pays £220 per 1,000 words, and that's based on printed, not submitted words. That is to say, if they ask for 1,500 words, and you write 1,500 words, but they only print 1,000 words, that's what you'll get paid for

– working out at £220 in total. And for what they call 'Fact' pages, which is the further information on how to get there, where to stay and what to eat, etc., *Wanderlust* only pays £90 per page, which works out at about 750 words. Fees, in other words, are not high.

Let's keep things simple, and suppose for the moment that you could average a fee of £250 per 1,000 words and that every article you managed to get commissioned was 1,500 words. That would mean you'd receive £375 per article you write. Doesn't sound too bad? Well, perhaps not, but now let's think about how many pieces you'd have to produce over the course of a year if you wanted an annual salary (before tax – and please remember that freelancers must self-assess for tax) of £20,000. You'd have to write more than fifty articles a year. If you wanted to make more like £30,000, you'd have to increase that to eighty pieces. It's also worth pointing out at this stage that freelance fees have barely increased in the past decade, arguably longer, and with newspapers and magazines facing an uncertain future thanks to the rise of digital publishing, few people envision them increasing much in the next decade either.

Now ask yourself, are you going to travel to eighty, or even fifty, separate destinations in a year? It seems unlikely, if not downright impossible – most travel writers would probably feel pleased if they managed eight separate trips in a year. Of course, it's perfectly possible to get two, three or even four articles out of one two-week trip (someone I know says that their record is eighteen). But, realistically, to do ten trips and get five articles out of each would be very, very good going.

There is one important caveat to this gloomy prognosis – every travel editor is also desperate for great photos, and while they have access to untold numbers of images of Barcelona, the Niagara Falls or the wildebeest migration on the Serengeti from photographic agencies, if you're writing about something a little bit more obscure – that Crown Green Bowls club in Riga, for example, or taking part in a contest to find the best imitator of a red deer stag 'roar' during the annual rut – then good-quality shots will be harder to come by. So if you can take half-decent photos (and with digital cameras it is a lot easier than it used to be) you can earn extra money. Indeed, for many travel writers, photography is a vital part of their income. Having said that, digital camera equipment is not cheap, and if you really want to sell your shots, you would also need to invest in expensive processing and retouching software, and the necessary computer hardware or online space to store the thousands of images you'll be taking.

So, you'll already have worked out (if you didn't know it already) that you're not going to make a fortune out of travel writing, and you'll do well, at least to begin with, to make enough to even pay the rent. Some people cut their costs right down (why pay for a house or flat if you're rarely in the country?), but most will simply make sure they have other sources of income: it could be that they are already established writers who have branched out into travel writing, but other jobs or professions that sit well with travel writing include teaching (plenty of spare time in the holidays), any job that allows you to travel anyway such as tour-leading, and any 'freelance' or self-employed career, particularly if you can earn a sufficient amount of money from your work to give you plenty of time on the road.

As I'll show in Chapter 4, the growth of digital technology has allowed some writers to develop a very different model. Bloggers don't rely on the usual format of doing a trip and then writing it up for a magazine or newspaper, but are constantly, or frequently, on the go. They earn their income through advertising and what's called 'affiliate marketing' (see p.22) on their websites – but that's only if their website is well-followed and advertisers will pay sufficient amounts of money to be on it. Some certainly do – Gary Arndt's 'Everything Everywhere' blog (http://everything-everywhere.com), for example, claims to have 100,000 unique users every month and, in the year up to December 2010, pulled in 1.5 million unique visitors and some 4 million page views. Those are fantastic figures and, on the basis that the vast majority of these people are going to have a similar passion for travel as Gary himself, you can imagine that sponsors would be falling over themselves to advertise.

Actually, that's not quite the case. Gary gets by on about

$50,000 a year (which is what his blog earns him, and which is still remarkably good), and says that the travel industry has been slow to appreciate the potential of bloggers. But not only that, he argues that traditional media companies have completely misunderstood what the internet is about, believing it is just another outlet from which they will somehow make money (at some stage). 'The promise of the internet is not and never has been making more money,' he says on his website. 'The power lies in reducing costs. Analog dollars are going to turn into digital dimes, and there is nothing that can be done to stop it. What people fail to realize is that even though revenues may shrink from dollars to dimes, costs are going to pennies.' The future, in other words, lies with low-cost, bargain-basement operations such as his. Readers are happy, the travel industry is happy, and bloggers are happy.

Working as I do for a 'traditional' media company (*BBC Wildlife* is actually owned by the Immediate Media Company and published under licence), I don't entirely agree with Gary. In fact, the 'death' of print has been greatly exaggerated, with many magazines – such as *BBC History* and *Dr Who* magazine – continuing to increase their circulation despite ever-growing volumes of free digital content. At the same time, it is true that many traditional publishing operations have not fully appreciated the editorial nimbleness that is needed in this new age.

WHAT IS TRAVEL WRITING?

IT IS IMPORTANT TO consider, firstly, what travel writing is and, secondly, whether there are different types of travel writing. The first question is worth thinking about but not necessarily worth answering. Travel writing encompasses such a vast range of genres, styles and purposes that it is very hard to pin it down – clearly, it involves someone taking a journey, generally a bit further from their front door than to the local newsagent and back. Clearly, too, it involves the writer trying to tell the reader something about the destination they have visited, but this could relate to any number of things. History, architecture, food and drink, landscapes, wildlife, hotels and spas and other types of accommodation are some of the most popular themes for travel writing, but there's plenty of scope for moving out of these traditional travel themes: KLM's inflight magazine *Holland Herald* ran a wonderful and quirky little piece in its November 2012 edition on great Dutch thinkers and scientists – true, the writer, Rodney Bolt, could almost have done it without moving out of Wi-Fi range, but he has spiced it up by interviewing a Dutch historian and art expert, so the feature doesn't read like the simple history lesson it is. Still, if you're on a plane to the Netherlands, knowing a little more about its rich intellectual past can be no bad thing. As I said earlier, that's one of the things that make successful travel writers stand out – the ability to find unusual angles on commonplace destinations. Most people probably don't know or care about Christiaan Huygens, but when you discover that he ground his own optical lenses, made telescopes, discovered – thanks to that telescope – the rings of Saturn and its fourth largest moon, Titan, and came up with the laws of refraction and reflection, well perhaps you start to care a little more. I certainly did.

Other subjects that are ripe for exploration by the bold and imaginative travel writer include music, sport, mystery, literature, technology and sex. I love this funny, clever piece by 'Vagabonding' blogger Rolf Potts (available on www.perceptivetravel.com and in his book, *Marco Polo Didn't Go There*) about going for tantric sex lessons in Rishikesh in the Indian state of Uttarakhand. This is how it begins:

> You spot The Girl on your first afternoon in Rishikesh. She is long-limbed and graceful, and she walks carefully along the path, as if not to disturb the dirt beneath her bare feet. She wears loose cotton pants, and tiny bells in her hair. She is smiling. Her stomach is browned and taut; the tiny hairs on her arms are bleached from the sun. When she spots a cow in her path, she stops to stroke its neck and whisper into its ear. You watch, and you wish you were that cow.
>
> You think to yourself: 'If I have come here to learn Tantric sex, I want that woman to be my partner.'

Rolf soon finds out that men and women are required to take tantric sex classes separately and that, in any case, the teacher Swami Vivekananda's objective is more spiritual than sensual. There's a wonderful short paragraph towards the end which shows the power of great quotes:

> Eventually, Swami Vivekananda becomes exasperated with ejaculation questions. 'Look,' he says, 'there are some pelvic muscles that can help control ejaculation, and the best way to strengthen them is to urinate in short, start-stop bursts instead of one continuous stream. But please. Let us stick to spiritual matters.'

The story is almost perfect – I won't give away the ending, read it for yourself – except for one tiny thing: Rolf strolls among the trees looking for lemurs, when he should have known that they are only found several thousand miles west on the island of Madagascar. He meant langurs. It's a small thing, but it demonstrates something I will be stressing again later in the book: always get your facts right.

This story also leads me to look at the second question I asked: are there different types of travel writing? Examine this story carefully, and there is very little practical information for any traveller who happens to find themselves in Rishikesh for an evening or a few days, so what purpose does it serve? What, indeed, is there to do in Rishikesh, apart from taking tantric sex lessons? Well, that's not the point of the piece, of course – this is more like a short story (read the ending, and you'll see what I mean) and it has a deliberate, albeit not very profound, literary aim, that goes beyond the scope of travel writing with a practical purpose – go here, see that.

It can be useful to see travel writing as being split up into four quite different types, though in many ways it is more like range, extending from one extreme to the other. First comes the practical type: guidebooks and an increasing number of websites fulfil this purpose. Someone going for a weekend break in Pisa or two weeks caravanning around New Zealand both want the same thing: information – where to stay, where to eat, what's good to do, great places to go. Providers of this type of travel writing range from the traditional Baedeker publishing house, which was founded in 1827 and is still going strong, to the empires that were spawned in the 1960s and 1970s such as Lonely Planet and Bradt Travel Guides and the proliferation of almost untold amounts of information on the internet – the Columbus-owned World Travel Guide, for example, which has short guides to just about every country on the planet.

The aim of this type of travel writing is almost entirely to inform the reader, so writers don't need to reach for inspirational descriptions and witty metaphors to transport their readers to the destination. Copy tends to be simple and succinct and picks out the most obvious details. Any guidebook on Quito, the capital of Ecuador, for example, is likely to tell you how the city is flanked by spectacular volcanoes or that the 'old town' has splendid colonial architecture. Narrow streets ride the hilly terrain like a rollercoaster, you will probably be told. Don't, in other words, expect a huge amount of originality.

This form of travel writing has its critics – it always has and it almost certainly always will. In E.M. Forster's *A Room with a View*, heroine Lucy Honeychurch – on her first morning in Florence – opens her Baedeker to find the location of the church of Santa Croce. The elderly Miss Lavish immediately remonstrates with her: 'Tut, tut! Miss Lucy! I hope we shall soon emancipate you from Baedeker. He does but touch the surface of things. As to the true Italy – he does not even dream of it. The true Italy is only to be found by patient observation.' Later, the pair become lost in Florence, and still Miss Lavish forbids Lucy to look at her faithful guidebook. 'We shall simply drift,' she says. When Miss Lavish abandons Lucy – and without her Baedeker – the young heroine is forced to enter Santa Croce on her own, enjoy the building and its people for what they are worth without much understanding of what she is looking for and, finally, to enter into conversation with the eccentric Mr Emerson and his son George. The message is clear – opportunities arise when we are not wedded to a narrow view of the world dictated by guidebooks!

Just as reading these more practical guidebooks can leave

something to be desired, it is also probably true that writing them is less of a joy. If you want to have space in which to express yourself even a little, only the more modern guides such as those produced by the sprawling Lonely Planet empire or Bradt really allow that. And even then, it's the cold hard reality of finding out where buses to Peluchuco leave La Paz, how often and at what time, that really counts.

Second in my list of travel-writing categories is articles – whether for magazines or newspapers. There is a massive range of outlets here, ranging from the Saturday and Sunday supplements of national newspapers to dedicated travel magazines. And then there are dozens of other even more specialist magazines – if you're interested in walking, for example, then try *The Great Outdoors* (if you're the slightly more adventurous type) or *Country Walking* (if you're more of a gentle rambler). There's a whole weird industry devoted to the world of spas and beauty treatments both in print form (*Spa Secrets*) and on the web (*World Spa & Travel*, www.theworldspa.com). There are wildlife-focused travel magazines such as *Africa Geographic* and the new kid on the block in the shape of *Wild Travel* magazine, which started as a one-shot 'bookazine', but has clearly found a readership because it is now being published twelve times a year. And remember that most glossy magazines, from the women's staples to food-based ones such as *Sainsbury's* to men's magazines and even specialist consumer titles such as *BBC Music*, run travel-based articles. The publishing world, as the old cliché goes, is your oyster. I'll be looking at this market in much more detail in Chapter 2.

There is a great deal of variety in what is expected of writers in this form of travel writing, and different types of magazine (as well as different magazine editors) will have different requirements. The fundamental point to be clear about is that most magazines are in the business of both entertaining and informing their audience, so that's what they want from their features. Travel articles are usually a mix of being an enjoyable and lively read with some practical details – often in the shape of a box or 'sidebar' or (in the case of the more specialist titles) a whole page. In this category of travel writing

I would also include in-flight magazines – while their business model is quite unusual in that they are not sold on the newsstands, via subscription or via the web, the quality of writing is mostly very high. Finally, there are also many trade titles that take different types of travel writing – some of this can be basic industry news, written by people who have a specialist knowledge, which I would hesitate to call travel writing. But for someone working in a specific sector, it may be a valuable source of income.

Third in my list comes the book – and by that, I don't mean the guidebook but the travel book, or travel literature. Wikipedia – ah yes, we all use it, just be careful *how* you use it – tells me that an early example of travel literature is *Description of Greece* by Pausanias, who lived in the second century AD. According to the Theoi Project website, this was a ten-book account of the author's travels in the Peloponnese and central Greece, and it 'provides a comprehensive catalogue of temples and shrines in the region, as well as frequent discussions of local myth and cult practice'. It sounds more like a second-century Insight guide to me.

I first became aware of, and intrigued by, the concept of travel writing when I stumbled across a history of the life of Sir Richard Burton, the Victorian explorer, writer and all-round polymath and polyglot, while studying for my degree. I can't say that Sir Richard's writing left any impression me, but the idea that someone might make a living by writing about his travels (though I suspect, in his case, other forms of income-generation were substantially more significant) certainly stuck with me. What a marvellous idea!

Sir Richard was part of a movement that proliferated in the nineteenth century. As empires expanded, the opportunities for travel opened up, while, at the same time, the middle classes were becoming better educated, so their interest in reading about these travels also grew. As already noted, the first major guidebook publisher, Baedeker, opened for business (however prosaically for Miss Lavish) in 1828. But in addition, many of the great novelists of the day such as Herman Melville, Mark Twain and Henry James produced travel-related books, while writers such as Robert Louis Stevenson were also famous for their adventurous, travel-themed novels.

The point about this genre – and this is still partly true today – is that it was being read by people who had little or no intention of travelling to the country in question or replicating the trip being described. These were books read purely for the vicarious pleasure in experiencing another person's triumphs and disasters, thrills and spills. And while it is true that many people will read one of these books about a place they plan to visit or are visiting, in the end, such works – more than guidebooks or magazine articles – stand or fall on the quality of their writing.

I have never read a truly outstanding travel book about Ecuador, one of the countries where I have travelled the most; one Christmas many years ago, I was given *Reality Is the Bug That Bit Me in the Galapagos: Trips in the Americas*, and I was initially delighted because it covered many of the countries of Central and South America (including, as its title suggested, Ecuador) that I too had visited and planned to visit again. That was until I opened the book to read the first chapter and found it to be, well, not my shot of pisco sour. It provided more information about the author and her travelling companion than it did about Latin American culture, and it was eventually used as lighting material for a much-needed fire while lost on a trek in the Cordillera Blanca in northern Peru.

On the other hand, many of my favourite books are about places I have yet to visit: *In Patagonia* by Bruce Chatwin and *Into the Heart of Borneo* by Redmond O'Hanlon, for example. Though I have subsequently visited Sabah on assignment for *BBC Wildlife* magazine, I hadn't been anywhere near that part of Asia when I read the book.

Fourth on my list of travel-writing genres comes blogging. Quite where this fits in is difficult to say, because it is still a relatively new and developing form. Many bloggers – of which more in Chapter 4 – that I have contacted in the course of my research admitted that they started their blog purely as a way of keeping friends and family up-to-date with their adventures, so you could argue that the blog started as the web equivalent of the letter home. Some – probably only a very tiny fraction – have acquired an audience that goes way beyond their immediate circle of acquaintances and, as a result of this following, have even managed to attract commercial interest from sponsors. Such blogs also tend to make money via affiliate marketing, which is when a site recommends a product, such as a book or travel-related gadget, and provides a link through to the producer's website. If a sale is made, the blogger receives a small commission.

That said, many of these bloggers appear to be recreating the spirit of the 1970s, which birthed the modern travel-guidebook empires. Lonely Planet was spawned from an underground publishing company called BIT, which ran from 1970 until 1980. One of the key figures in this 'movement' was a Yorkshire-born Englishman called Geoff Crowther, who I distinctly remember as describing himself in one of the guides he co-authored, *India: A Travel Survival Kit*, as someone who enjoyed smoking mushrooms and brewing mango wine. I liked the sound of him. Reading an extract from the last-ever BIT guide, published by Geoff's daughter, Ashley Crowther, on her Crowther Collective blog site (http://crowthercollective.org), gives a real insight into what it was like working there. What strikes me is that – just like today's bloggers – they were pushing at a frontier that had no known limits. Who knew where it would lead? When Tony and Maureen Wheeler started up Lonely Planet in 1972, they could not possibly have dreamed that they would later sell the publishing company to BBC Worldwide for a combined total of £130m less than forty years later.

BIT's first guide, *Overland to India and Australia*, which became known as the 'Bible of the East', 'consisted of half a dozen or so duplicated foolscap sheets stapled together with one staple and no cover', which were churned out using a second-hand, manually operated duplicating machine, after the guide had first been typed on 'an arthritic IBM electric typewriter that frequently threw fits.' It was responding to the demand from travellers for information, and the whole enterprise just, well, mushroomed.

By 1975, it had grown to 200 foolscap pages ('still stapled together with one staple and no cover'), and BIT was forced into a change of strategy. Geoff takes up the story:

In order to keep up with demand, we'd worn out two duplicating machines and were entirely reliant on the gullibility of successive IBM or Gestetner representatives who we could persuade to deliver us a new machine for a couple of days 'on trial'. No machines in the history of technology have ever been subjected to such a rigorous 'trial'. In the short time they were left with us, we managed, one way or another, to coax well over half a million sheets out of them. But that was only the start of the work since then the sheets had to be collated – by hand.

Ashley Crowther believes that today's guidebook empires have betrayed the original spirit of the early days of BIT, Lonely Planet and Bradt Guides because they have become too commercial. Her father, Geoff, stopped writing for Lonely Planet, she says, after it started reviewing five-star resorts, which clearly no budget traveller could ever afford. She says, 'All the popular mainstream guides like Lonely Planet and Rough Guides, for example, are aimed towards a traveller or "tourist" that is willing to travel more "commercially" so to speak'. Perhaps that's just the nature of travel – though costs have gone up a little in recent years, generally speaking going abroad is much cheaper today than it was back in the 1970s and has been opened up to a lot more people. Ashley also argues – and this is hardly a new point – that the need for guidebooks has diminished with the growing capacity of the internet to provide content free of charge, but nobody's going to rely purely on TripAdvisor and the odd blog, especially if they're off to somewhere such as Nicaragua. You are never going to make a fortune out of guidebook writing, but for many writers it can (partly) serve as a means to an end, allowing them to become expert in particular destinations.

None of this directly answers the question, 'Why be a travel writer?', of course. What it does show is the sheer breadth of opportunities out there and the many different reasons for becoming a travel writer. George Orwell, who dipped a toe or two into the travel-writing pond in some of his essays and books such as *The Road to Wigan Pier*, wrote an essay called 'Why I Write', in which he came up with the four main things, putting aside the need to earn money, that motivate people to write. First: 'sheer egoism', the 'desire to seem clever, to be talked about, to be remembered after death, to get your own back on the grown-ups who snubbed you in childhood'. Second, there is 'aesthetic enthusiasm', or 'pleasure in the impact of one sound on another, in the firmness of good prose or the rhythm of a good story'. Third comes 'historical purpose', the 'desire to see things as they are, to find out true facts and store them up for the use of posterity'. And finally comes 'political purpose', the desire 'to alter other people's idea of the kind of society that they should strive after', and no book, he claims, can be 'genuinely free from political bias'.

Orwell says that each of these motives will exist to different degrees in every writer, and that, in his experience, 'serious writers' tend 'to be more vain and self-centred than journalists, though less interested in money'. So where do you sit on the Orwell scale? Are you mostly writing to puff up your ego or to change the world? Do you love the act of writing itself, the creation of beautiful prose, or is it the setting down of facts for posterity that truly motivates you? For a travel writer, the investigation of the story, the travel itself – Orwell's 'historical purpose' – has to be one of the principal motives, but I still think it useful to establish in your own mind what your other main impulses are. As someone who comes from a journalistic background, I have always had the notion of laying down facts as a primary goal (though in an entertaining way), which is why I don't do a lot of hotel reviews – in fact, I've never done one. If your primary impulse is the poetry of the language, don't go into guidebook writing. If you don't care too much about the truth, don't do guidebooks or magazine or newspaper work. If kudos isn't your aim, don't write a travel book, because it won't earn you much money.

Finally, before you set off down the road of travel writing, ask yourself whether you truly enjoy the process of writing. If the thought of sitting down in front of a blank computer screen fills you with dread, or worse still, boredom, then are you cut out to be a writer?

Q&A WITH GEMMA HALL

GEMMA HALL IS A freelance writer 'specializing in natural history, heritage, travel and the environment'. She grew up in the north-east of England and – on the back of her inside knowledge of the area – wrote *Slow Northumberland & Durham*, which is published by Bradt. She was previously deputy editor of the National Trust's membership magazine and now writes regularly for magazines such as *BBC Wildlife* and *BBC Countryfile*.

Why did you become a travel writer?
Though I studied social sciences at Edinburgh University, for a long time before university, my passion was wildlife, but I didn't want to study biology or be a vet. After university, I started working for various conservation organizations, such as TCV (The Conservation Volunteers), which allowed me to travel a great deal within the UK. Then I started working for its international section and running projects abroad. This was perfect, because I wanted to do something worthwhile, and the skills I was learning were amazing. But I'd already decided that if I wanted to combine my interests in travel and wildlife, the best thing to do would be to become a writer.

What was the first piece you wrote?
The first travel piece I ever wrote was when I walked the Camino de Santiago, before I did my post-graduate course in journalism. I just jumped on the Eurostar and went off there with the intention of writing about it. I wrote the feature and sent it off to about forty publications, and I thought it was great, really witty, because it was all about me. But, of course, it was rubbish, and I realized this once I started doing my course.

Why was it rubbish?

Because it was about me, and I realized that people do not want to read about someone's holiday, they want to read about the place. It's much better if you can take yourself out of the piece. Another thing that I soon learned was that it was not very honest. There is a tendency in travel writing to exaggerate stories so much so that they are no longer true. When I'm reading a piece of travel writing these days and I wonder whether an anecdote took place in the way it has been related, then very often I stop reading.

Writers should be honest, then?

Yes, of course! Another thing that annoys me these days is this trend for self-deprecation, and I have been guilty of this, too. I once wrote a piece on wildlife crime, and I just came across as a bit stupid. There's also this tendency to tell stories about not understanding local customs, but I often wonder whether incidents happened in the way they are depicted. I do sometimes find myself lapsing into this sort of writing even now, but I am much more careful these days. With travel writing, you can be funny in other ways – it is about recording experiences as honestly as possible.

So, if it wasn't your piece about the Camino de Santiago, what was your big break?

After finishing my course, I was doing bits and bobs for magazines such as TCV's in-house magazine and taking any opportunity I could find. A lot of it was paid, some of it unpaid. Then I got a job on the National Trust magazine, and I did quite a lot of travel in the UK. My remit – well, I made it my remit – was to increase coverage of natural history in the magazine (before I joined, it was much more about homes and gardens), and that was perfect for me.

So, how did you do that?

I hung out with the people from the conservation department, and I'd pick up stories from them – about how there was a good bat roost at Tyntesfield or whatever. I'd then pitch stories to the editor. She was much more used to dealing with heritage and garden stories, so I had to convince her that these stories would not only be of interest to a birding or wildlife audience. It was a generalist audience, so you needed quite a light touch, and luckily I found that quite easy to do.

Why did you leave?

I was getting itchy feet and wanted to do other things. I was in the office a lot of the time and I had thought that I would be out and about more. I wanted the freedom to write about other things that I was interested in, such as environmental stories. But again I was lucky: my National Trust contacts gave me quite a lot of work in my first year of being freelance, copywriting and so on, which really helped. And the conservation department also gave me a nice job co-ordinating a wildlife survey, so I was doing lots of different things. Then I got some work off Kent County Council, doing walking guides for them. This was really enjoyable, because I didn't know the area very well at the time.

How did you get the Kent Council job?

Someone from the council had contacted *Country Walking* to see if they could recommend anybody, and I'd done a few pieces for them. I also did a piece for *BBC Wildlife* on the back of it. One of the key things to travel writing is selling several stories from one trip.

Who do you write for now?

I now write for *BBC Countryfile, Country Walking, Homes & Antiques, Natural World* and *The Great Outdoors*. My book,

Slow Northumberland & Durham, took up most of my time for a year or so over the course of 2011 and 2012, and I'm also now doing a part-time Geography MA which has allowed me to study urban ecology.

Why are you doing that?
I am always looking at ways to open up new avenues, different things I can do, and urban ecology is a growing area. People are much more interested in it than they were ten years ago, and this gives me more material to write about. I'm particularly interested in brownfield sites and the way in which government policies are creating pressure to develop them. I'd like to do more environmental writing, too.

What proportion of your work is travel writing, then?
In the past few years, about fifty or sixty per cent of my work has been travel-related in some way – mostly UK travel – but I've done plenty of international travel, too: the Italian Alps, Transylvania, the Channel Islands. But I tend to steer clear of many international stories because I can't make them pay. It's good for a jolly, but if you come back from a trip and have broken even, that's good going. I've managed to do a few trips by staying on after I've finished a conservation project abroad, so many of the expenses such as flights have already been covered.

So, where would you like to go but haven't?
There are so many, but I'd prefer to go to many of them – Finland, for example – on genuine holidays so that I didn't have to write about them. When you're away on travel pieces, you're working really hard and you're constantly on the go. Lots of people think you spend your time in an infinity pool drinking cocktails, but you don't, and there's a lot of boring stuff as well.

Boring stuff? When travelling?

Yes, if you're staying in a hotel, then the owners will want to have dinner with you and talk to you about their new conference facility, and I'll be there thinking, 'I've got this to do and I've got that to do', and I do find myself literally running to places.

Was it fun writing the book?

Yes, but it was extremely hard work, bombing here and there and sometimes getting only five or six hours' sleep a night. Originally, they only gave me four months to write it, but I said I wanted to revisit all the places I was going to write about and needed more time. It wasn't just about making money, it was about doing it well. I had been to a lot of the places before, but it was about seeing them with a different eye. I did have to do other work most of the time, but for the last few months I only wrote the book.

Will you make much money from it?

I only got a small advance for it, but if the book sells enough copies, I'll get some royalties, too. But I have also done other work on the back of it – pieces for *BBC Countryfile* and *Heritage* magazine.

Did Bradt ask you to write it?

No, I contacted them with the idea. I knew that they had this series of guidebooks (the 'Slow' series), and I thought that this was my chance. Writing a book was on my life list of things to do. I liked writing for Bradt: there's more room, than with other guidebook publishers, for your own personal views to come through.

2. IN THE DEPARTURE LOUNGE: GETTING STARTED

FIND YOUR PASSION

MANY YEARS AGO, I had a life-changing conversation with a then-girlfriend. She was living in Japan at the time, and I was in the UK, and I'd rung her from my dingy house-share in Tunbridge Wells to confirm what I'd told her in a letter (yes, it was *that* long ago) – that I'd met someone else and it was all over. It all seemed so serious at the time, and yet I was only twenty-two. Still, she'd been my girlfriend at university, and was the first person I'd had a vaguely adult relationship with.

At some point during that conversation she asked me the question that we were forever asking ourselves at that time: 'What do you want to do with your life?'

'I dunno,' I replied. 'Travel. And write.' Even at the time, I had the self-awareness to realize that it sounded a bit weak. I'd ended up in a town that epitomized middle-class security and I was working as a temporary admin assistant in a publishing company full of titles such as *Cabinet Maker* and *PrintWeek*. At some point, I even graduated to become the 'machinery correspondent' of *Packaging Week*. This was hardly the stuff that dreams are made of. I'd like to say that the day I acquired the dubious distinction of having something to say about vertical form-fill-seal bagging machines was the day I went home and started learning jujitsu or booked myself onto an ice-climbing course in Torres del Paine National Park in Chile, but I didn't.

Meanwhile, my now ex-girlfriend was living in Japan,

teaching English for the JET graduate programme and, while I sensed it wasn't easy, she was at least having some sort of experience that might shape her life.

'I've never understood,' she said to me rather pointedly, 'why you're so interested in travel but not in learning other languages.' This stung – it was true. Even though I was marooned in the doldrums of Tunbridge Wells, I still saw myself as a 'traveller'. I'd been to India and Nepal after I left school, hitchhiked through France, Italy, what was then Yugoslavia, Greece and Turkey after my first year at university and then travelled to Ecuador and Venezuela the following year on the back of some vague and frankly amateur 'research' project with three friends. But, despite spending the best part of two months in two Spanish-speaking countries, I could barely string two words of the language together.

My ex's comment had an effect on me and, within a couple of years, I set off on a nine-month trip through Central and South America, starting off in the Guatemalan city of Antigua to (finally) learn Spanish properly, having done a few evening classes while living in London. And while I am not a natural linguist, I became sufficiently adept at holding a drunken conversation in a bar, so much so that in 1996 I interviewed one of the candidates for the Ecuadorian General Election entirely in Spanish – something I would never have dreamed possible just three years earlier. Possibly more importantly, this trip showed me what my real passion in life was and, funnily enough, it wasn't pallet wrappers or case erectors, it was wildlife and wild places.

All that is another way of saying that the first thing you need to do if you want to be a travel writer is to find your passion. Some people, and indeed some travel writers, would probably say that it's enough to be passionate about travel, but when you look at the market, which we will in this chapter, you'll find that it is surprisingly fragmented. Of course, there are general travel magazines and websites, but it's by finding a niche, a specialism, that you'll make yourself valuable and find that editors come back to you on a more than sporadic basis, saying, 'Can you put together a quick round-up on the best places to learn to tango in Buenos Aires?'

HOW DOES PUBLISHING WORK?

For the moment, let's go back to basics. How does this strange business called publishing work? How do you go from being a keen, hopefully talented but as yet unpublished writer to one that has a few bylines to their name? And what the hell is a byline, anyway? (It's the bit under the headline of the article where it says: by So-and-so.)

The first thing to realize is that, unless you are exceptionally and uniquely brilliant, no editor is going to be interested in your account of the bareback yak ride you took across the Mountains of Mourne with your ageing great grandfather and his pet ocelot. Yes, some people have managed great success with concepts that are almost as ludicrous – *Round Ireland with a Fridge* by the comedian Tony Hawks springs to mind (it sold some 800,000 copies), but Hawks had already had some success as a comedian and actor, and besides, we're not even daring to think about books at the moment – we're thinking simple magazine articles that an editor believes his or her readers will enjoy.

Let's assume, for the moment, that you know what you want to write about and for whom. Let's say your passion is walking – it's not a bad place to begin. Millions of people in the UK love walking, and quite a few of them are prepared to spend some of their hard-earned cash on books and magazines that help them extract even more pleasure out of their hobby – these not only give them inspirational information about great walking locations in Britain, but they also set out specific routes for people to follow and sound advice on walking clothes, boots and other gear. As a result, there are plenty of writers employed, either as staff or as self-employed freelancers, by the companies that own these publications.

We will start with the walking magazines. There are three key ones, which are, in no particular order: *Trail*, *The Great Outdoors* (normally abbreviated to *TGO* in the business, so I will do that from now on) and *Country Walking*. First, take *Trail* and *TGO*, because they are fairly similar, and though they are both walking magazines they also stray into what I would call mountaineering territory, too. The February 2013 issue of *Trail* has a big feature on a winter skills course that involves ice axes and crampons, while there is also a profile of the legendary mountaineer Don Whillans. One of the adverts shows a climber ascending a vertical ice wall and cliff face. In the 'Routes' section at the back of the magazine – a standard section that all walking titles carry – the only 'route' that isn't in proper mountain territory is one for Dartmoor National Park. The rest are either in the Scottish Highlands, the Lake District or Snowdonia. Hopefully you get the picture. What you have to understand from it is this: you wouldn't, I hope, pitch an idea to the editor of *Trail* about a gentle ramble through the Lincolnshire Wolds, however lovely you found it.

TGO, meanwhile, is also pushing at frontiers. Its big feature of February 2013 has the assistant editor escaping to the Lake District for a weekend to spend a cold and lonely night in a bothy (a small, rural hut). There is also a 'How to' guide to winter skills: performing an ice-axe arrest, navigating in bad weather and a section on cold-weather injuries. One of its adverts – always a good indicator of the aspirations and interests of the readership – for Patagonia jackets shows a couple of gnarly chaps hacking their way up an ice-and-snow-covered ridge. Looking at the 'Wild Walks' section, however, suggests a very slight variation in the yearnings of *TGO*'s readers: they are more varied than those of *Trail*, and their walks include a bird-watching destination in the shape of Arnside and Silverdale in Lancashire and a fourteen-mile ramble down the west coast of the Isle of Man.

Country Walking, on the other hand (and as its name suggests) wears a quite different pair of boots to both *Trail* and *TGO*, and there is certainly no sign of any crampons here. Its February 2013 front cover, rather than showing a silhouetted figure striding across a high snowy plateau of the Cairngorm Mountains, has a t-shirted walker in the green and sun-kissed Malvern Hills. Rather than telling its readers how to survive in Scotland's most extreme environments, *Country Walking* has a feature about walking the length of the country's River Dee. The most 'out-there' feature is about the Yorkshire Three Peaks challenge. It's not hard to work out what sort of ideas this editor is looking for, and it might involve the Lincolnshire Wolds.

Those are the top three walking magazines, but there are others. The Ramblers has its own quarterly magazine called *Walk*, and you will find that this is much closer to *Country Walking* than the other two. Meanwhile, *BBC Countryfile* – a magazine that was launched on the back of the BBC1 Sunday night programme – while not being a specialist walking title does stray into some of this territory (though less than it used to). There's also a magazine called *Lakeland Walker*, for those diehard Cumbria enthusiasts but, rather than being monthly like the other newsstand titles, it is published six times a year.

If you want to contribute to any of these magazines, the first thing that you need to do is buy one (or several – better still, subscribe). It's not just a question of knowing what sort of articles they carry, but also of looking at how they are structured. If you're just starting out as a travel writer, it's unrealistic to expect any of them to run a 2,000-word article from you about walking in the Brecon Beacons (that would be *Trail* or *TGO*) or the Cotswolds (*Country Walking*), because they are going to have plenty of trusted experts who will also know these parts of the country well. But all three magazines carry much shorter 'routes', usually at the back, which are often little more than descriptions of a hike over a mountain or round a valley. Writing them doesn't require huge technical expertise or flair – though there is still a craft and style to be understood and learned – so if you come up with a decent idea and convince the editor that you know what you are doing and what you are talking about, you stand a chance.

The next thing I'd do is have a look at the magazine's website. Some magazines – though not all, and probably not even the majority – will have some advice about how to go about contributing editorial. *Wanderlust*, for example, has an excellent section on this. At the very least, you should find the names of the key editorial people, with the editor and features editor usually being the most important names to look out for. Of course, magazines will usually carry these details in the printed version, too, but many use their website for publishing information (such as how to contribute) that they can't fit in the magazine itself. At the very least, what you need before you send any idea to the magazine is a (correctly spelled) name, an email address and ideally a phone number, too.

The usual advice, at this point, is to send an email to a member of the team outlining your idea. Never send your pitch to a general magazine email address such as 'info@' or 'editorial@' or something along those lines. Even if the email doesn't fall into some completely neglected part of cyberspace, it just looks lazy, as if you can't be bothered to find out the name of the person you require. And if you can't be bothered with that, what else can't you be bothered to do?

If you're not sure who to contact, just ring up the magazine and ask – 'If I want to send ideas to your X section, who should I send them to and what's their email address?' In the case of *Trail*, its 'Routes' section specifically says who the editor is and how to contact them, so you won't need to do that. But if there's any doubt, there is no harm in making a quick call.

SENDING IN YOUR PITCH

So, HOW DO YOU go about making your pitch? First of all, commissioning editors have a lot on their plate: it's their job to come up with the ideas that make their magazine what it is, and many will have features of their own that they're writing or want to write. They also get a lot of emails. The last thing they want is 2,500 words of your personal history plus an attached CV and six examples of work you had published in your student newspaper. Keep it short – say who you are, what your idea is and why you would be the right person to write it. If you have had something published previously, there's no harm in giving a link to where the editor can find it on the web or attaching a PDF of the finished article. Don't send it in the Word version (because then there is no evidence that it has been published) and don't send in examples of your writing that have appeared in your local village newsletter – they are unlikely to have been well edited and won't show your writing talent in the best light.

The most important thing, by far, is the idea: that's the first thing your commissioning editor is going to consider. Is it any good and can they publish it? They will then look at who you are and what you have done up until now – they'll be wondering if they can take a gamble on you. The last thing they want is to commission a piece and find it unusable or find that they have to spend precious time telling you what's wrong with it and how to correct it or – as all commissioning editors have done from time to time – rewriting it themselves.

It can be hard to second-guess what the commissioning editor will think is a 'good idea', but the most important thing to remember is this: if you are sending an idea to *Trail*, then there is not much point in suggesting a description of a walk up Ben Nevis or Snowdon – if you have truly discovered a hitherto unknown route up the north face of the UK's highest peak then perhaps you're onto something but, in general, these mountains will be very well known to the people who work at *Trail*. Instead, look for a walk that can be found in some of the classic mountain or hill-walking destinations in the UK, but is slightly off the beaten path. Or perhaps you could devise a route in the Lake District that takes in some well-known peaks, can be walked in a day but has an overall ascent greater than Mont Blanc. *Trail* readers like to feel they are being pushed, so perhaps you can find some good, relatively unknown scrambling route? Even if you come up with a pitch that is a bit of a gimmick, you may get brownie points for being imaginative.

Don't expect to hear back straight away – your pitch isn't going to be top of the commissioning editor's list of concerns. But if you haven't heard anything after two or three weeks, you're entitled to send an email giving a gentle nudge. In my experience, it is much easier just to say 'No' to an idea than it is to say 'Maybe' or 'Perhaps', so no news can be good news. (Or at least not bad news.) You might think it's worth making a phone call at this point, though I would probably stick with email – the editor doesn't want to feel that they are being stalked. I have a few freelance contributors who will ring me if (when) I don't get back to them a few days after sending in their idea. I don't have a problem with this, as long as they don't try to push me into giving them a decision, but, in all honesty, at that point I may not even have read the pitch, and I almost certainly haven't reached any conclusion about it, unless it is simply brilliant or simply terrible.

Let's say that this time you do get a response – and it's a straight 'No'. There may be a bit more to it than that: 'Hi John, thanks for your idea but, after careful consideration, I've decided that it doesn't quite fit with what I'm looking for.' That's the sort of meaningless waffle that commissioning editors are very good at coming up with, and – if we're being honest – they might as well have said a straight 'No.' For a start, 'doesn't quite fit with what I'm looking for' could mean one of two things: first, it's miles off the mark, but the editor is too nice to say so. This is a perfectly reasonable scenario: there have been many times when I have been tempted to point out to wannabe contributors that they might as well have sent their idea to *World Arms Trade* magazine for all its relevance to wildlife, but have desisted at the last minute because it just felt unfair. Or it could actually mean that it's a perfectly good idea, but the editor had to choose between you and the writer who has been contributing excellent work for the past ten years, in which case there's no real contest.

At this point, you could try sending them another email. Again, don't make it too long, but perhaps you could turn it into a bit of a conversation. Comment on something in a recent issue of the magazine (particularly if it was written by the person you're corresponding with – a little bit of ego-massaging never went astray), then ask for feedback about the idea and what they feel it lacked, and perhaps try to get some idea of whether they would ever, in fact, commission someone with a relative paucity of experience as a travel writer.

When I get pitches from people who can a) clearly write and b) have good ideas, but I decide not to commission them, I will often point out that I get relatively few ideas for good travel stories within the UK. Everyone wants to get a commission from *BBC Wildlife* magazine to trek to see mountain gorillas in Rwanda, but very few people ever send in an idea for watching the first barnacle geese of the autumn coming into land at Loch Gruinart RSPB Reserve on Islay. Even the second of these isn't stunningly original, but the first is just lazy and pointless. It's a bit like offering a feature on Mozart to the editor of *BBC Music* or pitching an idea on Italian cooking to *BBC Good Food.*

If I think a writer has promise, then I will try to point them in the right direction, and many other commissioning editors feel the same way. The sad truth is that finding good, reliable writers who fully understand what your magazine is about is surprisingly hard. Again, I know a lot of other commissioning editors who feel the same way.

Before I go any further, I will make a very simple but important point: before you send that first email with your all-important pitch, do check that there are no mistakes, whether in your spelling, grammar or punctuation. Some people might feel, 'It's only an email, what does it matter?', but I hope it should be perfectly obvious to anyone who aspires to be a writer that anything you write matters. I say that, but it clearly isn't obvious – I get enough poorly written and punctuated emails from people I don't know to realize that.

That's not to say that your email should adopt the tone of an Edwardian country lady. 'Hi James,' or just 'James' is a perfectly acceptable way to begin your pitch to the travel editor of *BBC Wildlife* magazine, but you might want to think twice about the same approach to a senior publishing executive at Fodor's Travel Guides. Other basics of writing always apply: split your email into paragraphs, as you would in a letter, because it makes the whole thing more readable. I occasionally receive emails from writers who run what looks like the best part of 500 words into one paragraph, with everything from who they are to what their idea is and how they're off to Ulan Bator in three weeks so would I mind getting back to them pronto, crammed into an almost indecipherable block. As the *Test Match Special* team often say, as the first clatter of wickets starts to fall and the cream of English batting is sent trudging back to the pavilion (apologies to anyone who doesn't like cricket, but you will understand the point I'm making): you can't win a match on the first morning, but you can lose it. So it is with pitching stories as a novice: you can't guarantee you'll get a commission with that first contact, but you can probably ensure that you will never get any work from that publication if you screw it up badly enough.

Let's look on the bright side, however, and assume that your email is polite, well-written and perfectly spelled! The editor doesn't reply to you with some meaningless waffle or even send your pitch spinning sadly into the vacuum of outer cyberspace to drift disconsolately among the asteroid belt of other rejected ideas: not only do they like the idea, they're short of a few pieces this month. Hell – it's 5.30 on Friday evening and they really want to be going home, but wouldn't it be nice to get this section commissioned before the weekend? So they take a chance, they offer you a commission, they outline the brief, they give you a deadline and – hold your horses – they even tell you what the fee is. What now?

Well, I'll be looking at how you prepare for a trip and record information on it in the next chapter, and the technical aspects of writing are covered in Chapters 5, 6 and 7. For now though, for all those aspiring travel writers who have never knowingly put one foot in front of another if they could simply raise a hand and hail a taxi, for all those people who'd rather be sipping ginseng tea in their boutique hotel than shedding Gore-Tex in a bothy – for all those people who have no interest in writing for walking magazines, in other words – it's time to explore the rest of the world of opportunity that is travel writing.

THE TRAVEL-WRITING MARKET

Dedicated travel magazines

AT THE TOP END of the dedicated travel-magazine market in the UK are titles such as *Condé Nast Traveller* and the *Sunday Times Travel Magazine*. A quick flick through the pages of these publications will reveal a lot: there are plenty of adverts for Louis Vuitton jewellery and Rolex watches and articles including 'The Total Guide' to California and why the Caribbean island of Nevis is the go-to destination for such pioneers of the zeitgeist as Anna Wintour. This is glamour travel for seriously, or fairly seriously, affluent people who want exclusivity above all else. Take this short excerpt in *Condé Nast Traveller*.

Nevis is old Caribbean, easy-going and unsullied by mass tourism. It doesn't have the beaches of Antigua, but neither does it have the kinds of hotels that have chocolate fountains at the breakfast buffet. Its few hotels are small and stylish, built in the old plantation inns, or super-starred like the Four Seasons (and there are whispers of an Amanresort on its way).

You get the picture? If, like me, you don't have the faintest idea what an Amanresort is, then you're a) not the target readership and b) more importantly in the current context, an unlikely contributor to the magazine. Of course, you can resort to Google and discover that Amanresorts prefer to think 'Small. Intimate. Involving' and that they have 'an appetite for pampering and a deep appreciation of the creative and elegant' but can you write a brilliant article that way? Contributing to a brand such as Condé Nast requires you to have an insight into what makes for an innovative luxury experience – so if this doesn't interest you, it's advisable to pitch elsewhere.

The *Sunday Times Travel Magazine* is less overtly luxury-accommodation orientated, with just a smidgeon of adventure in some of the locations it includes in its editorial. You'd be unlikely to find a piece about the Peruvian part of Lake Titicaca in *Condé Nast Traveller*, for example, even though the *Sunday Times* piece (from May 2013) is nevertheless recommending hotels at £350 a night. Later in the same issue is a feature on 'The 50 most amazing hotels in the world (not a single one over £199)', which truly differentiates it from its competitor. Still, don't expect to find anything on backpacker hostels in Brighton in this title – and don't pitch such an idea to the editor.

So, that's the top of the range magazines in the UK. (Note that there is also a *Condé Nast Traveler* – with the American spelling – in the USA.) Next come magazines such as *Lonely Planet Traveller* and *National Geographic Traveller* (there's also a stateside *National Geographic Traveler*). I'm not quite sure what this obsession with 'traveller' is, though to refer back to the Paul Theroux quote of Chapter 1, it is fairly obvious why we don't have a *Condé Nast Tourist* magazine. Anyway, you won't find any adverts for Louis

Vuitton or Rolex watches in *these* publications; it's more likely to be 'Hello Vietnam' and 'Welcome to the Unesco Country of the Czech Republic'.

There is a greater diversity of destinations covered in these publications – anywhere from the Manu Biosphere Reserve in the Peruvian Amazon to the Greek volcanic island of Santorini – and no one worries whether Palermo's Le Terrazze B&B is the accommodation *du jour* or is frequented by the editor of American *Vogue*. There's more emphasis on natural, outdoorsy experiences, rather than sipping cocktails by an infinity pool trying to spot A-listers, particularly in *National Geographic Traveller*, but don't assume that because these magazines are aimed at mid-market travellers they therefore employ mid-market writers.

The writing in both these magazines is always good and often excellent – I like the intro to this piece about Budapest in the Jan/Feb 2013 issue of the National Geographic title:

> Budapest is like Brigitte Bardot with an eye patch. There's elegance in the arcs of its boulevards, there's grace in its illuminated bridges, and a whiff of perfumed Parisian chic hangs about the tables of its pavement cafes. But this isn't a place that's been buffed free of every blemish. Hungary has had a turbulent history and its capital bears the scars to prove it.

It's trying to bring a new light to bear on a well-documented destination, but in a tongue-in-cheek way.

How much chance do you have of being commissioned by one of these magazines? Reasonable, I'd say. Pat Riddell, editor of *National Geographic Traveller* (at the time that this story was published), told me that while they have a pool of contributors that they do use regularly, they will consider ideas from people they don't know: 'The pitch is the most important part for experienced and inexperienced alike,' Pat added. 'If it's a good angle or story there's a chance we might take it further – the blog is a good "testing ground" for trialing new writers.'

What Pat has to say about his readers is probably worth

repeating, too: 'They vary in age from teenagers to pensioners but all are passionate about travel and the National Geographic brand. That said, it's generally accessible, affordable travel we aim to cover and not as extreme or adventurous as *National Geographic* itself – attainable as well as aspirational.' Getting something – anything – published in *National Geographic Traveller* would be coup for any wannabe travel writer, but don't expect to become rich overnight: a rate of £210 per 1,000 words isn't hugely generous, even if you can boost your income by selling some photos to go with your article.

After these two titles comes *Wanderlust*, which is more obviously aimed at independent travellers. The *Wanderlust* website has extensive guidelines for contributors, which contain the following 'warning' at the very start: 'The vast majority of our articles are commissioned specifically for the magazine, and written by experienced journalists, guidebook authors or travel experts.' The guidelines go on to suggest that first-time contributors should target shorter slots such as a news story or consumer feature before pitching a full-length travel idea, and that 'Off-the-beaten-track destinations, secret corners of the world and unusual angles on well-known places are always of particular interest.' *Wanderlust* pays £220 per 1,000 words, about the same as *National Geographic Traveller,* and it says that it only pays for what it prints – so, even if it asks for 1,500 words, and that's what you submit, if only 1,000 words make it to the final cut, your fee will be cut accordingly.

There are also a lot of country-specific titles such as *France* magazine, published by Archant, which is best-known in the business for its range of slightly posh 'Life' magazines like *Cotswold Life, Somerset Life* etc. *France* magazine is classic travel-writing territory, combining aspirational writing (wouldn't you want to be 'sitting on the sun-warmed deck of the most beautiful boat in the south of France', sipping champagne with a bowl of olives within easy reach?) with practical details and useful, interesting local history. You might think that there have got to be plenty of opportunities for any writer with a passion for France, but I think that this could be an extremely hard market to crack.

I asked *France*'s editor Carolyn Boyd (remember – editors come and go, so always check that you have the most up-to-date contact details) if she used freelance writers and, if so, what she was looking for from them, and she pointed out that her readership was particularly loyal to the magazine, with some having subscribed for every one of its twenty-two years of existence. Even the average reader has been taking it for seven years. They know France very well, she said, so it is a constant challenge to come up with editorial that will surprise them. 'This means a research trip needs to be very thorough and in-depth, and will often take longer than the money is worth! For this reason, we do use writers who live either full-time or part-time in France, as they have this depth of knowledge about particular areas.'

Not only that, but she doesn't usually find that commissioning new writers pays off: 'In my six years in the job, I have taken a punt on many new/unpublished writers with good ideas, but they have rarely, if ever, been worth the risk.' And finally, if you still think that you've got ideas that could work for the title, consider the fact that it pays between £100 and £200 per 1,000 words: you'd barely pay for the morning croissants and a few glasses of plonkish red in the evenings on the basis of a fee at the lower end of that scale.

I would briefly make reference to another batch of magazines in this ballpark, too: *Travel + Leisure*, *Travel 50 & Beyond*, *Vacations* and *Budget Travel*. The reason that I allude to them only in passing is that they are all US titles, and I wonder just how many writers from further afield they are likely to use. *Travel 50 & Beyond* specifically states that it does not commission freelance writers, while *Travel + Leisure* magazine does not allow either its editors or contributors to accept free travel, an issue that we will come onto in greater detail in another chapter, but which is worth remembering.

Back in the UK, there's one other magazine that I'd mention – *Wild Travel*, which is aimed at the booming wildlife-tour and wildlife-watching industry. This is largely a practical magazine for people who want to know where and how to see some of the world's great wildlife spectacles.

In-flight magazines

ALL OF THE MAGAZINES mentioned so far can be either purchased at newsagents or supermarkets (so-called 'newsstand' titles), but if you think you'd have a good chance of getting something published in any of them, you'd be better off getting familiar with them by taking out a subscription. Shelling out £25 or so will not only ensure that you don't miss what features they are running on a month-by-month basis, it also isn't much of investment if you get even one £200 or £300 commission as a result. But there is also a whole other group of travel magazines that it's very easy to overlook, but which offers huge potential. Leafing through the handbook of the British Guild of Travel Writers reveals one thing very clearly indeed: few people who call themselves travel writers survive without having at least one airline magazine that they contribute to on a regular basis. Think about it for a moment: how many airlines are there in the world, and how many of them have their own in-house in-flight magazine? How often do they publish and how many pieces in each one? It's a huge market, but like the Faroe Islands or the Paraguayan Chaco, it is very easy to overlook.

It's also quite easy to be sniffy about magazines that nobody pays for and which most people flick nonchalantly through before the plane takes off and then barely glance at again, even if they're on a twelve-hour flight to Hong Kong. Your automatic assumption might be that the quality is going to be pretty poor, but you'd be wrong: there's a lot of very decent writing in these magazines, even if most features are fairly limited in their ambitions: take a city, obviously a destination that the airline flies to, and give a rundown on the bars, restaurants, cafes, hotels and other attractions that the average visitor might want to know about. Still, I liked this introduction to a piece in BA's November 2012 edition of *High Life* about the US capital by the journalist Viv Groskop:

> Until recently Washington, DC was not seen as a cool place to hang out. If anything, Aaron Sorkin's pre-Obama cult series *The West Wing* made it look nerdy, stuffed full of

over-educated political types who talk too fast, have doomed personal lives and work long into the night. But *The West Wing* was fiction. And ten years ago.

It's knowingly, snappily written and will entice anyone who said all along that *The West Wing* was geeky, while fans of the show will read the piece just to feel outraged. It's a nice teaser, too – you know it's going to tell you that Washington *is* now a cool place to hang out; the question is *why*.

I think there's huge potential for inexperienced travel writers to get themselves published in this market. Piet van Niekerk, editor (as of early 2013) of the in-flight magazine of Brussels Airlines, *B Spirit!*, told me that he is usually happy to try out someone with little experience. 'At times we do have to do loads of rewriting, but it's better to get copy from people "on the ground" with local knowledge (I deal with many African destinations) than a great writer writing about something he or she does not really know anything about,' he said. The decision will generally come down to 'how fresh and unique the proposals are and – of course – if the client (airline) approves of the idea and/or destination.' Readers on the long-haul routes into Africa and New York are mostly charity aid workers and business people working in the mining and mobile phone industry, and 'while the airline demands a strong focus on destinations, I push for business analysis and human interest [stories], too.'

A quick glance at *B Spirit!* shows how this approach manifests itself in practice: articles include a profile of the Batammariba tribe of Benin, a celebration of Africa's biggest cinematic event, the Pan-African Film Festival of Ouagadougou, and a report on how a new bridge across the Gambia River (in Gambia) will help traffic flow from northern to southern Senegal (if that makes no sense to you, try looking at a map of West Africa).

And on that note, I'm going to digress a little here. I can't point to anything specific, but I am in no doubt that a lifetime of poring over maps and atlases whenever I get the opportunity has served me well as a travel writer. In the previous instance, I immediately understood the story because I know that Gambia is a sliver of land entirely encircled by Senegal, like a maggot wriggling in an apple. It's one of those geographical oddities that you're unlikely to notice unless you happen to find cartography infinitely fascinating, or you took a holiday in the region once and happened to flick through the in-flight magazine before take-off. But, as the bridge story in *B Spirit!* suggests, this type of knowledge can be turned into cash with a little inspiration.

(While we're on the subject of geographical oddities, my favourite is the fact that the Panama Canal traverses the country from the Atlantic side to the Pacific in a south-easterly direction, which is very strange when you consider that, usually, to get from the Atlantic to the Pacific – by the shortest possible route, of course – you'd travel west. So how does that work? Have a look at a map!)

Newspapers

ALL THE NATIONAL NEWSPAPERS, including the down-market 'tabloids' of *The Sun* and the *Mirror*, have extensive travel sections these days. The main ones to consider when thinking about where you could pitch your ideas are the so-called broadsheets of *The Guardian*, the *Daily Telegraph*, *The Independent* and *The Times*, the 'mid-market' papers of the *Daily Mail* and the *Express* and even 'free sheets' such as the *Metro*. All of these use freelance writers, so there are plenty of opportunities for aspiring travel writers, and they tend to pay better (apart from *The Independent*) than many magazines, with both the *Telegraph* and the *Mail* traditionally offering the most – somewhere around £500 for 1,000 words is normal.

One of the principal skills of being a travel writer is to iden-tify what different publications are looking for, and that is even more true for newspapers than it is for magazines. (A publica-tion such as *National Geographic Traveller*, for example, has a more established identity than the travel section of a newspaper.) You have to assess the readership demographic of each travel section and consider what the editors are looking for – remembering that the travel section demographic may not necessarily be the same as the mainstream readership of that newspaper.

What follows is a quick run-down of the different types of

editorial that the publications are looking for, but one thing that struck me while researching this section was just how similar much of the content is these days, particularly that offered by the four broadsheets. Increasingly, they borrow each other's clothes and copy each other's ideas, but I think there are still some general rules to be outlined.

In no particular order, then:

The Guardian runs features on a wide range of destinations and types of travel. There are regular pieces on city breaks, yoga retreats and 'cool' camping locations. The type of article varies from a standard travel piece with the writer at its centre to 'top 10' compilations of the best seasonal destinations. 'Insider guides' to cities are often put together by local writers and bloggers – there may be opportunities here, but you'll see that the writing is much more along the lines of guidebook writing than feature writing. Arguably, *The Guardian* is the most technologically engaged of all the newspapers – it has started a concept called 'TwiTrips' in which writers set off on a journey while taking advice from readers on Twitter. Round-up features, such as the 'best tiny campsites in Britain', are compiled by writers with a specialist knowledge of this area.

You'd expect the *Daily Telegraph* to focus more on upmarket travel, and to a certain extent it does – a travel guide to Monaco, a round-up of the best new luxury resorts of Mauritius and a hotel guide to a country house hotel near Sandringham are typical fare. Like many papers – and magazines – it will exploit an anniversary as the peg for a big feature, so it's always worth trying to come up with those types of ideas. But it will also run counter-intuitive pieces – a piece on North Korea, while the world's attention was focused on a nuclear stand-off between the totalitarian regime and the rest of the world, is a good example. In some ways, I'd have expected to see this in *The Guardian* or *The Independent* instead.

One of the key sections in *The Independent* is '48 hours in . . .', a highly formulaic guide to destinations as diverse as Ibiza, Kathmandu and Kiev. These pieces are written to a blueprint, with standardized headings such as 'Touch down' (for flight information), 'Check in' (for hotels), 'Get your bearings' (finding your way around) and 'Take a hike' (walks). (The *Telegraph* has a very similar approach with '36 hours in . . .' – its readers are obviously time-poorer than those of *The Independent*!) Travel editor Simon Calder focuses on, well, independent travel, often to overlooked European destinations. There's also plenty of adventure and outdoor travel stories, but this is true of all the newspapers these days.

The Times has a lot of round-up pieces, such as '20 little British islands', '20 secret islands in the Mediterranean' and 'Sweden's 20 best beach houses'. It has a strong walking section, with a wide range of destinations from Canvey Island to the Clwydian Fells in North Wales, and has a section that is very similar to '48 (or 36) hours in . . .' called 'A weekend in'.

The *Daily Mail* has the most obviously upmarket editorial of all the newspapers, with lots of pampering-type pieces: 'Project babymoon: A pre-parenthood break in the Canaries' is quite typical. There's some family travel content ('Britain's favourite picnic spots', for example), but there's a greater emphasis on luxury. There's some adventurous travel too – Burma and a self-drive trip to Namibia, for example.

The *Express* is the most family-orientated of all the nationals, with a new attraction at Legoland getting the full-feature treatment. Even a piece on the Everglades in Florida features both alligators and children, though not with any unhappy results.

The *Metro*, as befitting its readership, is targeting a younger audience, so an Abba museum in Sweden and Glastonbury are both featured.

One other newspaper area possibly worth exploring is regional papers. While not all of them have travel content, some such as the *Yorkshire Post* do, and it's not just what to do in Leeds on a wet and windy night. There are features on Sri Lanka, Rwanda and Kangaroo Island off the south coast of Australia. The writing is not always of the highest standard, and the features may not impress a travel editor of one of the nationals – this partly reflects the readership, of course – but it is worth bearing these publications in mind nevertheless.

A couple of final points – clearly, newspapers vary their approach and the sort of editorial they run, so you need to look at the newspapers for yourself to decide which ones would suit the kind of travel feature you have in mind. Learning to analyze editorial and assess where you ought to pitch your ideas is one of the key skills of any budding travel writer. Unlike magazines, newspapers tend not to carry what in the trade are known as 'flannel panels' – boxes, either near the front or the back of the magazine, which have the names of all the staff members with job titles and (sometimes) a phone number or email address. Even online, where newspapers usually carry additional information, finding out who you need to be sending your pitch to is frequently a waste of time – it's far quicker to simply ring the offices, ask who the travel editor is and get their email address.

And the rest . . .

EVEN THOUGH WE HAVE covered dedicated travel magazines, including the in-flight titles, we've only just scraped the surface of the travel-writing market. Almost every magazine, from the nerdy reaches of *Airliner World* (a business magazine aimed at people working in the airline industry) to the effervescent hot springs of *Cosmopolitan* (cover line: 'Epic sex: Get it, give it & do it again!'), and from the extreme polar and desert environments of the Royal Geographical Society's *Geographical* to the pipe-and-slippers terrain of *The Oldie*, carries at least one or two travel features a month. *The Oldie* reminds me of an eccentric, ageing aunt, with articles on everything from the troglodytes of Cappadocia in Turkey to a ferry crossing to Northern Ireland.

At the beginning of 2013, I contacted *The Oldie's* then assistant editor Jeremy Lewis to get a steer on what they look for in their writers. 'Both [editor] Richard Ingrams and I enjoy publishing newcomers as well as old lags,' he told me in an email. 'We're not that interested in the blander type of travel piece: we like disasters, discomfort and blocked lavatories, plus odd/unusual adventures, as often as not involving oldies. We have an occasional series called "The World's Worst Dumps", and these have included, as far as I can remember, St Petersburg, Carcasonne and the Verona open-air opera stadium.' Fees aren't great, but if you could bash out 1,000 words on how, despite everything else you tend to read about Prague or Vienna, you can find cities teeming with awful decay if you scratch the surface, you might be onto something. In terms of tone, *The Oldie*'s editorial strikes me as being entertainment first, with any practical use a distant second. I'm not saying that the travel features are for armchair nomads only, however – readers may well be spending their final salary pensions on a globe-trotting existence, just not necessarily to Cappadocia.

Finally, here, in no particular order, are a few more titles that you might not consider when thinking about travel writing, but which could have a part to play: *Golf Monthly*, *Railway Magazine*, *VW Camper* and *The Lady*. Or what if canoeing is one of your great passions? Try looking at the raft of canoeing titles in a large newsagents, and pitching a few ideas to the editor. A quick glance at *Canoe & Kayak UK* shows that, while there is plenty of gear-focused editorial, there's space for some fairly standard if colloquial travel-based writing.

So as to give a full run-down of the magazine market, I will now turn, quite briefly, to the sex and celebrity world of women's glossies. A quick glance through these reveals little room for the freelance travel writer; according to those in the know, many of the women's magazines tend to keep any trips as perks for their staff. Looking at *Cosmopolitan* as a representative of the business, much of the travel-orientated editorial is verging on copywriting, (i.e. largely uncritical reporting of accommodation that could have easily have been written by someone who's not actually been there).

Now, it may be useful here to include a word or two on copywriting. This is essentially travel writing for corporate clients rather than publications, and it is usually much better paid. Unless you are an outlandishly successful author who shifts books in the tens or hundreds of thousands, the chances are that it will be the best-paid work you ever do. In contrast to editorial, this sort of work is often paid on a daily rate rather than a rate per word. In some cases you simply negotiate a flat fee for a particular piece of work. But, as a guide, fees of £400 a day are not beyond a copywriter's wildest dreams. Without doubt, my best-ever day's work purely from a remuneration perspective was a piece I did for a Tasmania Tourist Board-sponsored *Daily Telegraph* supplement – it was not, strictly speaking, copywriting, since I was paid by the *Telegraph*, but nor was it strictly editorial either. Certainly, the commercial element meant that I earned a fee well beyond remunerations scales I was (and still am) accustomed to.

Digital horizons

FINALLY, BEFORE WE LEAVE the labyrinthine recesses of the travel-writing souk, we should consider the opportunities of writing purely for the internet. It's a big generalization, but travel websites tend to fall into two distinct categories: big corporate sites such as Columbus Travel's World Travel Guide (www.worldtravelguide.net) and the virtually single-handed sites set up by specialists in their field.

The World Travel Guide definitely requires writers to leave some of their critical faculties at the door. And by that I mean that there is no room for negativity. A lot of travel writing, it is true, tends to emphasize the pros over the cons, but sites such as the World Travel Guide are supplying copywriting rather than the type of editorial you would read in almost any magazine or newspaper. I'm not saying that it's terrible, just that it requires the writer to recognize certain disciplines.

One of the guide's commissioning editors told me that she is reluctant, usually, to commission unpublished writers and said that new writers were asked to provide evidence of other online articles they'd had published. 'I would ask them to do a small, unpaid article to see what their writing style is like first, before I commissioned them,' she added. World Travel Guide readers are fairly adventurous, she told me, though I am not sure that necessarily means they'd go canyoning in Tasmania's Franklin River gorge, just that they might go to Tasmania in the first place. They are relatively affluent and (intriguingly, I thought) seven out of ten don't have children. The guide pays £200 per 1,000 words.

This is all very well, and the sort of pieces it publishes are probably quite easy to write, but personally I think the real opportunities on the web come from creating your own sites.

A quick look around reveals some intriguing opportunities – take something like 101 Honeymoons, a website started by Jane Anderson. As travel editor of *You & Your Wedding Magazine* for ten years, Jane has, as she puts it, 'been on more honeymoons than Elizabeth Taylor.' Funded by advertising, her website makes money in its own right, but it also allows her to set herself up as the honeymoon travel-writing guru, meaning that she is in demand from other magazines and newspapers.

Acquiring the mystique of being 'an expert' has to be the Holy Grail for any travel writer and, for some publications or websites, it is more important than being regarded as a highly talented writer. It is a moot point, and I am sure plenty of people would disagree with this, but to me it is undeniable that writing practical 'Go there, do this' articles, where readers are purely looking for information, requires less skill than the type of writing that is being read purely for pleasure.

I am not saying that it is completely without skill, of course – indeed Jane Anderson and the other people she works with (they have a whole '101' brand going, including sites such as 101 Short Breaks, 101 Family Holidays and 101 USA Holidays) are not just writing articles but developing entire websites, and there is great skill here in working out how they should be structured and who they should be aimed at. In essence, it's like creating a magazine. But it's nevertheless true that people go to 101 Honeymoons because it's regarded as being a reliable, trustworthy source of information, not because it will have them weeping with laughter into their cappuccinos like a Bill Bryson book.

I contacted Jane to find out whether she ever commissions freelance writers for 101 Honeymoons, but she said that there was no budget for external contributions. As she pointed out herself, this is increasingly a problem within the travel industry – magazines and newspapers (and websites, though she didn't say this) that see travel as a nice perk for a member of staff or a freelancer and no need to pay for the copy. There is some truth in this, but it's not the whole truth.

Another website in the one-man-band category is family-travel.co.uk, which was set up by freelance travel writer Kate Calvert, who has also written the *UK Baby Guide* and

London's Baby Guide, which essentially provide practical travel information for people with infants. Like 101 Honeymoon's Jane Anderson, Kate has cleverly set herself up as an expert in a fairly niche area, though a niche area that is going to appeal to a lot of people over time. Family-travel.co.uk has a different working basis to the 101 format, in that it is a subscription service, breaking the golden rule that everything on the internet has to be free. Arguably, of course, this makes it a more trustworthy source of information, for as Kate says on the website:

> We don't take commission from companies we recommend, we don't go on press trips organised by tour operators [and] we don't sell holidays. No company has paid in cash or kind to be included on the Family Travel web site. If a business is listed it is because it offers a useful service to parents, not because it makes us money.

This whole business of whether any travel feature is compromised if the writer has taken a 'freebie' is complex and divides opinion. Many US magazines, in particular, explicitly ban it, and *The Independent*'s Simon Calder is – famously – the man who pays his way. I'll be going into it in more detail later in the book, but for the moment I will only say this: all the travel I have done for *BBC Wildlife* has been done on the basis of tourist boards or tour operators offering me free travel, and yet I have never come under any pressure to change something I wrote. Some people will say that any pressure is more subtle than that – self-censorship, possibly, because you don't want to offend the organization that hosted your trip. Or, in the case of a hotel or restaurant review, the fact that you're on a 'freebie' will be known, so the level of service may be raised and not what a paying customer would receive. I'm not sure I believe that, but one thing is for sure: no company or tourist board can force a baby elephant to plunge joyfully into a water hole in a Sri Lankan wildlife reserve. Even though I accepted a free trip there, what I saw was one hundred per cent genuine.

Family Travel's Kate Calvert does have a different point of view about freebies, however, which for the sake of balance is worth repeating: 'Whatever anyone says, the journalist does feel obliged to be polite about what they have experienced, and the result is not a fair account of what's on offer.' Kate also has a pessimistic view of the travel-writing market: 'I occasionally write a travel piece for pay, but my experience is that rates have not increased in twenty-odd years, so it looks decreasingly viable as a way of earning a living rather than pocket money.'

However, as Kate herself has shown, there are other ways of being a writer these days; things change, and none of us can ignore the media industry's current, unprecedented state of flux. Hopefully, this chapter has shown that, whatever the rates of pay, whatever the state of the industry, there is no shortage of opportunities for the imaginative travel writer. I think the key is to be focused, to work out what your strengths and passions are and stick to those. You also have to be patient and learn to develop a skin tougher than the proverbial rhino hide, because – to start with, especially – you will get lots of knock-backs. But in my experience, it can merely be a matter of showing (the right kind of) persistence – eventually, a travel editor will give you a commission because you've come up with a genuinely great idea.

Q&A WITH MARK ROWE

MARK ROWE HAS WORKED as a journalist for more than twenty years, including a four-year stint as a reporter for *The Independent*. He specializes in travel writing and writing about environmental issues for a wide range of publications.

How did you start in travel writing?
Before I started my journalism training in 1991, I took a gap year to China, Vietnam and all over Asia. I immediately saw the potential for writing up the trips as travel articles, and *The Independent* and *The Guardian* took three or four of them. This was in the days when you printed something out and put it in the post.

What did you write about?

I was aware that I would not get anything published by doing mainstream articles. I was in China just after Tiananmen Square [the famous student protests took place in 1989], and I could have done something on what an amazing place it was. But what struck me was the amount of staring – the cultural differences, really. I called it the three 'S's of China – spitting, staring and slurping (their noodles). For *The Guardian*, I did a piece about travelling by rickshaw between Bangalore and Mysore, as opposed to their amazing architecture.

What happened after that?

I kept the travel writing going, even when I joined the *Grimsby Evening Telegraph* after finishing my journalism course. There, I was always on the look-out for potential stories, so when a big aid convoy was going out to the Ukraine, I got myself on that, and wrote a few stories on the back of it. In those days, I think it was easier to place articles about off-beat places in newspapers, but there are opportunities everywhere if you can think laterally.

Then what did you do?

I left the *Grimsby Evening Telegraph* and started doing news shifts for papers in London. I joined *The Independent* as a news reporter in 1996 and, while I was there, I did a lot of work for the travel section. I'd go over to the travel desk and say, 'I've just been to Bruges, do you want a piece about Belgian beer?' Another time, I came back from Iran and offered them something on the taxi drivers of Tehran. I made a real effort to get in with them, and then they actually started asking me to do things for them. And I made sure I went on interesting trips for them – Syria or the South Pacific, for example.

But then you decided to leave *The Independent* in 2001?

My partner [Lucy] and I had just got married, so we went

travelling for a year. I was able to fund a lot of that year
from travel commissions. We specifically went to places
that I thought I would be able to write about and that I
might not go to again – including Paraguay, Easter Island,
Laos and Samoa.

What was the most memorable piece you did?
In Paraguay, I wondered how I could possibly write a
travel article about its Nazi past. What fell into my lap
was that, in a city called Ciudad del Este, there was a Nazi
memorabilia market full of pictures of Hitler and all his
motley crew. It was weirdly fascinating.

**Did you send your stories back while you were
travelling?**
Yes, and that was in the days when you had to search
around for an internet cafe. In Ushuaia, in Argentina,
I had to use a coin-operated internet connection to file
my story – I was literally putting ten cent pieces into the
machine. I wrote twenty features in nine months, most of
them while we were away.

**What did you do after you got back from your year
away?**
It was around 2001/2, and the internet was really starting
to kick in, and this meant you could more or less live
anywhere, so we moved to Bristol. Since then, about
thirty-five per cent of my work regularly comes from
travel writing, and the rest is environmental, science and
wildlife writing.

Would you like to do more travel writing?
If you are going to succeed, you have to go with the
flow. I know very few people who have survived writing
only about travel – there used to be a lot more, but not
anymore.

How do you make travel writing pay?

When I go to most places, I make sure I have several commissions before I travel. The only exceptions I have made to this have been once-in-a-lifetime trips to Svalbard and the Galápagos. I have to have a hard, commercial approach to it. For example, I would expect to get three or four pieces out of one week-long trip. I once got eighteen pieces out of a ten-day-long trip.

You must work hard . . .

The point is not just to sunbathe on a beach or drink lattes all day – you are always thinking about potential stories. Generally speaking, I say to tourist boards, 'I have one or two commissions, and I know I can get more,' and they are usually happy with that.

How can you get more than one article out of one trip?

Let's say you're going to a place such as Frankfurt or Cologne. You might write a weekend-break piece for *The Independent*, but you could also do a different one for the *Telegraph*, so you have to make sure you 'have' both experiences. Then you might target a family magazine. But don't try and write up the same story for different publications – that will just annoy editors and they won't use you again.

How do you get your ideas?

Often, I think up them up in the bath. When I was at university, I lived in Belarus [Mark studied Russian for his degree], and around 2008, I noticed that England were playing a World Cup qualifier there. So, I suggested an idea to the *Daily Telegraph* on what the Wags would make of Minsk. To write the piece, I went looking for croc-skin handbags and drank champagne cocktails in bars.

What lessons has your career as a travel writer and journalist taught you?

Never assume anything and never get too comfortable. There is nothing more satisfying than getting a really good travel article into a national magazine or newspaper, but travel writing is the hardest thing to do properly. A lot of travel writing is pompous and self-important and tells you what a wonderful time the writer had but does not inspire other people to go there. If you are going to write good travel articles, you have got to have an interest in what you're writing about. If you have no interest in motorbikes, don't write up a road trip.

3. TAKE-OFF: GETTING THE TRIP

THE PERFECT STORY

STARING OUT FROM THE fourteenth floor of the *BBC Wildlife* office at the gull's-eye view of Bristol city centre early in January 2007, my thoughts started to turn to where I would like to go on my next trip. Though I had had an exciting two-week itinerary in Gabon lined up for February, it had fallen through at the last minute in late October, and I felt that I needed something else to look forward to.

But when thinking about where to travel to, you can't just think, 'Oh, I know, I've never been to Belarus.' If you try pitching that (or any other equally 'angle-less' idea) to an editor – and I've seen it enough times – most will turn you down flat. Actually, in my view, you'd be lucky to even get a rejection email. It would be like proposing a feature on sports cars to *Top Gear*. You've got to come up with something they haven't done or even considered.

So, I started to think, and my mind began to wander. What destination had been in the news recently, and not necessarily as a travel location but for some other reason? The ideal scenario was to be ahead of the curve, to find somewhere that wasn't on a beaten tourist trail but was still accessible to *BBC Wildlife* readers – people who aren't, generally speaking, going to rough it in the Altai Mountains of Kazakhstan for six weeks.

Then I remembered a short news story that I had written the previous year. The Shetland Islands were gaining a reputation as the best place in the British Isles to see orcas, or killer whales as they are more usually called. Not only that, but some contacts of mine were starting to call our most northerly archipelago 'Europe's Galápagos Islands'. It was suddenly very obvious to me – I'd go to Shetland in search of killer whales, and if I didn't encounter any there'd be plenty of other diversions to make a great feature – this was, after all, the best place in Britain to see otters and great skuas, had one of the most spectacular gannetries in Britain and was awash with thousands of other seabirds from Arctic terns to storm petrels.

But, as with most publications in the UK, my magazine wasn't going to fork out the air fare, car hire, accommodation and any other costs associated with, say, a week's stay on the islands, so I had to find someone who would. I had a contact at the Scottish tourist board, or VisitScotland as it likes to be known, so I fired off a quick email on the assumption that I'd then have to ring him in a week's time if I wanted anything to happen. As it turned out, I didn't have to wait a week, a day or barely even an hour. When would I like to go, my contact at the tourist office asked? This needed some thought – going over the data I'd used for my original news story the previous year, it was apparent that killer whale sightings slowly rose as the year progressed, only dropping off again around August and September. But if I wanted to see any of the seabirds for which Shetland is famous, I would do well to arrive before late July.

I emailed my contact for that original story about killer whales to see what he'd suggest, and I was pleased (again) to get an almost immediate response. He thought any time from mid-June onwards would give me an excellent opportunity for seeing arguably the ocean's most spectacular predator.

I got back to my tourist board contact – it was still that same day – and suggested a week outside of the hectic last two weeks of the magazine's four-weekly schedule, when time out of the office can be rather fraught. I then checked in with my editor to make sure that she agreed it was a good opportunity for the magazine.

The next thing I knew, the flight had been booked – Bristol to Shetland via Aberdeen – and the car hire arranged. Not only that, but this very helpful executive was suggesting they put me up in a self-catering apartment in the centre of Lerwick for the week, which I immediately liked the sound of – it meant that I could come and go as I pleased and therefore maximize my time searching for orcas and the other wildlife. Looking back on it, that was a very satisfying day's work.

So, why had it all gone so smoothly? How had I managed to turn one very simple idea – searching for killer whales in Shetland – into a flight to Lerwick in the space of about four or five hours? Well, the first thing to say is that I am in an extremely privileged position of being able to 'commission myself' to write travel features for the magazine, so I don't have to go through the awkward process of getting the promise from a tourist board to fund a trip only to find that no publication will take it.

Tourist boards will normally take considerably longer than they did in this case to weigh up the merits of investing in any journalist's idea – they want to be sure that the person in question can deliver what they have promised and that they will portray the destination in the light they're aiming for. That's not to say that tourist boards will try to influence what you write, but they will certainly ask themselves a question along the lines of, 'What's the agenda of the writer here? And does it align with ours?'

In this case, I had suggested a quest for killer whales. I might even have thrown in that remark about Shetland being the Galápagos of the North. Well, most tourist boards would charter an entire Boeing 727 if they thought they were going to get that sort of publicity. So it happened that my aim – casting a relatively well-known, though at that time undoubtedly under-represented destination in a new and, dare I say it exotic, light – happened to coincide reasonably well with theirs. From my point of view, I figured readers would love to know whether you could really see killer whales that easily in Britain, and the Galápagos tag was just the cherry on the top. If, on the other hand, I'd emailed with an idea of investigating whether the impacts of the *Braer* tanker disaster were still being felt by Shetland's marine wildlife, my man at the tourist board might not have booked those flights quite so readily.

From my point of view, what was also key was that the ball was in my court. While the tourist board did come up with some excellent suggestions for places to go and people to meet while I was in Shetland, it helped that I had made the initial contact with a simple, original angle. One place I hadn't planned on visiting was Fair Isle, the tiny island that lies about halfway between the southern tip of Shetland and the northern part of Orkney, but the tourist board organized a flight for me anyway.

It was great day out, even though it turned out that, just as I was flying back over Sumburgh Head in the south of Shetland at about 4 p.m. that afternoon, I was missing out on some killer whale action. I picked up my voicemail from my Shetland expert after I landed and rushed straight to the point where they had been seen, missing them by about an hour or two. Well, some things even tourist boards can't organize.

THE PR SPIN

THE SHETLAND VISIT CONTRASTS markedly with another trip I took for *BBC Wildlife* in 2004. On this occasion, I was contacted by the Heritage Lottery Fund (HLF) inviting me to write about some of the work they'd been funding on islands off the west coast of Scotland – Tiree, Mull and Islay. It sounded intriguing, but I was quite new to the game at this time, so I signed up to the trip when I probably shouldn't have done. The difference between this and my Shetland story was that all I had in this case was three completely unconnected ideas, involving corn-crakes on Tiree, white-tailed eagles on Mull and barnacle geese on Islay, with the only thing that they had in common being that the HLF had funded some conservation work in each instance. At the time, I just thought it would be fun to go – now I know that that doesn't necessarily make a story.

The press officer at the HLF had organized quite a hectic schedule that involved landing on Tiree on a scheduled flight from Bristol via Glasgow and spending a few hours there with the local RSPB warden before taking a tiny four-seater plane on to Mull. Here, we'd go looking for white-tailed eagles the next morning and then depart for Islay in the afternoon.

But the PR had planned this schedule without taking the weather into account. It was mid-October, just the time when pre-winter storms start to lash the already wind-whipped west coast of Scotland and, by the time we were getting ready to leave Tiree, the stiff breeze we'd been greeted by when we arrived had grown to practically gale-force wind. Our tiny, cobalt-blue charter plane – barely even four seats, from what I could tell – flew in looking like a flimsy, radio-controlled toy as it was buffeted by the wind, and our ageing pilot greeted us with the words, 'It's marginal, it's marginal. Come on, we'd better get going,' while looking like that was precisely the last thing he really wanted to do. The press officer looked at me quizzically. 'Is this a good idea?' It had already dawned on me that this was not a story that was worth dying for, but I just shrugged. The pilot wouldn't want to die, I figured. It wasn't quite the most terrifying thirty minutes of my life, but it wasn't far off it.

But, more important than the fear I put myself through is the fact that I fell for the PR spin, the allure of a few days out of the office. I should have seen it for exactly what it was and said, 'Thanks, but no thanks.' In contrast, Shetland was a great story partly because I had my own clear vision for it, which happened to align with the tourist board's goals.

THE PROS AND CONS OF THE FREEBIE

MANY PEOPLE FEEL THAT, by even taking a free trip, whether it's from a tourist board, which I've done many times, or from a tour operator, which I have also done frequently, you immediately hand over any claim you might have to being 'independent'. Indeed, this sort of person – and some of them are good friends of mine – would probably add that the whole travel journalism business is rotten to the core. I don't agree. It's true that I have rarely written negative stuff about any destination I've been to for a travel article, but that's because I research potential locations carefully and make sure that they will deliver the sort of wildlife experiences that our readers would also consider worthwhile. Killer whales in Shetland – what wildlife lover wouldn't want to know about that?

In fact, on occasions, I *have* reported places in a not-wholly-positive light – I was less than impressed with some aspects of Doñana National Park (in southern Spain) when I visited it for a piece I was writing about the quest for the world's rarest big cat, the Iberian lynx, and I said so; there are some well-known foibles among the people of north Cyprus (which involves them eating songbirds such as blackcaps and thrushes), and I wrote about that, too – but in neither case did I receive angry emails from the tourist board.

I think the only time I've had a negative reaction to something I've written was after staying at a luxury tented camp in Zambezi National Park in Zambia. In my piece for the magazine following this trip (which also included visits to Kafue and South Luangwa National Parks), I was critical of the way that the 4x4s went out at night in search of leopards, staying in radio contact and often tracking one single animal down to a particular thorn thicket. This didn't – it seemed to me – give that animal much chance of behaving normally. The owner of the camp wrote a long, defensive though ultimately good-natured email in response, but the boss of the tour operator that provided the trip certainly never complained, and remains a good friend to this day.

To many people who have never worked in travel journalism, however, the idea of a 'free trip' is probably anathema or at best slightly weird. As I work for *BBC Wildlife* magazine, I think many people assume that my trips are paid for by the BBC, but this is never the case. The magazine isn't even funded by the licence fee – until 2011 it was owned by BBC Worldwide, the commercial arm of the BBC, and the profits that the magazine made went back to the BBC and into film-making. In 2011, BBC Worldwide sold most of its magazines to a private publisher and now they are published under licence (so the publisher pays a fee to Worldwide). And despite the fact that there are some readers who appear to imagine that we share an office with Sir David Attenborough and the team of *Springwatch*, we're nothing to do with the BBC's natural history output and are actually a very small team – a total of about eight full-time members. So, we can't afford to send people off here, there and everywhere just to come back with a travel story.

Equally, when we pay roughly £500 for a travel story, a free-lancer can't afford to pay for a two-week safari experience and make any money. So, the vast majority of publications require trips to be provided free of charge for travel stories. But, as I said earlier, that doesn't necessarily mean that the journalist is automatically compromised. I think it's worth repeating here how *Lonely Planet Traveller* magazine is open and transparent about this issue, as well as being clear that it does not affect the honesty or accuracy of the reporting:

> [We] provide trusted, independent travel advice and infor-mation that has been gathered without fear or favour. We aim to provide you with options that cover a range of budgets and we reveal the positive and negative of all loca-tions we visit.
>
> Because we believe it is important that our journalists experience first-hand what they're writing about and because you require comprehensive information from every corner of the world, at times it may be necessary for us to seek assistance from travel providers such as tourist boards, airlines, hotels, national parks etc. However, when receiving such assistance, we ensure our editorial integrity and independence are not compromised through the following measures:
>
> By publishing information on all appropriate travel suppliers and not just those who provided assistance;
>
> By never promising to offer anything in return, such as positive coverage.

As I said earlier, not everyone agrees with this approach, and not just for ethical reasons. Here is what Simon Calder, the travel editor of *The Independent* puts on his website:

> I have the strap-line 'The man who pays his way' because I don't accept free transport or accommodation from the

travel trade. As a result of this somewhat curious and eccentric policy, I tend to meet a lot of very interesting folk. The people with the best stories to tell live life in the cheap seats.

This, of course, is absolutely true, and there have been times when I've been on an organized, free trip and I have longed to get off the carousel and just go it alone. But on trips tracking pandas in the Qinling Mountains of China, searching for proboscis monkeys, orangutans and other primates in Sabah on the island of Borneo, or whale-watching in the Azores, I wasn't going to have any joy if I didn't have an expertly organized trip and highly knowledgeable guides who knew exactly how to get results. I might have been able to sort something out for myself if I'd had six weeks to spare, but that's a luxury I no longer have – and nor do most freelance journalists (or our readers, for that matter).

Whether you can ask a tourist board or tour operator to organize a trip for you probably depends largely on the sort of publication you hope to be writing for. If its readers are the sort of people who wouldn't let a travel operator organize their break-out from Death Row, then the chances are that the publication won't be running pieces on a ten-day cruise to the Caribbean. However, if they are mostly senior and highly paid executives for whom taking a weekend out of the office is unusual, the chances are that they aren't going to be as interested in a piece about someone trying to overland it through the Darién Gap with nothing but a guitar to pay their way.

As with life, there is a spectrum to how people travel, and a travel writer has to decide where they want to be on that spectrum – completely independent of the travel business, completely engaged with it or somewhere in between. Personally, my ideal is to be somewhere in the middle: I've done fantastic stories, such as one about walking the length of the River Dart, without any assistance from any travel providers (I spent a couple of nights in a bivvy bag and a couple in cheap B&Bs), and I've done equally enjoyable stories, in places such as Tasmania, where the whole trip from start to finish was organized by the tourist board. Walking down the Dart, I could do exactly as I pleased, and there was an incredible sense of freedom – plus, it's proved popular with readers, and I still get emails from people who want to try and replicate it today, and this was back in 2005. But the Tasmanian Tourist Board really does know the best places to find and see its remarkable wildlife – on one trip, I went from eating my supper with eastern quolls (a small, vaguely weasel-like carnivorous marsupial) to watching duck-billed platypuses on a small pond within twenty-four hours. A few days later, I was in the north-east of the island spending a night with a couple of Tasmanian devils. I've been to Tasmania twice for the magazine, and it really is one of the best places in the world to get close to wildlife – the tourist board didn't have to organize that phrase, it's just how it is. If it weren't true, I wouldn't say it.

Of course, free trips are quite a different story in the USA, where there is more disapproval of the practice. The US version of *Condé Nast Traveler* (note the difference in spelling) has a print run of more than 800,000 and says it has 3.3 million readers every month, so it's got massive influence within the industry, and here's what it has to say about free trips:

> Travel sites often accept free or discounted trips and accommodations—not to mention gifts, products, and even outright payment—in exchange for editorial coverage. *Condé Nast Traveler* never has and never will. The magazine's editors and reporters pay the same prices you do and travel unannounced, except in rare cases where it's impossible to do so. This ensures that we experience travel the way you do—with no special recognition, treatment, or obligations—and are free to report our findings honestly, with no conflict of interest or ulterior motives. Although some of the contributors to our Daily Traveler blog engage in work outside *Condé Nast Traveler* that does not always follow these rules, when writing for us they adhere to our standard and are transparent about any of their affiliations and sponsorships.

It seems entirely plausible, I think, that writers who are paying their way will have a more authentic experience than someone whom it's well-known is writing for a leading national newspaper or travel magazine. But, equally, this is going to be truer where what they are writing about is directly connected to what is being provided free of charge. So, if a key part of your article is going to be about how soft the Egyptian cotton sheets were, how relaxing the spa or how good the food, then it stands to reason that a hotel might make an extra effórt in these areas than it might with an average paying punter. But when the place you are staying at is incidental to the experience – say, when visiting a historical site – then the fact that you are having your accommodation paid for becomes less of an issue.

But there's also the question of whether having something provided gratis makes a writer obliged, in some way, to the hotel or tour operator. What if the PR who organized the trip comes with you (this happens, particularly on group press trips)? You might find you get on really well – PRs are excellent at getting on with journalists, usually; it's their job – but does that mean you'll be less likely to highlight negative issues about the accommodation or another part of the experience? This is such a difficult area, and there are no easy answers. The solution is to remember that, as a travel writer, you are an independent and impartial observer of everything you see and hear – your 'duty', if you like, is to the readers of the article you're going to write.

It's worth saying here that, generally speaking, most magazines and newspapers do not take payments from tour operators or tourist boards for coverage, and where they do this it is made absolutely explicit – either such an article would be branded 'advertorial' (and though advertorials can resemble features, they are also sufficiently different in design to the publication's normal editorial to signal to the reader what's happening) or would be a clearly sponsored supplement.

It's also worth saying that the idea of journalists being bought off with gifts and products in return for a favourable piece is largely fantasy – I'm sure it happens now and again, but speaking for myself, I've never been given anything more valuable than the odd t-shirt. And, of course, that's just as it should be.

CONNECTING WITH COMMISSIONING EDITORS

IT'S PROBABLY WORTH CONSIDERING what is likely to work as a story and what is not. What will a commissioning editor go for and what will they turn down? This is far from an exact science, and part of the skill is getting to know the commissioning editor well enough so that you can, if not exactly read their mind, then at least have some idea what they might be thinking.

I know one freelancer who rings me about every two to three weeks and we get on very well and always chat at some length about what we've both been up to. Many of his ideas aren't quite right for the magazine, and he's not top of my list of 'Five Star' writers. So, is he wasting his time? Absolutely not, because he certainly gets commissions out of me, though usually for conservation news stories rather than travel features. In other words, time spent 'networking', even on the phone, is time well spent.

Then again, I know another freelancer – in fact, I can think of several – who rarely contacts me, but every so often comes out with an idea so brilliant I wonder why he hasn't mentioned it before. We get on well, which helps, but he can be elusive and you can be fairly certain he won't hit the deadline. But I love his work, and he writes for us on a regular basis. He appears to have plenty of work, and therefore doesn't see the need to network with the travel editor of *BBC Wildlife* magazine.

And I can think of occasional freelancers who I have found it extremely difficult to get on with, even when dealings were done, in the case of one writer, purely by email (this particular person lived in the Far East). The point is that it is worth making an effort with commissioning editors, unless you are already swimming in work, and sometimes even then. Remember – despite how some may appear to you or wish to present themselves – they are human, too. And if you can work out what makes them tick, you'll have a better idea of which stories they might commission and those they definitely won't.

DEVELOPING STORY IDEAS

So, WHAT DOES MAKE a good idea? There are a number of ways of thinking about this. The first, as previously mentioned, is to think of a country or a destination that's in the news for some reason that isn't necessarily anything to do with its potential as a travel destination, and see whether you can sell something on the back of that. At the time of writing, the big news stories were the general election in Pakistan and the ongoing civil war in Syria, while unlikely 'holiday' places such as North Korea and Mali had been hitting the headlines earlier in the year. None of these make for obvious trips – but if you'd already visited one of them, you might be able to sell something on the back of that.

For example, I spotted a piece in the online magazine *Sabotage Times* (which, to give you an idea of the sort of content it's looking for, was started by the former editor of *Loaded*, James Brown) by the freelance writer Jim Shelley about a trip to Timbuktu, headlined: 'Timbuktu: Misery in Mali's Mythical Slab of Sahara', which was perfect for a website that prides itself on taking a more anarchic approach to travel writing than most newspapers. If you weren't clear from the headline that this story wasn't going to be recommending the five-star hotels that offer the greatest massage in the Sahara, then the opening paragraph made it clear:

> A one-eyed terrorist-cum-smuggler responsible for the hostage crisis in Algeria; the jihadist group 'Al Qa'ida In The Islamic Naghreb' that exiled him; the enigmatic Tuareg nomads; the Malian military that was overthrown by their various, fractured alliances; and now troops from the French military with, David Cameron admits, British forces inevitably joining them ... It's hard to believe so many disparate, powerful forces are fighting over Mali. One of the poorest countries in the world, Mali is twice the size of France, but more than half of it is sand.

No one – or almost no one – is going to be reaching for their passport while reading this, and that, of course, is the point.

This is pure entertainment, the vicarious thrill of travel to a diverting and dangerous place.

But other events can be used to peg a story on: my killer whales, for example. Another classic pitch is a TV or movie 'tie-in'. So, at the beginning of February 2013, *The Guardian* ran a piece about Brooklyn in New York, because that's where the HBO hit series *Girls* is set. The peg was that the DVD of the first series was due to be released in the UK the following Monday, which feels a bit flimsy to me but clearly worked for the travel editor.

Another destination that has had a massive amount of exposure thanks to a TV series is Copenhagen – in this case, its fame springs from the gritty and huge crime hit *The Killing*. The *Daily Mail* ran a big piece about it in September 2011 – but this idea was so obvious it was nabbed by the travel editor of the paper. If *you* want to grab a travel editor's attention, you may need to be more imaginative: I'm sure someone somewhere ran a piece about Puducherry (or Pondicherry as it was previously known) after the UK release of the film *Life of Pi* came out (it's where Pi's family lives before they decide to emigrate), but I didn't see one – *The Guardian* ran a photo gallery, but that barely counts. I was intrigued to see a short piece in the free newspaper *Metro* about 1920s-style bars, pegged to the release of Baz Luhrmann's film *The Great Gatsby* in April 2013, almost a month before the film was due to hit British cinemas.

Another very obvious angle is where there is a new tourist 'product' on offer – new accommodation is one thing, but what's more likely to whet a travel editor's appetite is some sort of tour or experience that's just opened up. For example, I went on one of the early panda-tracking trips in China – I wasn't the first journalist to go, but our readers wouldn't have known much about what was a relatively new experience at that time. In any case, these sorts of travel products open up all the time: there could be a tour of Ireland's whisky distilleries or a week herding mustangs in the American mid-west. There was a time when the Earthwatch conservation volunteering 'holiday' was relatively novel and exciting, and newspapers and magazines wrote about them in their hundreds. Today, they are commonplace and, unless you come across something that is startlingly original, I don't think they will really excite most travel editors.

There is also another problem with the 'new product' idea. If you're relying on a press release for this sort of information, then the chances are that any half-awake travel editor will have seen it, too. Or, if they can't be bothered with press releases (which is not unfeasible, if they're anything like me), other freelancers may well have spotted and already pitched the idea.

At *BBC Wildlife*, I don't tend to commission ideas on this basis because we very rarely do 'products' in this way. I mostly delete any email from a PR company representing a tour operator the moment it enters my inbox, but I do keep on top of conservation charity and NGO news feeds, even if I don't necessarily use them for our conservation news pages (which I also edit). I'm always slightly amazed by freelancers who offer stories based on one of these press releases, particularly when it comes from one of the really major groups such as the WWF or the RSPB – I wonder why they don't think that I will have seen it as well. This approach strikes me as a bit lazy – when I get a pitch, I want to read something that I genuinely won't know about.

Another approach might be to think of anniversaries. Towards the end of the decade there will, no doubt, be a rash of articles featuring the Isle of Wight to coincide with the three great festivals that were held there between 1968 and 1970– incredibly, half a century will have passed since then by the time we get to 2018. It's always good to be thinking ahead (although pitching an idea five years in advance may look a bit keen!). Or you could go down a more serious historical route – the tearing down of the Berlin Wall in 1990 (it started in 1989) no doubt produced a slew of articles about the city in 2010 to coincide with the twentieth anniversary.

Another idea is to follow in the footsteps of another great traveller. An obvious example is Charles Darwin's trip to the Galápagos (done a million times, I'm afraid, if you fancy a trip), but really there are plenty of others. For my part, I'd love to recreate the journey Peter Matthiessen took with the eminent field biologist George Schaller for his iconic book *The Snow Leopard* (even better, I'd love to take the trip *with* George Schaller, though I suspect this is unlikely). I have ten years to prepare for the fiftieth anniversary of the trip, or I could aim for 2019 and the fortieth anniversary of the book's first publication in the UK. Again, there are any number of famous journeys to be recreated.

But it's also true to say that the majority of travel articles you see in national newspapers and magazines don't have any of these pegs, and you may be wondering why I think it is necessary to try and create one. To a certain extent, of course, it is possible to write in with a pitch that doesn't have a specific peg, other than it is a really interesting destination with great things to do. But if you're not an established freelancer, then you need something to make you stand out from the rest of the crowd. One approach might be to send in two or three ideas to a travel editor, one really standard, one with an interesting angle and one totally outlandish – that way, they will hopefully remember who you are when you ring up ('Ah, yes, you're the person who's going to swim *up* the River Amazon'). Don't pitch too many ideas at once, however – I've had people put nearly ten ideas in a single email. It smacks of a scattergun approach and even desperation, and it also suggests that the person isn't really wedded to any of them.

AND YOU'RE OFF . . .

So, LET'S ASSUME THAT you not only manage to persuade a magazine or newspaper travel editor into taking your idea, but you're also successful in getting a PR for a tourist board or tour operator to get you to your planned destination for free. You've done it – you've achieved the Holy Grail of travel writing, the free trip. What now? Check your passport's still valid? Pack the factor fifty sun cream? Well, possibly both, depending on where you're going, but I'm going to assume that you know both how to travel and what to take. We'll go through a few of the particular things that a travel writer might want to have with them later, but, for now, a few thoughts about pre-departure preparation.

You will already have done a fair bit of research about the destination, otherwise you wouldn't have sold your story, so you might think that there's nothing more you can do on that score. I'd disagree – at this point, my first instinct would be to go out and read something – a travel book, a history, anything – about the country that is nothing to do with what you're going to be writing about. If you have sold a piece about the hitherto unheard of thermal spas of Belarus, why not read something about its history – its devolution from the USSR, for example? You never know, it might give you an idea for another story you can sell, either before you go or perhaps when you get back. Not only that, but it might add something to the story you are already writing. You can never know too much about a country.

As I've said, I'm going to assume – I think it was a review of a Lonely Planet guidebook that said this – that you know how to get your backpack off the luggage carousel and that you arrive at your chosen destination safe and sound. What next? The most obvious thing to say is you need something to keep notes in. Everyone has their own preferences here, but I personally prefer something that is small enough to keep in a shirt or back pocket, so it's always with me (I rarely keep it in a daypack – it's more likely to be stolen or lost) and can be taken out at any moment. I wouldn't rely on tapping notes into a phone – it would be really annoying if the battery died on you just as you were getting some juicy quotes.

Again, people will have different ways of operating, but I'm quite an obsessive note-taker – descriptions of people and landscapes, records of brief conversations, even writing down funny or revealing signs. Most of what I write down never gets used, and on many occasions I will start writing a piece without actually referring to my notes. I might read them through once, just to remind me of my trip, but not every time. The point is – they're there. One thing I've always found is that just by taking a note of something, it sticks in your memory better, so you don't actually need to refer back to it.

I can still remember some notes I took of a menu at a tiny restaurant on Kovalam Beach in Kerala in the south of India in 1986. Though it doesn't sound terribly funny now, my travelling companions and I were delighted to find some of the items on the menu – 'banana filters' and 'scrab salad', for example, though without doubt my favourite at the time and to this day was 'green peace soup' – it wasn't long after the famous incident of the *Rainbow Warrior* being sunk in Auckland Harbour in New Zealand, and I remember joking about whether this particular soup came with little croutons of French security agents. I might have recalled these details anyway, but the very act of recording them in my travel diary probably gave my memory an extra shot.

Nevertheless, I think there's a certain skill to taking notes. When you first reach a destination, whether it's a big city or a vast and endless rainforest, one's first instinct is to notice quite general things – there's lots of people and it's very noisy or there are lots of trees and it's quiet. Perhaps a hundred years or so ago these might have been valid and interesting, but it's safe to say that times have moved on.

Actually, perhaps the fact that rainforests do tend to be very quiet *is* interesting – people might think they are full of the noise of large mammals crashing about in the undergrowth and monkeys and birds screeching and calling up in the canopy, but that isn't the case. One of the best descriptions I have read of a person's first experience of rainforest is contained in the foreword, written by the eminent tropical ecologist Thomas Lovejoy, to a book called *Tropical Nature* by Adrian Forsyth and Ken Miyata. There was no great obvious variety as he had been expecting, Lovejoy said; everything was just green and looked the same. It wasn't unbearably hot (it rarely is in forests of any sort) and the only things he could see moving were ants.

Not only is it spot-on, it is also a great example of someone who's paid attention to what they are seeing (and hearing) rather than what they expect to see (and hear). I particularly like the way he has focused on just a few details – the quietness, the green-ness, the ants – to produce a picture of the rainforest in very few words. In this situation, a travel writer might home in on the ants and describe them in greater detail or start walking through the forest and picking up on other things they see.

So, when you're taking notes, try and pick out these details, because you might forget them if you don't. These days, almost wherever you go in the world, you'll be writing about a place that people already know about, have preconceptions about and have seen photos of – indeed, there's a good chance they've been there themselves. Somehow, you've got to make your portrayal of a destination appear fresh without being misleading, and your ability to achieve that will, in part, be dictated by your ability to pick out details from a scene that other people might have missed – but still make your description of it ring true.

Descriptions of people are equally important – almost no piece of travel writing is complete without some human component, unless you happen to have gone to a part of the world that is completely uninhabited or are specifically writing a piece about spending two weeks entirely on your own in the middle of the Gobi Desert. What do they look like, what are they wearing? What does it say about them? Again, it's a question of finding some details that make this person stand out, and sometimes you may not know what those details are until later, perhaps until you've got home and are writing the piece, so it's better to have more information than less.

For example, I bet Zach Unger didn't have this second sentence in mind when he met the pre-eminent polar bear scientist Steven Amstrup for a piece he was doing for *Pacific Standard* magazine entitled 'The Fuzzy Face of Climate Change', but he certainly wouldn't have been able to write it if he hadn't recalled the particular details:

> With sandy-blond hair, a square jaw, and broad shoulders, no wonder the cameras loved Amstrup. To this day, he remains the only person I've ever met who can look suave while wearing thermal underwear and a hat with chinstraps.

Of course, I can't be sure that Unger methodically noted down that Amstrup happened to be wearing thermal underwear and a hat with chinstraps, but it would certainly have helped if he had.

TAKING QUOTES

NATURALLY, YOU DON'T JUST describe what people look like, you also record their conversations. This is vital, but how do you do it and are there any rules? The first thing I'd say is that there are two types of quote that you might collect while on your trip: the first, and most obvious kind, is from a pre-arranged interview or conversation. This might be with a guide or expert who knows that you are writing an article, and it could be that you specifically sit down over a meal or cup of coffee to conduct the 'interview'. The second type of quote you might record is the more casual remark of someone who doesn't know who you are or what you're doing, and this could be anybody from the person serving you a beer to someone you run into at the museum. The distinction between the two types of quote is not always as clear-cut as that but, for the moment, let's assume that it is.

The first type of quote – from those who know what you're doing – sounds reasonably straightforward, but there are all sorts of potential pitfalls here. First of all, much will depend on how long you are spending with this person – an hour or two or four or five days? If you've only got an hour, then it's vital that you mine this seam as deeply as possible. If they are a key expert for your story, you've got to make sure that they are prominent, well described and come through clearly in the piece. You might want to sit them down straight away, so that you can get the interview (and relax), but it's equally possible that they're showing you round a particular quarter of a city, a castle or a museum. Can you walk and write at the same time? Probably not. I can't.

You might, then, ask this person if you can sit down at the end of the tour for half an hour so that you can take notes, but what if they don't have time? And then there's the other thing – people often say the most interesting things while showing you things. Sometimes, you just have to try and hold a particular quote in your head and write it down later. The travel writer Don George – who has also written an excellent guide to being a travel writer published by Lonely Planet – describes his approach to this problem:

> Whenever I have a conversation I want to remember, I imme-
> diately jot down as much of [it] as I can. It's often awkward
> to start writing in front of the person I'm quoting, so if I'm

talking to someone over a meal in a restaurant, for example, I'll excuse myself and go to the restroom, then write feverishly. Paul Theroux once told me that he uses this technique. Now, whenever I'm waiting interminably for someone to vacate a restroom, I imagine Paul Theroux is inside, scribbling.

At journalism school, this was called 'doing a brain-dump' (as a journalist, of course, the whole point was to take notes as the person talked, and this was only to be used in a situation where, for example, a dictaphone had failed to record a conversation). Don George and Paul Theroux are quite right in advocating it as a way of operating. But George's book was first published in 2005, and personally I think a lot of the time you can avoid this situation by using a digital recorder or even your smartphone (as long as you keep the previously mentioned battery issues in mind!).

I have an Edirol recorder, which is small, easy to use and can be turned on and off very simply as you're walking around. If I'm with someone who knows what I'm up to, I will show it to them when we meet and say that I'll be recording our conversations. I find that as long as I hold it within four to six feet of their mouths (assuming there isn't a lot of background noise), it picks up perfectly what they are saying. It's great for a situation where taking notes would be problematic or where, for example, you feel it particularly important to capture every nuance of what they are saying (which isn't always possible if you are taking notes). To date, I have stayed with the Edirol over my smartphone because the recordings are good enough to be used in podcasts, which I also do for the magazine, but it does mean carrying an extra item. You need to find out what you are most comfortable using and make sure you understand exactly how it works before you set off. You don't want to be reading the instruction manual and inserting batteries just as your expert tells you they've got to go in ten minutes.

Before we move on, I have two words of warning about recording conversations in this way. The first is that you can end up with a lot of material that you then have to wade through when you get back from your trip. You have to decide whether you are going to transcribe it all, so that you have a written record of everything or whether you just pick out the bits you want. You also need to keep a permanent copy of the sound file, so that you have proof that the person said what you quoted them as saying, just as you should keep all your notebooks. In many ways, it is more efficient to take notes and highlight the good quotes later that evening or on the flight home.

The second thing about recording conversations is that you might run out of space to store the files, unless you have a laptop with you onto which you can download the audio files. I used to take my laptop on long trips – anything more than a few days – because I needed to download photos, but I try to avoid doing it these days, particularly since flashcards have a much bigger memory than they did when I first started using a digital camera around 2004.

Another basic but easy-to-overlook thing to consider is spare batteries – some rechargeable batteries let me down for an interview I was conducting for a podcast once, but luckily I was, quite literally, in the pub about fifty yards from my front door, and was able to sprint back home and get some more while my interviewee sipped his pint. Of course, that won't usually happen, so if you decide you want to record interviews and conversations, spare batteries are something you'll have to carry with you.

The other thing to say about taking quotes from people who know you're a writer is that, if you are spending several days with a person, there are clearly going to be many conversations covering all kinds of territory. Can you regard anything they say as fair game for your article? What if they confess to having had an affair with the receptionist at the hotel? Well, hopefully, you'd have enough of a conscience to feel that that was out of bounds and irrelevant anyway. What if they told you that the famous painting in the museum was a fake, but the director of the museum didn't want to admit it? That could be a fabulous scoop for your article, but the chances are that they don't want it appearing in print (not to mention the potential libel issue if you did print the accusation against the director, but that's another matter). Personally, in such a situation, I'd show interest and then ask (the classic question), 'Can I quote you on that?' If they suddenly realize what they've done and are horrified by the idea, you should just forget it.

Remember this: you're a travel writer, not Woodward or Bernstein uncovering the truth behind Richard Nixon's bugging of the Watergate building, and a simple maxim to remember when thinking about quotes is, 'Would this person happy to be quoted saying this?' If you're not sure, have a think about it – why not, what's awkward about the quote? If you're any doubt, in these days of email, you can always check back with the person. The chances are, whether you've spent two hours or two weeks with this person, a certain level of trust and friendship has developed between you. Do you really want to damage that friendship because of how you portray them? If you're still not convinced, think of it like this – what if the person in question complained to your editor about the way that they had been quoted? Even if, on balance, your editor felt you had been justified in what you had written, they might think twice about using you next time. It's not a question of censoring the truth, it's a question of taking a human, thoughtful approach to the way you report things.

As with everything, there are, of course, exceptions to even this. If you have sat down and are doing a very formal, recorded interview (or even if you are just taking notes), particularly if it is with someone who is used to talking to the media, then to a certain extent whatever they say is fair game. I have heard some journalists take the view that if an interviewee says something, and then tells you that it isn't for quoting, you can ignore their 'request' – only if they say beforehand that something isn't for quoting, and you agree, is it valid. I disagree, however. The key thing for me is to remember who you are talking to and why, and to take that into account when writing your piece. As a writer, you are in a certain position of power, and you should use that power carefully and conscientiously.

Now we come to the second type of conversation, with people who don't know who you are and probably don't care. They can, of course, say interesting and revealing things, so it's always worth looking out for them. They might be hotel receptionists, barmen, people in the street or other travellers or members of your tour group (who may know who you are but wouldn't necessarily expect you to be writing down what they say). You're most likely to be quoting them to add some colour to a scene, and it's not necessarily important to identify them by name. Indeed, if it's a casual remark, such as 'Don't go wandering about the hotel grounds at night, you might run into a hungry elephant,' then it would be distinctly odd to start taking out your notebook and then ask the person for their full name and age.

Instead, remember the quote – if you think it might be useful in your piece – and write it down later. If you find that you strike up a nice rapport with the receptionist, and you find out he's called David and other details about him, then you might feel it's worth saying a bit more about him – he might become part of the story. But again, if it's possible that a quote that you use could embarrass the person (particularly if you identify who they are), think twice. How would you feel if someone did that to you?

TAKING PHOTOS

THE THIRD CRITICAL WAY of recording your trip is, of course, taking photos. There are dozens of books about being a travel photographer, and it is certainly a very useful skill for any writer to have because it can increase your earnings greatly. Many magazines will pay almost as much for photos as for the words, and I've been to many destinations that are not well-photographed (many parts of the Cayman Islands, for example, have been routinely ignored by travel photographers, as has much of North Cyprus), so it was important that I came back with some. But taking good travel photos is a skill in itself, and though I don't pretend that I am anything more than a workman-like snapper, there are a few things to say on this matter.

The first thing is that just having a photographic record of your trip can be useful when you come to write it up. Sometimes looking back over the pictures can trigger a few memories or thoughts, though images are largely inferior to written notes. You might be able to use a snapshot to later identify a particular flower or bird or it might be a way of recording a particular sign or interpretation board at a historical site. But if you're only using your pictures for this reason, you don't need anything more than a cheap-ish, easy-to-use, fits-in-your-pocket digital camera.

The second thing is to think very carefully about whether you really have what it takes to make the photography side of your travel-writing business pay its way. It sounds like a great idea, but if you're going to take photos that newspapers and magazines want to buy, you'll have to invest in a DSLR camera and probably a couple of lenses, and while you will probably have a laptop and/or desktop computer on which to download and store your images, ideally you will need a software package such as Photoshop to process and improve those images. You'll also need to know how to use it. It's a lot of extra time, effort and money. My guess is that a lot of writers see it as a nice hobby that may bring in a bit of extra money over the years, while I think that bloggers regard it, rightly, as essential. Of course, they can afford to have a cheaper, lower-quality camera because their images are only appearing on the web.

Q&A WITH SUSIE DE CARTERET

SUSIE DE CARTERET HAS worked in the tourism business as a public relations consultant for nearly twenty years. She runs her own business, Juicy Communications, which handles publicity for the Cayman Islands, and she recently launched her own tour operator, Tasmanian Odyssey.

How did you get started working as a PR in tourism?
I started in the hospitality industry, working as the marketing manager for a five-star London hotel. At some point, I had to employ a PR company, and for various reasons, I ended up moving to the agency. Around the same time, the agency picked up the accounts of two or

three quite high-spending tourist boards – the Cayman Islands, Arizona and Indonesia. This was around 1994.

Then what?
That gave me access to some quite high-powered travel editors and journalists, and on the back of Indonesia, we picked up Tasmania, so by now we were working for ten or fifteen different destinations or their tourist boards. Then I moved to Jersey, and though I was quite happy being a director of the agency, I decided to set up my own company.

What's the secret of good PR?
As long as you employ basic common sense, the rest of it is about relationships. You have to have certain skills – I can write a press release in two seconds flat and that helps. You've got to be able to get your head around a subject quickly. It is all about communication, whether written communication or talking with people. It's not rocket science. You need a certain amount of marketing nous, but that's just instinct.

What do travel writers need to know about the PR business?
Our job in PR is to deliver increased bookings for the places that we send writers to. If that doesn't happen, we're wasting our time. Journalists have to understand that there are people who are hoping to benefit from what they write, but most writers do not appreciate that. And, so, if their piece fails to carry the appropriate information in the factbox, the travel editor of the newspaper or magazine will have the PR moaning at them down the phone. The travel editor doesn't necessarily care, but they certainly don't want that hassle.

What makes a great piece of travel writing?
Whether it really zings or ticks the box. The best pieces

make your heart soar and you want to read them again and again and again. You can always tell if somebody loved the place they visited or if they didn't.

What pieces are you really pleased to have been involved with?
I remember one time when I read a film review of *The Hunter*, a film about searching for the Tasmanian tiger in Tasmania, in the *Daily Telegraph*. I tweeted the reviewer, Tim Robey, and then contacted the travel editor of the *Telegraph* to see if they'd be interested in running a story about the Tasmanian tiger from Tim. And that's what happened – and it was a great piece, a double-page spread in the paper.

Any others?
Well, I'd wanted to get Robin Lane Fox, the gardening correspondent for the *Financial Times*, down to Tasmania to see some of its gardens for ages. So I asked him if he'd be interested in going, and it turned out it was his life-long ambition. The pieces that he wrote made me cry, and I never cry about gardens. Since they appeared in the newspaper, I've had calls from people all over Europe saying that they want to go to Tasmania.

What about bad pieces?
Well, there was quite a well-known writer who wanted to go to Tasmania and see a Tasmanian devil, but she only wanted to stay in five-star hotels during the trip. It was a nightmare to arrange. She got a double-page spread in a national broadsheet, but all she did was rave and rave about a place that cost $2,000 a night. Now, that's not going to appeal to a normal visitor to Tasmania.

You have to deal with quite demanding people, then?
Yes, there was another time when we were due to send A.A. Gill [a well-known critic and columnist] and his

partner [Nicola Formby] to Tasmania. A couple of months before they were due to leave, I got a call from Nicola saying, 'Is there any reason why we can't go to Tasmania in March?' And I said, 'No, there isn't, but you're going in February.' And she said, 'A's just been offered a week on a yacht in Barbados and doesn't want to go any more.' So, I said, 'Well, go to Barbados, because if he goes to Tasmania now it will just rain for the entire time he's there.' In fact, as we found out, there is a very good reason why you shouldn't go to Tasmania in March – that's when devils are mating, and they disappear. We took A up to see the devils, and it was nearly a disaster, because for the first half of the night, nothing turned up, because they were all down their dens, well, mating. Eventually, two did turn up, so it was OK in the end.

Do you work with journalists from specialist magazines, or just national newspapers?
I love working with specialist magazines. OK, the circulation tends to be smaller, and the readership tends to be more disparate in the way that they book their holidays, which can be problematic for us. It can be harder to get a fully funded trip as a result, so it can be more expensive to set up. The benefit is that you are dealing with a more informed audience and you have got a writer who knows what they are talking about.

What don't you like about working with journalists?
I hate it when I get approached by people who say, 'I see you do PR for Turquoise Holidays, have you got any trips going out to the South Pacific soon?' I wonder who they think I am – they must know that they must have a commission before I send them anywhere and they have to know what they are talking about. They also have to realize that the PR exec will know what's already appeared in the press. Getting a story together is a collaborative effort, but not all journalists realize that.

What advice do you have for travel writers just starting out?

Well, it's important that a journalist says, 'Thank you' at the end of a trip. You never know when you may run into someone again. One thing that journalists may not realize is that we are being judged by auditors, not people who appreciate the lovely column inches we've achieved as a result of our PR campaigns. Your beautiful prose will mean nothing to the guy who is auditing the government accounts and has to decide whether that PR campaign was money well spent or not. And these days, the travel industry is becoming more scrutinized and harder to work in every day. Even when travel is a major part of a country or destination's GDP, it is heavily scrutinized, more so than ever.

4. DIGITAL WORLD: BECOMING A TRAVEL BLOGGER

In May 2011, *The Atlantic* – a US-based political, cultural and literary magazine and website – published an interview with the writer Paul Theroux, one of the true fathers of modern travel writing. Theroux had just published a new book *The Tao of Travel*, which is a sort of miscellany of observations and insights from the author and other writers ranging from Mark Twain to Pico Iyer. The interviewer – a noted travel writer himself, Rolf Potts – had the temerity to describe the 'aggregated aspect' of the book as being 'a little blog-like'. In his article, Potts does not comment on exactly how Theroux took to this suggestion, merely printing his response in simple, reported speech, but there's little doubt that Theroux wasn't impressed.

> You could say blog-like, but I think 'blog-like' is a disparaging term. I loathe blogs when I look at them. Blogs look to me illiterate, they look hasty, like someone babbling. To me writing is a considered act. It's something which is a great labor of thought and consideration. A blog doesn't seem to have any literary merit at all. It's a chatty account of things that have happened to that particular person.

One suspects that many established writers may share his view. Blogging can seem rushed, ill-thought-out, poorly structured, self-indulgent and frankly trite at times. With the best will in the world, most blogs are probably best left to the blogger's family and friends to read so that they know what they're up to. But Theroux dismissing all blogs in this way misses the point: it would be a bit like Salman Rushdie sounding off about the literary failings of chick-lit. For a start, chick-lit has proven to be enormously successful, so some writers must be doing something right and, secondly, it's not really aimed at him. The crucial thing is this: if you aspire to be a travel writer, don't immediately dismiss the possibilities of blogging. Gary Arndt didn't.

Gary had already written a few 'trial blogs' before he set off on a round-the-world trip in 2007, and there was never any doubt that he would do so again. 'About nine months into my trip I was in Hong Kong and I began thinking seriously about what I was doing online', he writes on his website. 'Not many people were reading my site. I probably knew the names of most of my readers because they were friends and family. I decided to rethink how I was doing things and began to take the site more seriously.'

And it worked. As of January 2012, he says that his website Everything Everywhere (http://everything-everywhere.com) has 100,000 visitors each month, and he has more than 15,000 RSS and email newsletter subscribers. In 2010, the blog was named by *Time* magazine as one of the top twenty-five blogs in the world. Not bad for a boy from Wisconsin who didn't see salt water (as he puts it) until he was twenty-one. Having previously owned a business that he sold in 1999, the blog is now Gary's business, and it allows him to travel virtually 365 days of the year. In the six years since he started travelling full time, he's visited seven continents, 116 countries and territories, all fifty US states, nine of the ten Canadian provinces, every Australian state and territory and more than 180 Unesco World Heritage Sites. Gary is a well-travelled man.

What struck me about Gary, apart from the fact that he's making enough money from his website to fund full-time travel, mostly through advertising and affiliate marketing, is that this is now what he does, as opposed to it being a path to a more conventional travel-writing model. 'I have no desire to be a mainstream travel writer,' he told me by email from Barcelona while attending a tourism digital marketing conference at which he was due to speak the next day. 'I don't see the point in it. Right now the value in what I'm doing is the fact that I have my own audience, and that audience is growing. Writers do not have a personal following. Most people have no clue who wrote a given article in a magazine and, even if they do see the name, they know nothing about the person.'

This, by the way, is pretty much spot-on. I occasionally get emails from people who comment on a particular piece I have written, and every now and again I am pleasantly surprised when someone tells me that they enjoy what I write, but unless you have a regular column with your name in seventy-two-point type or there's a photo of you accompanying your article that's more than just a tiny thumbnail, the chances are nobody knows and nobody cares who actually wrote it.

'Right now,' Gary continued, 'I make more than ninety-eight per cent of all travel writers and that will only go up as my audience expands and the industry warms up to bloggers. Having no background as a writer, I don't view writing for prestigious publications to be the pinnacle of my career.'

So what makes Gary's blog successful? I think what he does is to combine what I would call classic magazine craft with a straightforward no-nonsense style of writing. Take this post from October 2012 called '9 ways I break Conventional Travel Wisdom', in which he describes some of the ways he defies the sort of advice frequently found in travel books. There is nothing especially revolutionary here – he doesn't travel light, he says, he doesn't have a frequent-flyer credit card, he doesn't use hand sanitizers and he doesn't bother with guidebooks. Here's what he has to say about that old staple of the backpacker, the moneybelt:

There are easier ways to foil pickpockets than wearing a special undergarment just for your currency. Just buy pants with deep front pockets and that will pretty much solve the problem. Likewise, I don't use a passport holder that goes around my neck. I keep my passport in a pocket of my Scottevest jacket. If you do get mugged by someone with a weapon, your money belt isn't going to fool anyone. It isn't as if money belts are a secret [that] muggers in other countries don't know about.

It's pretty prosaic stuff, so you can immediately see why a literary master such as Paul Theroux might not take to blogging, and Gary has plenty more in this vein, including 'Seven tips for Visiting an Art Museum', 'The Single Biggest Travel Safety Tip' ('Stay away from nightclubs'), 'Gary's 20 Immutable Laws of Air Travel', '8 Things You Might Not Have Known about South Africa' and almost any other place Gary has visited. And so on.

It's a shame that some of his posts are let down by inaccuracies: South Africa, he writes, is home to the world's largest mammal (the bull elephant), the smallest mammal (the dwarf shrew) and the fastest animal (the cheetah) – actually, he's wrong on all three counts (the largest mammal is the blue whale, the smallest is Kitti's hog-nosed bat and the fastest animal, though this can be debated, is the peregrine falcon). Many of his posts, however, are refreshingly novel and thoughtful. 'The Futile Quest for the Authentic Experience', for example, runs counter to much of the travel writing that is published in print or on the internet. Here's an excerpt:

> When an ethnic restaurant opens up in a western country, that's diversity. When a western restaurant opens up in a non-western country, that's cultural imperialism. If diversity is good for us, why isn't it good for others? Preservation of culture is considered an asset when practised by other countries, but a liability when practised at home. There are more Chinese restaurants in the US than McDonald's, Burger Kings, Wendy's and KFCs COMBINED. I don't think anyone is worried about a Chinese cultural takeover of America. A few McDonald's and Starbucks overseas is hardly an invasion.

Everything Everywhere is largely funded through three key sponsors: the adventure tour company G Adventures, the travel app TripIt and the travel clothing company Scottevest. Gary is effusive in his praise for all three sponsors. This may sound suspiciously like he's being bought, but Gary denies it. 'Even before becoming an official sponsor, I was singing the praises of Scottevest to anyone who would listen,' he writes. On balance, I believe him. (His unrequested vocal enthusiasm probably helped to attract his sponsor.)

Gary also does gear reviews (which is where the affiliate marketing comes in – basically, he recommends a product and, if you go and buy one after clicking away from his website, Gary gets a commission), but I think the main attraction of the site is his 'man-on-the-sun-lounger', 'Honest John' approach. There is plenty that is wrong with it, but he's got something to say and he says it loudly and clearly. As we will see, this is one of the keys to being a well-read blogger.

There are many other bloggers like Gary out there. Take Ayngelina Brogan, who – again in her own words – 'left an amazing job, boyfriend, apartment and friends to find inspiration in Latin America. I'm creating a new life choosing what I want instead of what other people think I should do.' She's doing this via a website called 'Bacon is Magic' (www.baconismagic.ca), a gastronomic guide to Latin America, with a few European destinations such as England, Germany and Austria thrown in. Most of her posts use photography as much as they use words, and that's a crucial aspect of many successful travel blogs. Here's a post from January 2013:

Dear London, I was wrong about you. I thought that you were just an expensive, boring city with bad food. But now I realize I wasn't giving you a proper chance to show me your good side. Tonight as I exited my apartment in Camden I saw someone getting a mohawk and asked if I could come in and take his photo. I ended up having a great conversation in the barbershop and realize you do have a more interesting side. And you know the funny thing is I think Toronto suffers from the same issue. The city is terrible for tourists unless they know someone . . . It turns out your interesting side is far away from the museums and tourist attractions but in the neighborhoods. I'm calling a truce. I will no longer say bad things about you – except about your food because you haven't proven me wrong about that – yet.

There is nothing stunningly original or insightful about this piece of writing but, like Gary Arndt, Ayngelina has a devoted following, including nearly 10,000 'Likes' on Facebook, and that means she has a product – her blog – that is valuable to sponsors and advertisers. I contacted Ayngelina to ask her the same questions I asked Gary, and I got very similar answers. 'I am purely a blogger,' she told me in an email. 'I also blog for other sites from time to time but I do not consider myself a freelance writer or journalist. Blogging requires many different skills than simply writing and while I think I am a very good blogger, I will never win a Pulitzer [Prize] for my writing.'

She also goes on to say that the blog is really a kind of online CV or showreel, demonstrating what she can do for people who may want to hire her: 'I have no desire to be published elsewhere unless it addresses a need for my site, but blogging is basically an online portfolio and it has opened up opportunities for me in marketing consulting work, particularly in Latin America.'

To a certain extent, Ayngelina is not a helpful example of a successful blogger, because writing is not her primary motive. All she's really doing is shouting from the digital rooftops, 'Look at how I draw attention to myself – I could do it for your business, too', while making some money from the website at the same time. Some people might consider this anathema to the whole principle of writing, the idea that it's all about attracting attention rather than the ideas expressed or the stories told. I even think that myself, but clearly there is a lesson here for all of us: there's no point in writing a blog that's only read by your partner and your mum, whatever your ideas.

The problem you've got as a blogger is that you're not just a writer. If you're writing for a magazine or newspaper, there are many other people in the chain that help make your article a success – there's the commissioning editor who gave you the brief, there's the sub-editor who sharpened your copy, corrected the spelling mistakes and checked the facts, there's the picture editor who selected the images to go with the piece (and the photographer who took the shots in the first place, unless you supplied your own) and the designer who laid out the pages to make the reader stop at the first spread and decide to read the piece.

As a blogger, you have to be all these people. You have to

consider what sort of platform you use or whether you pay someone to design a website for you. You have to take the photos yourself and then select the ones that will go up on the site. You have to proofread every word yourself, and eliminate as many mistakes as possible (some are bound to slip through if you're doing it all yourself).

But, above all, you've got to devise a compelling reason for people to read your blog. Given the sheer limitlessness of the internet, what will make your blog stand out from the crowd? There are three key things you have to do.

First of all, like Gary and Ayngelina, you have to develop a clear, strong and likeable voice. In the same way that reading such modern masters of travel writing as Bill Bryson and Chris Stewart (of *Driving over Lemons* fame) is like taking a trip with them yourself, your blog's readers have got to enjoy your company.

Second, try to develop a purpose to your blog. If you're just travelling around the world having fun, however well written it is, it's going to be harder to attract readers. Some blog-sites, such as WildJunket (www.wildjunket.com) have specialized in adventure travel, while Jodi Ettenberg's Legal Nomads blog (www.legalnomads.com) describes itself as the place 'where culture, food & travel intersect'. Both blogs are very clear about the sort of readers that will enjoy them and that's a great start.

Third, be opinionated. Subtlety simply doesn't work as well on the internet, where every voice is shouting out to be heard. In 2013, we still read books and magazines (even if on a Kindle or other e-reader) differently to the way we 'consume' content on the web. We scroll through pages on our computers, tablets or iPhones, barely giving anything more than a few seconds to attract our attention before moving onto the next site, while we sit down with a novel with the notion that we've got half an hour to invest in it and we'll stick with it even if we have to wade through a paragraph or two that we don't really enjoy.

As with any form of travel writing, read around plenty of sites before you start, and get a feel for what other people are doing. There are a number of bloggers who can help with marketing and – if you feel you want to try it – with 'monetizing' your site. One is Nomadic Matt (www.nomadicmatt.com) who's written a book called *How to Make Money with Your Travel Blog.* Matt says that he makes $8,000 a month from his, so he knows what he's talking about.

Or, there's Chris Guillebeau, who's been on a mission to visit all 193 countries that are recognized by the UN. Chris also makes money from his blog through selling 'e-zines' (magazines that are only available in digital form), affiliate marketing and some consultancy work, and he is even prepared to share the secrets of his success for nothing through a downloadable PDF called *279 Days to Overnight Success.* This is Chris' six-point strategy for making your blog a success:

1 Create a Compelling Story and Be Remarkable
2 Clearly Answer the 'Reason Why'
3 Prioritize Writing and Marketing Over Everything Else
4 Be Bigger than I really Am
5 Build Long-Lasting Relationships
6 Carefully Introduce Products and Services

So, ignoring the creative use of capital letters and a tendency to waffle (what exactly does 'Be Remarkable' mean here?), here's what's being said: points one and two I referred to earlier – these are about creating a purpose for your blog and telling people about yourself. Point three is – well, if you're writing a blog, make sure you write a blog on a regular basis. Chris says his goal is to write at least 1,000 words a day, though this isn't always for his blog. He updates the blog at least twice a week, and some of his posts are 2,000 words long. So, it's quite a schedule he's trying to keep up. Most bloggers go in for shorter posts (with lots of photos), and I would say that this is more usual. Point three, marketing, involves connecting with people via social networking sites such as Twitter, or working on a product launch, perhaps for something like an ebook. Point four is to write as if your site is read by more people than it really is. Even if you've only got 100 readers, assume you've got thousands, he says. I think point five is interesting – in the same way that a magazine editor must correspond with readers (particularly the tricky, vocal ones), a blogger must communicate with readers. Publishing, whether on the internet or in print, is not a one-way relationship, and just as a reader listens to what writers or bloggers have to say, so they expect to be listened to as well. Point six is the 'monetization' part. Remember, as a blogger, you're a solo publishing operation – writer, editor and advertising sales executive rolled into one.

Chris says that you only need to attract 1,000 followers or subscribers before you can start making money from your site, which doesn't strike me as an impossible number. In *279 Days to Overnight Success*, he says:

> Remember, people follow other people to be informed, entertained, and inspired. Generally, your content must clearly address at least one of these needs. Some of the best advice I heard for going from an average site to a remarkable one came from John Wesley over at 'Pick the Brain'. This is what he said: 'With our site there was definitely a turning point where it went from being about what I wanted to what the readers wanted. This attitude has been a big part of our success in growing the site.' Since John first said that in a round-up interview I did, I've thought about it at least a couple of times a month when planning my new content.

One thing that may be becoming clear by now is that the vast majority of bloggers who make money from their sites are from North America and particularly the United States. It seems clear to me that, with their arguably greater entrepreneurial zeal, Americans have understood and exploited the new digital opportunities of the web to a much greater extent than people in the UK.

But there are some Brits out there bravely pioneering their own, eclectic way through the online jungle. One of them is Mike Sowden, who blogs at Fevered Mutterings: Misadventures in Travel & Storytelling (http://mikesowden. org/feveredmutterings). Like the other bloggers, I've looked at so far in this chapter, Mike is successful because he has clear points to make, which he does in an entertaining and mostly straightforward way. There's a quite a lot of material on the site that analyzes how to be a successful blogger.

One typical post is headed 'These 3 Stories Can Kill Your Blog'. It describes the three most common mistakes that bloggers make, which often result in them abandoning their blog entirely. Mike cites a survey, published in 2008, which found that ninety-five per cent of all blogs have not been updated in the past 120 days and are therefore inactive. An article in the *New York Times* quoted Richard Jalichandra, the chief executive of the company responsible for the survey, as saying that while there are between 7 and 10 million active blogs on the internet – this is back in 2009, remember – somewhere between 50,000 and 100,000 (so 0.01 per cent, give or take) are generating most of the page views. While the number of active blogs may increase over time, you can probably assume that the percentage of those that are attracting most of the attention will not. 'There's a joke within the blogging community that most blogs have an audience of one,' Jalichandra said. There are two points to learn from this: first, that it's really easy to start a blog, but much harder to keep it going; and second, that unless you do something special, by the sheer laws of probability, it's most likely that your blog will end up being read only by your mother.

So, what will kill your blog? Mike relates three well-known stories to make his point: first, the 1989 American film starring Kevin Costner, *Field of Dreams*, about a farmer who digs up his cornfield to build a baseball diamond. 'The message is timeless and resonant: if you have a dream and you hang onto it hard enough and long enough, that dream will come true,' Mike writes. But he suggests that in the real world, and in the world of blogging, this is nonsense and will lead to a 'digital malfunction': nobody will read your blog. How often? 'Oh, probably about ninety-five per cent of the time.' So point one is that just having a dream isn't enough.

Mike then uses the analogy of *The Wizard of Oz* – 'A bunch of lovable screw-ups [who] walk a long, long road in search of someone who will magically fix all their problems in ways they never, ever could' – to say that you can't rely on magic to fix the problems with your blog.

Finally, he takes the story of *The Road*, Cormac McCarthy's dystopian tale of a father and son wandering the highways of the USA in a post-apocalyptic world to satirize pointless blogging:

> Everything is dying around you. You don't know why you keep going – there's no plan, nothing to guide you, and you've given up looking for guidance – but you keep going anyway. Day after day. Nothing really improves, but that's not the point – it's about basic survival. You have nothing to look forward to, nothing to aim at and nothing you really want to say. All you have left is just keeping going.

The film analogies might be a little overcooked, but the main thing to take away from them is that, if you want to blog and be taken seriously, think about it like you would any other business. What are you trying to achieve and how are you trying to achieve it? What are you trying to say? Why do you think people will listen to you? If you can't answer those questions, then stop right now and don't start again until you can. Otherwise, you too might get stuck on The Road without even reaching first base. If you're dreaming of a home run, forget it.

As with the other bloggers, I contacted Mike by email to ask him a few questions (and also spoke to him on the phone for the interview at the end of this chapter). The first thing that was immediately clear was that, unlike his US counterparts, he's making very little money from the blog, but it does act as a way to help him find freelance work. He gets somewhere between 400 and 1,500 visitors a day, which clearly isn't on the same scale as Gary Arndt or Nomadic Matt, although he does get name-checked by a number of these more wide-reaching bloggers.

All this suggests that the British market for travel blogging just isn't as developed as it is in the US or Canada. Even though, clearly, the internet does not recognize national borders, perhaps there is still a certain tribalism to the way we follow blogs. Though Mike's blog has enabled him to become a full-time writer, he has struggled with his motives for doing it. 'I've spent years struggling with defining my reason for having a blog,' Mike admitted in his email. 'At various times, it has felt like a business, an addiction, a waste of time and the best thing I ever did with my writing.'

In the US, travel blogging has even gone mainstream. *National Geographic* has its own full-time blogger, Andrew Evans or the 'Digital Nomad' as he is monikered (http://digitalnomad. nationalgeographic.com). Andrew is a more thoughtful, less shouty blogger than some I have quoted, though his writing is still quite simple. Here's an extract from a piece he wrote about travelling in Scotland in January 2013:

> The beauty of East Lothian makes me stop the car again and again. I jump out, shut the door, then stand on the banks of the Forth, listening to the gulls cry out, watching the slow tankers as they slide across the horizon. I pass old manor homes and walled estates, old forests alive with pheasants, and the cemeteries of Scottish men lost in foreign battle.
>
> My hopeful travel takes me through a vein of Scottish history (and natural history), leading me to the concave shoreline of North Berwick, littered with piles of dead brown kelp. No matter the winter, the boats in dry dock and the joyless beach—boys and girls bundled in coats and scarves explore this bit of wilderness with terrific energy, gathering shells and urchins and scaring up birds. Stevenson would approve, I thought.
>
> Once upon a time, the man who wrote *Treasure Island* [Robert Louis Stevenson] once explored the same beach and stared out at the same mountainous lump that is Bass Rock. The huge boulder of an island raised out of the Forth like a monster rising from the sea. Though forlorn and severe, Bass Rock glistens with a white lighthouse built by Stevenson's own brother, David.

Here you can see just how National Geographic is attempting to exploit the full potential of the web (and has the resources to do so) in order to maximize its 'brand'.

While my suspicion is that North Americans are more open

to the possibilities offered by new technology than the British and that they may have a greater entrepreneurial nature, too, Mike Sowden feels that there may be other reasons why US bloggers are more prolific (or at least more successful). It comes down to British cynicism.

> I think that folk from the US and Canada are more receptive to connecting with people and making friends, which underpins a lot of travel blogging online and offline. The famous British reserve – it's a cliché, yes, but one with some truth behind it. It's certainly a fact that the people making real money in the travel and blogging sectors are across the Atlantic. This may also reflect a more business-like attitude to it all over there.

There is no doubt that travel blogging requires very different skills to straightforward travel writing. As Kate McCulley, a traveller who blogs under the title Adventurous Kate (www. adventurouskate.com) and whose 'ultimate goal is to show women that solo travel can be safe, easy and a lot of fun', points out on her website, 'Writing for the internet is different from any other kind of creative writing you've done before. You're writing to engage people with a short attention span who are reading your blog while being bombarded by major distractions like Facebook' (and, though she doesn't say this, anything and everything else that's out there on the net). This is one of the reasons why travel bloggers resort to devices such as '12 Ways to Get a Free Meal in Budapest' or 'Why I'm Never Going Back to Copenhagen'. It's also one of the reasons that their websites tend to be a bit loud and abrasive: he or she who shouts loudest is most likely to be heard.

If you think you can write as though you're talking through a megaphone to a crowd of people who are also being distracted by everything from circus acts to chefs, then great, but you're going to need a whole host of other skills, too. You need to become adept at regularly using social media to promote you and your blog – if you're on Twitter, make sure you are posting something every day, if you can. Tweet other people (with a large following) and, with luck, they will 'retweet' or 'favourite' you, but don't forget to return the favour to other people. Think of it like running into a writer you really admire at a conference or party and saying how much you admire their work – basic social networking, but from the comfort of your own home. You probably don't need to update a Facebook page every day, but you should be on your site at least once a week. The main thing is to find out which social media sites you like and which work for you. Ideally, you'll be able to take photos, as well, that perform the same function as your writing – you certainly don't want to shy away from putting yourself in the frame.

My judgment is that the British travel blogging 'business' is running a few years behind that of the US (and Canada, to a lesser extent), so if ever there was a time to get ahead in the business, it's now. As Adventurous Kate notes on her website, you should not expect to make money for about a year and, given the relative callowness of the market in the UK, perhaps longer. But in the spirit of blogging, here are James Fair's Top 10 Ultimate Rules to Making Your Blog a Complete and Total Barnstorming Success:

1. Have an angle to your travel blog – don't just set one up and call it Josephine Bloggs' Blog (though you could do something clever with that particular pun, I suppose). Travel writing, in any case, is about identifying your passion– for a blogger, it's much the same thing.

2. Create a persona. In this case, it's probably best if it's relatively close to the person you really are, but you can act up a bit. All the best bloggers suggest that in their title: *Nomadic* Matt, Mike Sowden's *Fevered Mutterings*, *Adventurous* Kate and so on. Eventually, you're aiming to turn your blog into a brand.

3. Be opinionated. Half-hearted views don't come across well on the internet: nuance doesn't work.

4. Post on a regular basis and have plenty of content. Before you

go live with your site, write plenty of material that can be put up on a weekly basis or as and when you need it. If you are going to bring people back to your site on a regular basis, then they need something to come back for.

5. Take photos. You don't have to be David Bailey, but you must have some idea of how to use a camera. Clever, snappy 'traveller-on-the-road' type shots and street scenes work well on websites – there's certainly no point in taking endless scenics and panoramas. You need people, action, views from crowded buses or busy streets.

6. If you feel you can invest the money, employ a professional to design your site. You want it to look fantastic but also be easy to manage. You want areas where you blog in different ways – not just about travel – and you want your readers to be able to add their own comments. You also need to be able to put your photos up easily.

7. Use Twitter, Facebook and other social media sites. Send out newsletters and RSS feeds. Different people will access you and your site in different ways. Make sure you give each of these different avenues the amount of attention they need.

8. Understand Search Engine Optimization. Think about it like this: once you've worked out what your 'angle' is going to be, you need to have an idea of the sort of people who will want to read what you're saying. But how are they going to find you? The chances are that they may stumble across you through Google or some other search engine, but you need to be aware of the words that they are most likely to use while doing searches, and to use those words in your blog, and elsewhere (headlines, intros and the metadata) as much as possible. There's a lot of advice about Search Engine Optimization, or SEO as experts call it, even whole websites about it – Search Engine Journal www.searchenginejournal. com is just one. There are also websites solely devoted to listing blogs, and you can register your blog on one or more

of these. Examples include Best of the Web Blogs (http://blogs.botw.org), Bloggeries (www.bloggeries.com) and BritBlog (www.britblog.com). Some of these you may have to pay for.

9. Think about what sort of commercial activity you want on your site, if it ever gets to that stage. Depending on how well you are doing, this will range from full-scale advertising and sponsorship to affiliate marketing or hosting Google ads and so on. It may be that your site is only ever a self-promotional marketing tool, but that's fine, too.

10. Do lists. People love lists. Ten ways to make your blog a success – everyone will read that. Thirty-seven ways to travel from London to Laos, 142 reasons why New York isn't all it's cracked up to be. But don't overdo the lists or you might end up (ahem) blogging a dead horse.

Q&A WITH MIKE SOWDEN

MIKE SOWDEN HAS BEEN blogging since 2004, and in 2011 his blogsite, Fevered Mutterings (http://mikesowden.org/feveredmutterings), was nominated by the Huffington Post as one of the 'top travel blogs to discover', with the comment: 'If you like travel writing with an insightful and thoughtful slant – and also with British sensibility – Mike is your guy.'

Did you always want to be a writer?
I always loved writing and was always submitting short stories to magazines, but I never thought of turning it into a career, because I knew enough writers who were struggling to make money. Then I decided to go to university to study archaeology, which is ironic, because it is one of the few careers that is less reliable than writing.

How did you start blogging?
The blog has had a variety of incarnations. I started in 2004 as a hobbyist blogger, but by 2009/10, it was starting to attract attention. I started to learn marketing skills that I could see other people using and, around the same time, I started to re-engineer it so that it was more travel related.

Why did it become more widely read?
Around 2008, I started freelance writing for a number of web magazines, and I was also getting involved in

the social media marketing and SEO ('Search Engine Optimization') side of things, and I learned the basics of writing for the web in a way that gets people clicking and sharing. I started applying those tactics to my own writing, and worked hard on a few, broadly travel-related posts that I hoped would get shared.

And that happened?
I wrote a post called 'The Human Scale Of Too Cold: How We Freeze (And How We Thaw)' [essentially about what happens to the human body as its temperature goes down]. It took me four or five days to research and write, and ended up reaching 40,000 people through Stumbleupon. That gave my site the boost it needed to reach a wider audience – that said, chasing traffic is useless if you have no idea what to do with that traffic.

Are you now writing full-time?
I did have a part-time job at the University of York, and I was writing for a number of [non-travel-related] websites the rest of the time. Then I was lucky enough to win a prize in a travel innovation competition, and it allowed me to put some money aside so that I could leave my job. That was April 2012, and I've been writing full-time for a year.

How has it been?

It has been an enormous learning curve. If I had known what I was going into, I would have saved more money. Sometimes I was very close to the wire. Now I am making most of my money from copywriting for websites and various online publications and doing some editing. I am starting to diversify my income streams – consultancy, online marketing and so on. You have to watch out you don't put all your eggs in one basket – when I first started, sixty-five per cent of my income came from one website and, after four months, it tanked.

So, what's your plan?

My dream would be to travel somewhere, write about it and then use the money I made from that to fund my next trip. It is interesting to see how many travel writers succeed in doing this, and most don't. A lot of people are making money from travel writing, but not many of them are doing it exclusively. I am looking at all the ways I can make money from writing full-time, but I acknowledge that I may never quite do it.

What is blogging to you?

It's an offcut of memoir writing, I think. When I see the really successful travel blogs, there is always somebody at the centre of it, a real personality. They have crafted a brand around themselves and their voice, without compromising their writing. 'Roads and Kingdoms' is a good example – a collective of established journalists who are trying to bring journalistic quality into a blog. You could also see it as the equivalent of going down to a coffee shop 100 years ago – it's a place where stories are being shared.

What don't you like about blogging?

A lot of travel blogging is just marketing for sponsors, and that's certainly not what I want to do. I grew up reading writers such as Eric Newby and Jan Morris, and that's the complete opposite of sponsored travel writing. I am interested, however, in how good-quality work can come out of working with sponsors – Alain de Botton showed that it could be done with *A Week at the Airport*, but I am not really seeing anyone else following that model.

Do you make money from your blog?
Very little, though indirectly it has helped me to find freelance writing work and get the attention of web-based editors. What I want to do is to move into electronic publishing – thanks to e-readers such as the Kindle and so on, I think self-publishing isn't vanity publishing anymore. It is very meritocratic in many ways – people who succeed have clearly worked very hard on what they do.

What will you write about?
I have one ebook I want to write on the 'why' behind blogging and why ninety-five per cent of blogs are abandoned. I am also very interested in the issue of the quality of travel. Alain de Botton writes about this in *The Art of Travel* – that our expectations often end in disappointment in ways that we cannot articulate.

Some bloggers make money out of 'self-help' ebooks – writing about monetizing your blog is one favourite. Is that something you think about doing?
That's how a lot of travel bloggers get started, but the internet is moving too quickly for this to last. I think it's short-sighted, and there are too many doing it. There are cleverer ways of making money out of blogs – for example, one couple I know who run a blog called Never Ending Voyage (www.neverendingvoyage.com) have developed a budgeting app for iPhones that's specifically aimed at travellers. They've stripped it right down to the only things that are needed. Other people are using their travel skills to set up food and city tours. People are branching out in ways that play to their strengths.

Do you see blogging as an end in itself or a way to get published in print? Are blogging and the internet the future and newspapers and magazines the past?

I think this sort of talk is blinkered. The *New York Times* is successfully transitioning to a subscription-funded service, and it's a news service that is filled to the rafters with blogs – and those blogs are being written by the so-called 'obsolete voices' of the previous generation. The tools and the formats are changing, but the people and the content are going to endure because, at a fundamental level, the work they do – reporting, storytelling, striving for quality and meaning, all the things that have defined 'content' for the past few hundred years – are not going to change, and that's because that's how humans are wired up. There used to be a much clearer divide between the online world and print, but now *Newsweek* is completely digital. For today's travel writers, both worlds are in such a state of flux that you can't close yourself off to one or the other – you have to look at both. But it is, nevertheless, true that print generally still pays better.

5. SEARCHING FOR SHANGRI-LA: WHAT MAKES GREAT TRAVEL WRITING

WRITING FOR THE READERS

THE TITLE OF THIS chapter should probably have a question mark at the end, because no one can pretend that they have the complete answer. Everybody likes different things. While a random group of travel literature fans could probably – *probably* – agree on what's truly awful writing, I doubt that there would be the same level of consensus on what's good, great or truly brilliant. But, having said that, there are some very basic rules that we can establish, and some more subtle points about what works in writing and what doesn't. The important thing is that you understand these rules, even if you end up breaking or ignoring them on occasions.

Perhaps the most basic, important thing you must do is to match the writing to the readers of the publication. You should have some idea of who the readers are and what their interests are. Even if you are writing a book (so it doesn't have an already established readership like a newspaper, magazine or even website), you should at least have a reader in mind. Successful travel books don't veer wildly in style, appealing to a 25-year-old art student one minute and a 65-year-old retired postman the next. This also comes back to the point I've already made in earlier chapters: reading and knowing the publication you have pitched your idea to are *essential*. If you're writing a piece for *The Great Outdoors*, for example, you should be aware that readers will know roughly where Ben Nevis is and that it's the highest peak in the British Isles; if you're writing for KLM's in-flight magazine, you may not be able to assume such knowledge.

Assuming you are writing a piece that has been commissioned, the publication's commissioning editor will already have given you a thorough steer in what they are looking for. Indeed, the chances are that you wouldn't have even got the commission if you didn't already have some insight into what the publication was all about. But if you're not sure, there's no harm in double-checking. You should also know whether your piece will be read mostly for practical reasons ('Ooh, a piece about Torres del Paine, perhaps that would be a good place to go this winter, darling?'), out of a vague interest in going there ('Ah, a piece about Torres del Paine, I've always wondered what it's like down there') or wholly vicariously, with readers experiencing your travel adventures through your writing ('This idiot spent two weeks in Torres del Paine; you wouldn't catch me doing that').

Why does this matter? Well, in straightforward terms, if it's mostly a practical guide you might want to weave into the piece how glad you were that you had on your thermal underwear and your Gortex jacket, or include advice on needing to get up early if you want to see condors. If, on the other hand, your reader wants to be informed about the place, then something – in the case of Torres del Paine – about the scrubby ecosystem or the rare, camel-like *guanacos* might be appropriate. If it's more of a vicarious read, then perhaps you can afford to put more of *you* in the story. If it's an amusing experience that doesn't necessarily depict you in a good or favourable light, well, that may not be a bad thing. But this is a tricky thing to handle – writers such as Bill Bryson handle self-deprecation brilliantly, and I think it's fair to say that many an aspiring hack writer has tried to use the same device (I certainly have) with varying degrees of success. When it works, it can be both funny and illuminating; when it doesn't, it can just sound like someone is more interested in themselves than the place they are writing about.

CREATING A STORY

SO FAR, WE'VE BEEN tinkering at the margins of travel writing, so I really want to begin to address the meat of the business. Most travel editors and writers would say that the most important effect of travel writing must be a sense of place ('Take me there!', as I have heard people say) and while I would not disagree, in my view, it is equally important to create a compelling narrative. Put simply, you need to tell a story.

I say this for two reasons. First, while someone might be able to depict a particular city or area of a country with great resonance, if they give the reader no reason to continue with the piece, they may stop. Second, it's often the case that writers achieve this sense of place but think that that's enough (if I now know from the fantastic introduction what the centre of Berlin is like on a Friday night, do I really need to read any more?). I might have got some enjoyment from the description of its street life, but will the piece really stick in my memory? Will I think I must read this magazine or newspaper again? That's what a commissioning editor wants from a travel piece.

A great example of a piece with what I would call a compelling narrative is a feature headlined 'A Tropical Brew' by Alex Bellos, a freelance writer who was previously the South America correspondent for *The Guardian*. In this lengthy article for *Intelligent Life* magazine (which is published by the *Financial Times* and is an excellent magazine, by the way, if you've never read it), Bellos opens with this paragraph:

> Rio Branco is the capital of Acre, Brazil's most westerly state and its most Wild West one too. A congressman was jailed there in the late 1990s, accused of slicing off an enemy's arms and legs with a chainsaw. I visited the city shortly after. I had recently arrived in Brazil, a freelance writer from the other side of the globe, and when an acquaintance invited me to a church service at which psychoactive drugs would be consumed, I jumped at the chance.

Bellos is clearly signalling his intention to tell a story in this introduction – we know that something is going to happen. He's going on a 'trip', but not the normal sort you associate with travel writing. The anecdote of the congressman, and the way it is told, is communicating that the story will be a bit mad but enjoyably gruesome.

The story goes on to talk about the drug 'ayahuasca', a long-established part of Amazonian culture that got taken on by a small Christian sect with whom Bellos was going to try it. The story quickly moves into the writer taking the rank 'muddy-looking concoction' and his feelings of sickness, vomiting and distorted reality that left him unable to remember whether he was straight or gay, a man or a woman, British or Brazilian, before he returned to his hotel room to sober up.

He continues:

> The experience did not feel at all spiritual. It was the most tormented five hours of my life. When I returned to Rio de Janeiro I was left with a respect for ayahuasca and a faint embarrassment for not having deduced *a priori* that it is inadvisable for Jews to take hallucinogenic drugs in bizarre jungle churches. Several years later, I tried again.

IN SEARCH OF A QUEST

THE FIRST SECTION OF 450 words is like the introductory paragraph of a normal-length travel piece, but the whole feature is some 4,000 words, so Bellos has extra space to entice the reader in. Nevertheless, he's used the space brilliantly to set up the *raison d'etre* for his journey. Most readers will be asking themselves, 'If he had such a bad experience first time round, why go back for more?'

Searching for an ayahuasca experience is really an adaptation of the classic travel narrative – the quest. Most people travel in search of something, whether it be Inca ruins if you're Hiram Bingham, a strange mythical creature called Mkele Mbembe if you're Redmond O'Hanlon or, of course, oneself. Arguably, it is the *only* way to create a travel narrative. If you're ever stuck for a way to create a narrative, try the quest format, because it will never go out of fashion. But what Bellos has done is devised a story where he is questing for something he's done before. It's the equivalent of Theseus going in search of the minotaur, not killing it, retracing his steps thanks to the ball of thread, and then going back to do it all again a few years later.

So, nine times out of ten, or probably ninety-nine times out of 100, you'll be creating your narrative as a quest – I went to Andalucia in search of Iberian lynx, but you could be heading to the Netherlands in search of clog manufacturers or Bhutan in search of happiness.

STARTING YOUR STORY: HOOK AND ANGLE

So, I'VE STARTED WITH the idea of creating a compelling narrative, partly because I consider it so important and partly because I think it's one of the biggest failings of a lot of travel writing. But perhaps, now, I should go back to the beginning: how do you start your feature? This is vital: if you don't create an entertaining and enticing opening, why should anyone read on? It's worth spending as much time as you can thinking about how you are going to do this. With pieces that I don't have to write up for several months (even up to six months) I have the luxury of being able to mull over possible openings for all that time, and it means that I can experiment with ideas (often just in my head, while I'm on the train or whatever) and – quite frequently – discard them, too. Often, it helps me get the wrong opening out of the way before I even start writing.

Jonathan Lorie, who runs well-respected travel-writing workshops called Travellers' Tales (Jonathan is interviewed at the end of this chapter), says he teaches his students that you need a 'hook' and an 'angle'. The hook is what it sounds like, the first few sentences or paragraphs must be so entertaining, exciting or intriguing that they require the reader to read on; the angle puts the hook into context, so that readers know what to expect of the rest of the article. As with most rules of writing, you definitely need to understand these concepts, and it's certainly worth using them (possibly most of the time), but you don't have to stick to them slavishly for every single piece of writing you do.

There are numerous examples of these concepts being employed, but here is a simple, short and sweet one from an article published in a Jan/Feb 2013 issue of *National Geographic Traveller*, entitled 'Welcome to the jungle' by Emma Gregg. First of all, here's the hook:

> We're squelching through the rainforest in single file, chatting as we go, when Leo, our guide, suddenly stops. Turning to face our party of six, he gestures us to halt behind him.
>
> 'Switch off your lights,' he whispers urgently. *'Escucha* – listen!'

Then comes the angle:

> With hearts pounding, we turn off our head torches, then wait, rooted to the spot. Only one of us has ever ventured into the Amazon rainforest at night before. We're ready for anything – but we don't know what to expect.

From the hook, you've got a vague idea of where the writer is (the rainforest) and you know that the guide has heard something. You're drawn into the story because you want to know what it is. From the angle, you learn that the writer is somewhere in the Amazon and it is night-time, and that's about it – but it's enough. The story doesn't quite progress as you expect (the hoot of an owl might be the obvious next step, or perhaps branches or sticks cracking). Instead, the writer describes how all the tiny noises of the forest are magnified by the absolute blackness. Somebody then asks the guide what he has heard.

> Leo switches his torch back on. 'I wanted you to imagine how it feels to be an animal in the forest at night,' he says. 'There's information in the tiniest of sounds, smells and vibrations. By day, we rely on our eyes. But by night, we have

to focus every sense. Now let's start exploring properly, but slowly, carefully and very, very quietly.

You could argue that we're still in the 'hook' at this stage, and it's not until we hit the ninth paragraph that we reach the angle:

The spot we're exploring lies within Manú, a wildlife-rich part of the Amazon basin and the largest protected area in Peru. Draped like a green carpet at the foot of the Andes, Manú is famous for birds, with more species than Costa Rica and a greater concentration than anywhere else in the world.

This is more like a classic angle, because the writer has finally nailed where exactly she is and has given you a bit of context to the place. Being hypercritical, I'm not sure it's really helpful to casual readers to say that Manú has more bird species than Costa Rica and a 'greater concentration' than anywhere else in the world. I often see such claims made for other national parks or reserves (usually, it's true, in tropical South America), and while it sounds good, it's rarely as much of a simple truth as it seems.

Overall, however, the opening 300 words or so have set the piece up perfectly. You know that you're in the Amazon Basin at night, and that this piece will try to describe what it's like to be there and what you see and hear.

Here's another classic example of the hook and angle, though for a very different type of travel feature about a very different type of place. It's an article by Harry Pearson for the February 2013 edition of *Condé Nast Traveller*, a magazine that mainly deals in 'high end', luxury travel.

There are few creatures in life more baffled than a praised Belgian. Like a dog that's had a lifetime of kicks, the citizens of Belgium approach any proffered compliment with an air of caution. 'Thank you,' they say with obvious pleasure, then the smile gives way to a narrowing of the eyes, a tilt of the head and the enquiry, 'You think so?'

I'm sitting in a bar in Bouillon on the banks of the River Semois, which curls – slow, black, speckled with the gold and orange of beech and hazel leaves – through the narrow gorge below the great castle of Godefroy, leader of the first crusade.

The chances are, if the reader has taken in the headline ('Fun & Game') and what journalists call the 'standfirst' (the bit of text underneath the headline that provides a one- or sometimes two-sentence précis or 'tease' of the article), then they will know that this is about the best foods of Belgium's Ardennes region and will be able to guess that the opening paragraph has something to do with a meal. It's still intriguing, however, and also conveys that this piece is likely to be as much about the people of the Ardennes as its wild boar and beers. The second paragraph then transports the reader to exactly where we are, by the banks of a river in autumn.

You're still not quite sure who the writer has been talking to or what he's been eating, so you could argue that we haven't quite encountered the angle yet. And as it is, the piece continues:

The elderly man beside me lights up a cigarette, then asks if the smoke bothers me. I tell him it's not a problem, adding that in England smoking in public places is banned. 'In Belgium, too,' the man replies. He gives a rueful shrug and draws in a lungful of nicotine.

Being critical, you could argue that this little aside interferes with the business of contextualising the hook. We still don't know who the writer has thanked and for what reason. It does give a little bit more insight into the people of Belgium – slightly anti-authoritarian, nonchalant, nostalgic perhaps – but, personally, I'd have been tempted to move this back a paragraph or two.

Next comes the real angle:

I've just had dinner – beef carbonnade stewed in Orval, a

lazy, honey-brown beer brewed a few miles away at the Abbaye Notre Dame by Cistercian monks. The meat had been cooked slowly, breaking into flakes the moment the knife touched it. It came with a big bowl of double-fried chips and a token lettuce leaf. As dishes go, it was the perfect example of the great American football coach Vince Lombardi's favourite dictum that nothing succeeds more surely than a simple plan precisely executed.

There we have it, the nub – the star – of the piece: the food. It's simply told, but I like the way the writer has echoed the slow-moving river speckled with autumn leaves in the image of the 'lazy, honey-brown beer'. I also love a writer who can draw comparisons with places or ideas far removed from where they are or what they are talking about – the Lombardi dictum works because Belgian cooking and American football are polar opposites, and yet, we learn, there are similarities, too. And, as it turns out, the person the writer is complimenting on the food is not the chef or restaurant manager but the elderly man who has lit up a cigarette, so it turns out that his intrusion into the angle, which I was critical of, is warranted.

'The food in Belgium is always good,' I say to the smoker. He grins. 'Yes, I think so,' he says, then his eyes narrow. 'Really?'

This mini-exchange comes after the writer has described in loving detail his *café creme* and the additional dishes served with a meal at a different restaurant, and this highlights something else that is worth examining for a moment: it's not entirely clear when the conversation with the man takes place, and in particular whether it was after the beef carbonnade or while he's drinking his coffee. Does it matter? Probably not. But would it have mattered if the writer had manipulated the order of events to achieve a more coherent narrative? In my view, no – as long as he doesn't do it to make a point that is not valid, then I think that it is completely justified. We'll examine this in more detail later on.

CREATING A MORE ELABORATE HOOK

I THINK IT'S WORTH pointing out that the 'hook and angle' approach can work with features that aren't wholly or strictly travel writing. It's useful to know this, partly because it's unlikely that you'll make a living purely out of travel writing, but also to see how being on the road can give you ideas for publications that aren't pure travel magazines. I often pick up a copy of *Geographical*, the magazine of the Royal Geographical Society, because it frequently contains the sort of articles that inhabit this sort of publishing 'no man's land' that could, perhaps, be better called reportage and which I enjoy.

This story, headlined 'Gold's Dark Secret' and published in the October 2013 issue, was written by Matteo Fagotto, and it's about how the discovery of gold in north-west Nigeria is transforming the lives of the people of a tiny village in the region.

Every day, a lean figure dressed in white wanders among the gold miners of Bagega, a small village in northwestern Nigeria. His black-and-white leather shoes stand out in stark contrast to the bare, dusty feet of the miners as he inspects each piece of gold they've extracted.

Nothing escapes his watchful eyes. 'If someone gets caught stealing gold, he's first caned and then thrown into a wooden cage in the jungle,' explains Hassan Haruna, the overseer's secretary and right-hand man as he nonchalantly swings a large wooden club by his side.

Around the pair, in a square space as big as two football pitches, hundreds of young men crush, grind and wash gold ore, sheltered from the scorching tropical sun by makeshift wooden sheds. Aged between five and fifty-plus, they work from 8am until sundown, all of them united by a common dream – to hit the jackpot and become as rich as the White Ghost, Alhaji Adamou Tsiko, chairman of the Bagega Gold Miner's Association.

Until five years ago, Bagega was just one of the many villages dotting the countryside in Zamfara, one of the most northerly and poorest states of the Nigerian Federation.

There's lots to admire here – from the one detail the writer picks out to distinguish the miners from the so-called White Ghost (their bare feet as opposed to his shoes) to the implicit sense given by the writer that these villagers are similar to slaves, albeit slaves who have an outside chance of buying their freedom. The first three paragraphs are the hook and, though it's quite long, it's simply and concisely told. The angle comes in the fourth paragraph, where we learn that Bagega was just an ordinary Nigerian village until five years ago.

My one criticism of this piece would be that nowhere in the opening few paragraphs is there any indication as to what this story is really about – the reader believes it will be about how the discovery of a precious metal has precipitated the human exploitation and suffering frequently seen in the developing world, but in fact it is much worse than that: about one third into the feature, we discover that the real 'dark secret' is that children living in Bagega and seven other local villages have died, or been permanently handicapped, from lead poisoning, as a result of the processing of the ore in which the gold is found. As the writer (or editor), I would have been tempted to give some hint of this upcoming revelation in one of those opening paragraphs, but it is nevertheless still a fine piece of writing.

ANOTHER WAY OF LOOKING AT OPENINGS

THERE IS ANOTHER WAY of looking at openings, however. You could say that there are four main ways of starting a travel feature and that, if you read any well-written piece, it will fit into one of the following categories. You can find exceptions to this rule, of course, but I always find it useful to consider whether my 'opening' can use one of the following 'formatted' openings.

The first opening format is one that creates atmosphere and a picture of the place. Because one of the main jobs of a travel writer *is* to write about places, this is one of the most obvious ways to begin, and a good bet if all else fails. Here's a fine example of this opening style by the novelist Marcel Theroux, from the December 2012 edition of *Lonely Planet Traveller*, head-lined 'In the Saddle'.

> The scene is like something from a Biblical epic: 2,000 sheep are being driven across a desert of black lava. The sky overhead is bright blue and filled with the sound of bleat-ing. Every now and again, a sheep breaks loose and heads up the rocky hillside, from where it has to be coaxed back down. Herders, some on foot and some on stocky Icelandic horses, surround the flock, yelling and gesturing to keep the animals in a bunch. A support group of four-wheel drive vehicles is rumbling slowly behind us, but the main actors in this drama haven't changed in over a thousand years: Icelanders, sheep, horses.

You've got a very good idea of what's going on here and, if you haven't by the end of the paragraph, the writer repeats it one more time: 'Icelanders, sheep, horses'. It reminds me of some advice I was given many years ago on how to write a feature: you should start it by telling the reader what you're going to talk about in the piece, then you should say it and then – to wrap it up – you should tell the readers what you've told them. This may sound silly but it's very good advice and, while it doesn't apply in full to travel writing, it's worth bearing in mind.

Look at the article paragraph again: Theroux repeats the word 'sheep' three times and 'horses' twice, and he makes ref-erence to how far back this tradition extends on two occasions – first at the beginning with the Biblical reference, and then at the end when he says how this scene hasn't changed in 1,000 years. If you're being strictly accurate, of course, something that goes back 1,000 years couldn't be described as being like a 'Biblical epic', but I don't mind the licence with the truth that's been taken here, because you know exactly what he means.

The second classic opening places the writer at the heart of the piece, often in a situation of drama or suspense. Here's a good one by the BBC's security correspondent Frank Gardner, from the *Daily Telegraph* in December 2012:

In the damp, cool air halfway up a volcano in equatorial Africa, I smelt an odour I had never encountered before. Musty, pungent, tangy, hard to describe yet definitely over-powering. 'We are close now,' whispered Augustin, the khaki-clad ranger assigned as our escort. 'Please be very alert.' Every one of us who had trekked up the valley that morning was on tenterhooks, aware that something big was about to happen.

There are two things I'd say about this: first of all, note how Gardner has put himself right at the centre of the story and consider how that compares with Theroux's opening, where he has not used the first person pronoun 'I'. These days, Theroux's opening is the more unusual, and I think that it is technically harder to do well. The second point I'd make is that Gardner's opening is also very simply told, and the only sense that he is making reference to is the sense of smell, which makes the prose just a little more unusual. (Theroux, on the other hand, is describing both the sights and sounds in his opening, so that it is almost cinematic in feel.) Finally, look how similar Gardner's opening is to that written by Emma Greg in her piece about Manú National Park – both say that something is about to happen, they just aren't quite sure what it will be, and neither, of course, is the reader.

One other thing I'd say about this type of opening is that there is a tendency these days towards self-deprecation. Whether this is entirely down to the success of writers such as Bill Bryson, who used it to great effect in many of his highly popular travel books, I don't know, but I suspect that he has played a part in it. You could argue that it is a reaction, too, against the travel writer as the 'expert', and a way of making travel writing more naturalistic (and funnier). In fact, there is no self-deprecation in Frank Gardner's opening, and I think it is better for it. On the whole, the 'Aren't I an idiot?' form of travel writing has arguably run its course.

The third type of opening is information-led, often historical (though it doesn't have to be), providing a context for the piece as a whole. In a sense, this is like going straight into the 'angle' without providing a 'hook', and it can seem rather drab and safe and even dull. It is certainly used less frequently than the first two openings. Personally, I think it can work really well, but it is harder to do. I really like this example from the February 2013 issue of *Country Walking* in a piece headlined 'Walk the Line' by Hanna Lindon.

> This March marks the fiftieth anniversary of the Beeching Report, a notorious government hatchet-job that signalled the end of the line for Britain's rural railway system. Ten years after its publication, a third of the country's 7,000 stations had been closed and 5,000 miles of track were gone for good. The brutal cuts took 70,000 jobs and saw Dr Richard Beeching stigmatised as the most hated civil servant of the 20th-century – but the man who gave us National Rail was unwittingly creating a rural legacy.

What I like about this is that it works up to the 'hook' at the end of the paragraph, the fact that we do have something for which to be thankful to the infamous Dr Beeching after all. Indeed, it works perfectly as a hook and angle opening, with the second paragraph giving the context for the opening claim:

> Today, most of the lines that were felled by the Beeching axe have been reopened as public trails. From the thigh-busting hike along Scotland's 60-mile Speyside Way to the gentle scenic bimble that is the Cuckoo trail in East Sussex, some of our best national walks run along the routes of old train tracks.

You may find it better to use this type of opening where you haven't been asked to write very much. This piece was part of an extended series of inspirational features called 'Your Best Year Ever!', a classic device used by all sorts of magazines in their January or February issues. The box information aside, the piece is only about 400 or so words long, so the writer hasn't got room to indulge herself (and us) with a long drawn-out anecdote about walking along a former railway line. In this case (by happenstance, perhaps), she's got a really nice peg on which she can hang the story – the fact that it is fifty years since the Beeching Report was published. As I say, it is hard to make this sort of opening work well, and I suspect that many travel editors don't like it but, done well, it can be an interesting and (certainly these days) unusual way to open your piece.

Here's another, very different example of this type of opening. It's from a piece by Vicky Baker headlined 'Riding with Cowboys on a Mexico Ranch', published in *The Guardian* in January 2013:

> There is a certain look people give you when you say you are taking a trip just south of the US/Mexico border. The word 'border' triggers reflex panic. Eyebrows rise and eyes dart apprehensively. Even when I assure people I won't be back-packing into the notorious Ciudad Juárez and will instead be staying at an isolated family-run ranch in the middle of the Sonora desert, the look of unease doesn't fade.

This is a slightly sideways approach to the 'information-led' opening – it's telling you something about the country (Mexico – it's not safe), but it's also tapping into what people generally feel about it (unease). Baker goes on to virtually repeat all this in the 'angle', just in case you didn't get it the first time round:

> Mexico is as big as western Europe, yet it dominates international news for one reason only. There's no point pretending the country doesn't have very serious problems and that some areas certainly need to be avoided; however, not everywhere on or within a few hours' drive of the 2,000-mile border deserves to be blacklisted.

Again, there's no problem in repeating information, which is what she's doing, but this opening primarily works because it taps into people's own perceptions of and thoughts about Mexico. It's asking them to consider their views.

There's one other opening I am going to consider. I will give you a good example of it, but I would not recommend that you use this format on a regular basis – or at all, especially if you are not an established writer. I call it the 'checking in at the airport' opening though, as you will see, this piece doesn't start in the airport.

People often write badly when they take the idea of 'travel' too literally, and start their story with them handing over their passport at the check-in desk at Heathrow – something that (as I will point out in Chapter 7) is of minimal interest to most readers. But, in the following example, this works, partly because it seems so incongruous in the magazine it appears in and partly because it is well-judged. You already know from the opening photo covering a double-page spread (or DPS, as we say in the business) that this is going to be a piece about someone spending a weekend in a Lake District bothy, so when it opens in a quite different and unexpected location, the reader is intrigued. The piece was headlined 'House on the Hill' and it was published in *The Great Outdoors* in February 2013.

> We ground to a halt at Moorgate. A fire alert at Kennington. The Underground train would go no further. 'Passengers wanting to go beyond this point will have to proceed on foot.' A huge collective sigh ran through the carriages and the train's cargo of commuters disgorged itself on to the platform. I'm compressed with hundreds of other people into a shuffling swarm that proceeds slowly up the stairways, squeezes through the barriers and fans out on to the street, a process not made easier by the incongruous-feeling bulk of the 70 litre rucksack on my back. It contains all my gear for a weekend in the snow-bound hills of the Lake District, but right now, in the thick of this chaotic London rush hour, they seem very far away indeed.

In truth, you're much more likely to use this way of opening a piece of writing if you are writing something considerably longer – a book, for example. Redmond O'Hanlon exploits it to considerable comic effect in many of his books. Both *In Trouble Again*, which is about a trip to Venezuela, and *Into the Heart of Borneo* start with the writer still in the UK – in the case of *In*

Trouble Again, he is pondering, among other things, the natural threats he faces while in South America. These include the notorious candiru, the tiny catfish that can reputedly swim up a stream of urine (should a man be careless enough to pee while swimming in an Amazonian or Orinoco Basin river), enter one's urethra and lodge itself inside the penis with the aid of a set of spines. Nasty.

O'Hanlon is also looking for a companion for his trip, so he goes to see the poet James Fenton, who went with him to Borneo, to ask him if he'd fancy another excursion into the unknown. Anyone who has read the Borneo book will know that arrangements didn't always go according to plan there, but you don't need to know this to laugh at Fenton's response that he wouldn't even consider travelling with O'Hanlon to High Wycombe.

The extract below is another excellent example of the 'checking in at the airport' introduction. This is from a book about Robert Mugabe called *Brothers Under the Skin: Travels in Tyranny*, by Christopher Hope, and it begins in 2002 with Hope about to enter Zimbabwe from his home, South Africa. The book is set at a time when Zimbabwean civil society was breaking down to such an extent that people were fleeing the country in their thousands. The opening chapter develops a sense of menace (but never overplays it) that lays the foundations for the rest of the book:

> Once I had driven across Beit Bridge on to the Zimbabwean side of the river, I waited in a holding area, a bureaucratic limbo, where the dozens of truckers who shunt food and petrol into Zimbabwe from South Africa spend hours waiting to clear customs. Two men in caps and badges directed me to a quiet spot where they offered me the relevant customs form for a 'fee', pointing out that without these papers it would be dangerous to proceed. The forms were useless, the men were thugs, but it was an offer hard to overlook. These highwaymen were working with increasing desperation since South African tourists had stopped visiting Zimbabwe. I paid up and then went into the passport control office to get my permit, paid again, and went on

paying up until finally I reached the old iron gate which the guard opened just wide enough to allow one car at a time to squeeze through. I was in.

There is no sense of hyperbole here, and the only emotive language used is when Hope resorts to describing the customs officials as 'thugs'. I like the sense that he is being constantly obstructed, right up to the point where the iron gate is opened 'just wide enough to allow one car at a time to squeeze through', and then the final, ironically triumphant, 'I was in'. It's a great example of writing that delivers more by saying less.

DETAILS AND PACE: THE ACCORDION THEORY OF TIME

RETURNING BRIEFLY TO Redmond O'Hanlon's *In Trouble Again*, we can see another important aspect of travel writing. The anecdote of O'Hanlon's dinner with James Fenton begins in a leisurely way, with a map of Borneo hanging from the wall reminding the two men of their previous trip together. They down half a bottle of whisky, lulling the reader into a vicarious drowsiness, so there's no hint of what is to come with O'Hanlon's innocent-sounding invitation to come to Venezuela. O'Hanlon reports the absolute minutiae of their conversation, ending with Fenton's exasperated (but funny – to the reader, anyway) final response.

Of course, O'Hanlon has only reported a tiny fragment of his meal with James Fenton. He hasn't said what they ate, what else they talked about, what colour the curtains were or whether they listened to any music. Why not? Well, clearly, because it's not necessary – as a travel writer, you don't report every last thing that happened, firstly because it would make your article unfeasibly long but also because it would make it painfully dull. In his excellent guide to travel writing published by Lonely Planet, Don George calls this the 'the accordion theory of time', and I quote here directly from his book: 'You expand the accordion to full arm's length in order focus closely on a moment in time, then you push it in to skim over whole days; then you draw it out again to focus on the next significant experience, then push it in to jump over more days.'

Put like that, it sounds easy, but it's not. How do you know when to dwell on the details and how do you know when to rush through the story before pulling the accordion open again? I think that, to get this right, you have to consider who your readers will be and why they will be reading your feature. If it's a piece about bungee-jumping in Moldova, then you want to concentrate on the details that make the adrenaline-surge vivid in the minds of the readers. There are all sorts of things you could include in such a piece, but an account of having the rope attached might work, as would a description of the view from the 'jump' spot. The journey to the jump site might make for interesting material, as might a conversation you had on the way there. On the other hand, are you going to write about what you had for breakfast? Or what your hotel is like? Probably not.

It may not be obvious when you are travelling exactly what will be relevant to your story and what won't, and this is the main reason for taking detailed notes at the time. Something that appears trivial at the time could acquire a whole new significance later, and having notes of what happened can only be helpful.

This was very apparent in the winning entry in *BBC Wildlife*'s Travel Writer of the Year competition in 2008. The winner, Diane Butcher, wrote a piece in which she contrasted she and her husband getting hopelessly lost in the streets of Lima with the miraculous ability of a hummingbird to find flowers. After opening her piece with how they got 'sucked into the maelstrom of Lima's traffic', Diane launched almost immediately into a lengthy argument about her map-reading skills:

'Avenida Tacna,' Richard would bark. 'Do we want that?'

Me, peering at the tiny print on the map and playing for time. 'Ummm . . .'

'Jiron something leading onto . . . Tinga something.'

'Well . . .' (too terrified to say I can't find it on the map)

'. . . Jiron just means street.'

'I don't want a Spanish lesson. Avenida Arica. Can you find that?'

'Not yet. What's this big road up ahead? Take that! Take that one!'

'I can't. It's a ruddy one-way street.'

'Don't shout at me!'

'Do you know how difficult this is? Do you have any idea?'

'Why don't we stop and ask?'

'Zepita. We're on Zepita. Where does that take us?'

'Ooooh, I've got Tacna ... were we going up it or down it?'

'Don't you know? Do I have to do everything myself? What's that bus doing?'

And so it continued. As we discussed when judging the competition, there are many things wrong with this piece of writing, not least the fact that it was entered in a competition run by a wildlife magazine, and yet Diane was about three-quarters of her way through the entire 800-word allocation before she even mentioned an animal. But there's something almost timeless about the bickering over the navigation, with the man driving and the woman desperately trying to locate their position on the map. (I say this as someone who witnessed my parents' worst arguments when we were in a car, with vivid memories of one of them – usually my mother – suddenly wailing, 'Turn this music off – I can't hear myself think!') One of the judges said he would have put a red pen through the entire first section of the argument, but it won anyway, perhaps a little surprisingly.

When Diane and her husband finally see some wildlife, they're filling up with petrol and stocking up on bottles of water on the edge of a town. Diane points the hummingbird out to her husband, who dismisses it as 'just an amazilia – they're common along the coast'. Nevertheless, Diane feels a mini-wave of optimism ('I began to remember why I had come to Peru'), and then she concludes with these final two paragraphs:

A flicker of wings and the bird was gone. She flew directly

towards some houses as if she knew exactly where she was going. Did she carry a star-map in her head where flowers were scattered like constellations across her urban universe?

I climbed into the car and chucked our map into the back seat. The cartographer's runes would remain a mystery, but the road ahead looked pretty straight.

It's a brilliant and funny ending, self-deprecating in just the right way, but there are two particular points I want to make about this. The first one is that, in truth, Diane breaks the rule of the accordion of time, because there's too much focus on the initial argument, too much dialogue. It's entertaining, but it could have been cut in half or more and still had the same effect. The second is that Diane clearly didn't take notes at the time, and one wonders whether she ever did. Was the conversation so intense that it stuck in her memory or has she recreated it as best she could from the 'clips' that she can remember? In this case, I don't think it matters: in my view she has even very subtly signalled that this isn't a verbatim transcript of their argument by the use of '"Avenida Tacna," Richard *would* bark'. To me, it suggests, 'This is roughly what was said.'

And the main lesson for an aspiring travel writer? That you can use apparently 'marginal' material in very powerful ways if you can just see how to.

If anyone ever mastered 'the accordion of time', it was Bruce Chatwin, the author of revered travelogues such as *In Patagonia* and *The Songlines*. I've always loved the opening chapter of *The Songlines* for its description of the main character in the book, Arkady Volchok, the son of a Russian émigre whom Chatwin meets in Alice Springs and who is an expert on Aboriginal 'songlines'. There's lovely detail in his description of Alice Springs ('a grid of scorching streets where men in long white socks were forever getting in and out of Land Cruisers'), and in his portrayal of Arkady as a 'tireless bushwalker [who] thought nothing of setting out, with a water-flask and a few bites of food, for a hundred-mile walk along the Ranges'. Here, the accordion is compressed, with the focus on the minutiae – scorching streets, white socks and water flasks.

And then Chatwin describes how Arkady threw in his job as a teacher on an Aboriginal settlement in Walbiri after a row with an academic and went abroad.

> He saw the Buddhist temples of Java, sat with saddhus on the ghats of Benares, smoked hashish in Kabul and worked on a kibbutz. On the Acropolis in Athens there was a dusting of snow and only one other tourist: a Greek girl from Sydney.
> They travelled through Italy, and slept together, and in Paris they agreed to get married.

Now, the accordion is at full extension as Chatwin skates rapidly over a prolonged period of time, perhaps several months or a year or more, and yet he still finds room to put in the odd tiny fragment of detail – 'the dusting of snow' on the Acropolis stands out for me. It's unexpected (most people visit the Acropolis in summer, when there wouldn't be snow) and gives a nice visual touch to the narrative.

FINDING AN ENDING

IN THIS CHAPTER I'VE looked at great openings, great narratives and how to change the pace of your narrative. You should have the basics of starting your travel feature now, though I want to end, briefly, on how to come up with a satisfying conclusion. There is no golden rule on how you should do this, and many travel writers, even well-established, experienced ones, can be quite lazy when trying to create a memorable ending.

The first question to ask is: does the ending matter? Well, clearly, it matters less than the opening or the overall narrative structure, because your goal is to lead the reader to the end of the article. But, equally, a clever, well-spun ending can leave the reader feeling nicely sated – it's the mint chocolate or espresso at the end of the meal, the reward for making it this far. It also makes an editor feel that you have worked on your feature right up to the last full stop, and that's no bad thing.

One of the laziest ways to end a travel feature is to invoke the 'I loved it so much, I can't wait to go back' conceit. I've seen this dozens of times, and I've even done it myself, much to my shame. Unless, there's a very, very good reason for it, avoid this at all costs – it's too obvious and horribly clichéd.

Most of the time, writers try to finish their feature so that the ending summarizes the themes of the piece. Here's a nice example from *National Geographic Traveller*, a piece about South Korea headlined 'Finding Enlightenment' in which Mark Stratton explores beyond the high-tech veneer of its large, modern cities. He concludes the piece with two paragraphs describing a home-stay, organized by the tourist office, with a woman and her son, who take him to eat pancakes and mung beans in the local market.

> Amid the Central Business District's gleaming glass edifices, appetising tradition is once again wedded to South Korea's fast-paced future.

It's short, simple and neatly picks out the ancient and modern of South Korea, so that the reader doesn't have to think too hard for themselves.

I would also go back to Diane Butcher's piece about the hummingbird, where she discards the map in the final paragraph. Though her navigation skills have not improved, it's as if the tiny bird has showed them the way. 'The cartographer's runes would remain a mystery, but the road ahead looked pretty straight.'

In this chapter, we've looked at three aspects of constructing your travel article – openings, endings and the development of pace and structure in your story. But of course there's a lot more to writing than that and, in the next chapter, we'll be looking at some of the more detailed aspects of travel writing that are equally important.

Q&A WITH JONATHAN LORIE

JONATHAN LORIE HAS BEEN running travel-writing and travel-photography courses through his company, Travellers' Tales, since 2004. He was formerly the editor of WEXAS *Traveller* magazine, he writes for *The Independent on Sunday* and *Condé Nast Traveller* and he has been a judge of the Thomas Cook Travel Book Award.

How would you define travel writing?
It is a crossover genre that combines the functional reporting of journalism with some of the techniques of fiction. For example, it uses characters, it has a story arc and it needs to have an emotional pull – often, the writer needs to learn something from the journey. All these are fiction techniques. But travel writing also reports on how the world is, which is journalistic. How far you can fuse these two things depends – if it is an article for a magazine or newspaper, then you are going to be doing more straightforward reporting; if you are writing a book, then you can be more creative.

What inspired you to set up Travellers' Tales?
As an editor, it was heartbreaking to see so many submissions come in that were not right but could have been or should have been. I felt guilty about turning down work and had a feeling that if only they had got to do one other thing right, then it would have been OK. Most people can get to a publishable standard in this game if they only know the ropes.

What sort of difficulties do people have with travel writing?
Some of the people who come on our courses are quite reticent about putting themselves in the story. They may be used to writing business or academic reports and

having to be objective, so I try to encourage work where they put themselves in the story more. It helps give their writing structure and focus. And then there are people who are poets, for example, and they are really used to writing about themselves, so you have to make sure that they include enough external focus to keep the interest up. It is about balance.

What are the main traps for travel writers?
One of the issues is how writers should present themselves. Should they be the 'expert' advising the reader or the innocent abroad? As the reader, we enjoy seeing them fall off the surfboard, but the temptation is to get too embroiled in your own story and then you become too big for the piece. I always advise people to read the story aloud to somebody else and get their reaction.

Why do people want to read about the writer, surely they want to hear about the place?
If you look at the best-selling travel writers, such as Bill Bryson and Chris Stewart, half the pleasure is the feelings and thoughts of the writer and the comedy that ensues from that. Because most places have been written about, what any writer can bring to a place to freshen it up is them – their perspective and personality. So it's about understanding a place from that person's point of view, with their baggage and so on.

What advice do you have about starting a piece?
We teach that an opening must have two functions: it must grab the reader, which we call 'the hook', and it must signal to the reader what the article is going to be about, which we call 'the angle'. That's true whether it's a book or an article. In an article, those two things will happen in the first few paragraphs, with the first one being the hook and the second being a very direct statement of what the article is going to be about – I am in Paris to find the

perfect cup of coffee. In a book, you might spend a whole chapter doing this. With the angle, the more direct and upfront you are, the better. The hook is where you get to play some fancy tricks.

What's a good hook?
The classic hook is to choose the most exciting moment of your trip and put that in the first paragraph. You describe it so that you are right in the middle of the action, where you are catching the fish or finding the tiger. Another one is to start with a quote, which can be intriguing. A third one is to start with an opinion, but this is a high-risk strategy, because most opinions have been heard before. Just describing a scene is an option, but this might be considered a bit quiet these days.

What about the angle?
It needs to be strong and simple. You need to be able to express your angle in a single sentence to a commissioning editor. If you need a paragraph, then the idea for the article is probably too complicated. We tell people on our courses that they need to work out the angle and then buy the air tickets, and beginners find that a bit of a shock.

Let's move onto structure . . .
Most travel articles are quite a short, say 1,200 words. The way you tell the story is not the way you would tell it to a friend in the pub, so it's slightly unnatural. For a start, you're not telling the whole experience and you zig-zag between the experience and other bits of information. A lot of people have a problem with how they leave out experiences that were enjoyable but not relevant to the thrust of the story. Some of the skill is in building the links between different episodes in the story so that it flows smoothly.

Are people important in travel writing?

You almost never get a travel article that's empty of people, because otherwise it would be a still life. When you introduce a person, you have action and the possibility of drama. Quotes should be used sparingly. One interview could be boiled down to a couple of killer quotes. As a writer, you should be talking to loads of people and you should be nosy – in fact, if you say you are a writer, then that gives you an excuse to be nosy and doors suddenly open.

Past or present tense, what do you think?

This is a really tricky area. If you are not sure, just put the whole thing in the past and you can't go wrong. You can put bits of the article into the present tense to make it more vivid, but you can't drift between tenses for no reason. You can go further and write the whole thing in the present tense, which can be very vivid, but some editors don't like it and will change the whole thing back. It might be a case of looking at the publication and seeing what they usually do. The present tense can be quite wearing, and it can be used to cover up for deficiencies in the story.

Is it important to do research and further reading?

In specialist interest titles, where readers are quite knowledgeable about the subject, then you need to be an expert like them or it will show. For national newspapers or more general travel writing, you don't need to be an expert, but you do need to be able to relate your story to something. I've just written a feature about Hemingway's Paris, and I had a stack of more than ten books on the subject, and I used them all in the piece. It ensures you don't make any howling errors and it may also give you some fantastic material. For this piece, I knew that there was a Hemingway bar at the Ritz, but I also knew that it was closed, but thanks to my research, I knew there was another bar called Harry's Bar that Hemingway also drank at, so I went there instead. It's where they invented the Bloody Mary, and they were bloody good.

A final bit of advice?
Most travel writing is not literature, it's functional journalism. You don't have to be the most brilliant writer to get published. If you are persistent and professional, then you can get published. It is easy to be put off by how hard it is.

6. AT THE END OF THE DAY: PUTTING ALL THE PIECES OF YOUR TRAVEL JIGSAW TOGETHER

YOUR PLACE IN THE STORY

PUBLISHED IN 1988, JUST a year before his death, Bruce Chatwin's collection of short travel stories asks the question that every vaguely adventurous traveller has been asking since Odysseus took a decade to come home after the Trojan War: 'What am I doing here?' (The book, slightly intriguingly, I always think, doesn't actually have a question mark and is called *What Am I Doing Here*.) The title of the book puts Chatwin right at the heart of the story, which implies that we really care what happens to him. By 1988, with the likes of *In Patagonia* and *The Songlines* behind him, many people probably did care for Chatwin, particularly as it was reasonably well-known by this stage that he was dying. One thing you can be sure about, however: your readers probably won't care too much about you – not to begin with, anyway.

Does that mean you should never use the first person in any travel piece? Should you seek to eliminate your place in the story entirely, and construct the piece as a dispassionate, fully objective piece of feature writing? Well, no – because, then it wouldn't be travel writing. Travel can be as much about the journey inside someone's head as it is about the literal journey over land or sea. There is a place for 'I' in the story, but exactly what that place is will depend on what you are writing and for whom.

To take an obvious example, if you're writing a 500-word spa review, the journey inside your head is going to be minimal, at best. Having said that, your spa review still needs to be as light and fluffy as the towels you wrapped yourself in while enjoying the experience, and one way to do that is to give your own subjective reaction to the things you see, hear or smell. Your readers aren't going to be able to imagine what the spa is like very easily unless you can describe these things vividly.

Nevertheless, I am always impressed by writers who can hold off bringing themselves into the story for a decent length of time, because it shows that they have sufficient faith in their material, and it requires greater technical virtuosity and expertise than immediately reaching for the first person singular.

Take this memorable prologue to Joe Kane's book *Savages*, which is published by Pan Books:

> Though Moi hit the streets of Washington, DC, at the evening rush hour, he walked in the city as he does in the forest – in slow, even strides. He kept his eyes to the ground and his knees bent, and he planted his broad feet deliberately, heel and toe, yet lightly as raindrops. It was the walk of a man accustomed to slippery terrain. I found myself stutter-stepping all the way down Pennsylvania Avenue, but Moi slid through the pedestrian horde like a fish parting water. He stopped only once, to study a squirrel climbing a maple tree: meat.

There is only one person centre-stage here, and it's not Joe Kane – it's the eponymous 'savage', Moi, who has come to Washington from the rainforests of lowland Ecuador. As the beginnings of a character profile, I have rarely seen this bettered, and if anything Joe Kane's prose becomes even more compelling: next he describes the traditional Western clothes – dark trousers, starched white dress shirt and brown shoes – that Moi is wearing and how they contrast with his unusually high cheekbones and muscular, broad shoulders that hint at the distance he has travelled to get here:

> His journey had begun deep in the Ecuadorian Amazon, in

the homeland of his people, the Huaorani, a small but fearsome nation of hunter–gatherers who have lived in isolation for so long that they speak a language unrelated to any other on earth. It had taken Moi nearly two weeks to reach Washington. Travelling by foot, canoe, bus, rail, and air, he had crossed centuries.

What's particularly impressive about this writing is that *Savages* is, in many respects, a deeply personal work. Writer Joe Kane abandons his comfortable life in San Francisco to seek out the Huaorani, whose territories are being threatened by oil exploration. He joins Moi and other members of the tribe on a tour of their lands doing a census of exactly how many people live there. He becomes deeply involved in their fight against the oil companies. And yet he still manages to resist making himself centre-stage in those opening two (and indeed more) paragraphs, because he wants to make Moi the real 'star' of his book. It's a lesson for all travel writers – who is the 'star', the key actor, in your story? Is it the hotel, the barman, the guide, the wildlife, the scenery? Whatever it is, perhaps you should begin with that, and not you.

PAST OR PRESENT TENSE

I HAVE JUST SPENT half an hour scouring the books on our bookshelves for a travel book – or indeed almost any book – that's been written in the present tense. Clearly, the most obvious way to write about an experience that has happened to you is in the past tense, because that is how the past tense is intended to be used. And yet I am constantly amazed by how many writers try to put their pieces in the present. Writing, 'I am meandering the streets of Moscow' does, superficially at least, have a greater sense of immediacy than 'I was meandering the streets of Moscow', and that presumably is why many writers experiment with it – however, one ought to proceed with the present tense only with great caution.

Nature writers often prefer to use the present tense, because,

I suppose, it helps to lend a sense of eternity to their observations – the frog they saw hopping in the long grass will be doing it again and again and again (or other frogs will), so to write 'the frog is hopping in the long grass' suggests this. One section of *BBC Wildlife* called 'What to Do in One Weekend' showcases a short, 550-word piece of travel writing focusing on a particular British species (gannets, say, or boxing hares), and there is a strong element of nature writing, so putting the whole thing into the present tense can work well here.

Remember the intro I looked at in the previous chapter about exploring a Peruvian rainforest. Let's read it again:

> We're squelching through the rainforest in single file, chatting as we go, when Leo, our guide, suddenly stops. Turning to face our party of six, he gestures us to a halt behind him.
>
> 'Switch off your lights,' he whispers urgently. *'Escucha* – listen!'

Because this piece is all about Emma Greg's first proper rainforest experience, she has decided to create a greater sense of immediacy and urgency by putting it in the present tense. It works perfectly well, I think, though I do wonder just how much would have been lost had she written it in the past tense.

> We were squelching through the rainforest in single file, chatting as we went, when Leo, our guide, suddenly stopped. Turning to face our party of six, he gestured us to a halt behind him.
>
> 'Switch off your lights,' he whispered urgently. *'Escucha* – listen!'

Some people may think that the original version in the present tense is more powerful, but it is marginal at best. Interestingly, this piece throws up one of the challenges of writing in the present tense, though in this case Emma Gregg deals with it well. And that challenge is? If you're in the present tense, it is harder to convincingly go backwards or forwards in time – usually, it means you have to adopt a more strictly chronological approach in your article. Often, as previously discussed, you may not start a travel article at the beginning, but with an especially pertinent or noteworthy anecdote that happened halfway through the trip you are writing about. At some point in the article, you then go back to the beginning, which is fine if you are in the past tense already, but more problematic if you are in the present tense.

In Emma's case, it works fine. She concludes the first part of her rainforest adventure thus:

> Fascinated, we watch closely, until Leo strides on and we follow, senses primed for our next sighting.

At this point, the magazine's designer or sub-editor has inserted what we call a 'crosshead', which is often just a few words, written in a different font and usually a larger point (i.e. type) size. This splits up the text so the reader is expecting some sort of natural break in the flow of the article. In this case, it simply says 'An expedition' (in my experience, few sub-editors will spend too much precious time dawdling over what to write for a crosshead), and the next part of the text continues as follows:

> A few days earlier, as we begin our day-long journey from Cusco to Manú, it's impossible to guess we'd have the confidence to walk through the Amazon rainforest by night.

So, the transition back in time works absolutely fine here, but that's not always going to be the case and it's worth keeping an eye out for any complications that might ensue from starting in the present tense. It could be argued that the present tense works better here, because had the whole piece been set in the past tense the writer would have used the following, slightly awkward construction:

> A few days earlier, as we began our day-long journey from Cusco to Manú, it was impossible to guess that we *would have had* the confidence to walk through the Amazon rainforest by night.

I'm still not entirely convinced, however. Later in the same paragraph, we hear:

> I'm intrigued to see if the Crees Foundation – the charitable body behind our trip, which supports sustainable development and conservation within the buffer zone adjacent to Manú National Park – can make first-timers like us feel at home in the extraordinary surroundings of the Amazon Basin.
>
> And I'm particularly keen to find out whether its team can summon those crucial ingredients – a dose of danger, a brush with the unexpected and the chance to make discoveries – that can turn an ordinary trip into something exceptional.

The use of the present tense jars slightly here, partly because what she's hoping for so closely matches what appears to happen. Was she really having those thoughts a few days before the expedition into the forest, or is she merely constructing these ideas in retrospect? In a sense it doesn't matter – most readers probably won't question it – but it does sound contrived, and that is something every travel writer needs to be aware of. Whenever I receive a piece of travel writing in the present tense, nine times out of ten I probably end up changing it back into the past, and not thanking the writer for giving me an extra ten minutes of editing to do, so bear that in mind, too.

As a final thought, I did find one book in which the writer uses the present tense for occasional 'excerpts'. It's called *A Place in My Country: In Search of a Rural Dream* by Ian Walthew, and it's a book about how a publishing executive and his wife abandon their high-flying careers to buy a cottage in the Cotswolds. Chapter 2 opens like this:

> I am lying in our London bed, listening to the garbage trucks starting their engines. Han sleeps next to me.
>
> *What have we done?* I must have been drunk. We'll be living in a tiny cottage in a country I hadn't wanted to come back to (why is that?), career thrown away, drowning in debt.

In the *countryside.*

What are we going to do with a bloody Aga?

Han will resent me and my weakness, my 'career' will be finished, my life unrecoverable, my friends and contemporaries living in a world I once had a grip on but which would now be forever out of sight.

The publishers then put in a small graphic crosshead-like device, and it carries on:

It was a long wait between the 'sale' and actually getting the keys and our joint decision to buy Lettem Cottage looked increasingly moonstruck.

I think it unlikely that many magazine travel editors would allow a writer to jump between tenses like this, and I can't think of many circumstances where I would. To give Ian Walthew credit, the device does work here but, in my view, contrivances of this nature can backfire because they suggest you are striving to make an impact. Italicizations are the same – in most of your writing, you shouldn't have to italicize words to create emphasis. In general, my advice would be to avoid the present tense – it cannot mask deficiencies in your writing, and it adds little to any skills and technical expertise you do possess.

USE OF DIALOGUE

WE'VE ALREADY SEEN HOW good travel writing must contain memorable characters, since people are as much a part of a country as its culture, scenery or anything else, and the most obvious way to make them memorable is to give them great lines. I say give – you are, of course, reporting fact, not fiction, so they do have to say them in the first place, but you've got to recognize them as great lines and then remember to write them down. That's the idea anyway.

As a way of starting, I'm going to look at a great writer of dialogue from any era, Gerald Durrell, whose most famous book, *My Family and Other Animals,* recounts the years he and his family spent living on Corfu before the outbreak of World War II. Here's an extract from the book in which the family, living in Bournemouth, are contemplating their future. It's raining outside and brother Larry is fulminating about the situation in which they find themselves.

> 'And, if it comes to that, look at us . . . Margo swollen up like a plate of scarlet porridge . . . Leslie wandering around with 14 fathoms of cotton wool in each ear . . . Gerry sounds as though he's had a cleft palate from birth . . . And look at you: you're looking more decrepit and hag-ridden every day.'
>
> Mother peered over the top of a large-volume entitled *Easy Recipes from Rajputana.*
>
> 'Indeed I'm not,' she said indignantly.
>
> 'You *are*,' Larry insisted; 'you're beginning to look like an Irish washerwoman . . . and your family looks like a series of illustrations from a medical encycylopedia.'

The dialogue is wonderfully succinct and effortlessly funny, too, and manages to paint both a picture of the people Larry is describing and – most importantly – Larry himself. Dialogue can be about what people say and the information they impart when they talk, but the very best writers use it to reveal something about the person speaking. In this case, Larry (in reality, the writer Lawrence Durrell) reveals himself to be short-tempered, impatient, rude and pompous, which is pretty much how Gerald Durrell depicts him throughout the book but, despite these character traits, Larry is always depicted in an affectionate way. This was probably Gerald Durrell's greatest strength as a writer: his ability to make apparently unlovable people, well, loveable.

My Family and Other Animals was written some two decades after the actual events Durrell is describing took place, and he was only ten years old when this scene I quote from took place, so it seems unlikely that he was secretly taking notes while Larry held court. (Indeed, Durrell only wrote his books at all so that he could raise funds for the conservation work of his Jersey

Zoo, and, generally speaking, loathed the whole process.) In other words, I think we can safely assume that the words quoted above are not verbatim transcripts of what Larry actually said at the time, though what similarity they bear with actual reality we can only guess.

Most of the time, however, you will not be depicting ogre-ish members of your own family in your travel writing, and – for the most part – you will have to have some record of what they said in order to use a quote. We've already looked (in Chapter 3) at how you might record quotes, whether by taking notes at the time, recording a conversation or rushing to the toilet or some quiet spot to make a hurried note of something you've heard or something that has been said to you), so I won't go into that again. I would only repeat the most important piece of advice: you can never be absolutely sure what will make a great quote for your article, so err on the side of recording too many rather than too few.

A quote – or dialogue – can be used for a number of reasons, so let's just run through what those are. The first and most widely-used reason for a quote is to impart information. You have an expert telling you something, and that information is given greater reliability if it comes direct from your source, rather than you.

I used a quote for this purpose in a piece I wrote about the cranes that have been recently introduced to the Somerset Levels. On a bitterly cold February morning in 2012, I went out with an RSPB guide called Matt Brierley (and other crane enthusiasts) to see if any of the cranes had begun the courtship dance for which this group of birds is famous.

They're some 200m away, where they blend remarkably well with the silvery-green hue of this winter wetland. Indeed, they look like grey ghosts, their identity given away mostly by the bustle of tail feathers.

Then Matt spots something. 'Look, he's dancing,' he says. One bird is flapping his wings and pecking at the ground in slightly demented fashion. It's intriguing, but hardly the apogee of grace and elegance, and he's certainly no

143

contender for this year's *Strictly* title.

'What, the one flapping his wings?' I ask. 'On his own?'

'He's getting off the ground, and kicking his feet forward,' Matt insists. 'Think of it as a warm-up exercise.'

The point is that I wouldn't have recognized the 'slightly demented' wing-flapping as 'dancing', so I have used the quote from Matt to demonstrate this, rather than pretend that it was obvious to any numbskull who happened to be watching. I have also used my reaction to introduce an element of humour. 'What, on his own?'

But, as I mentioned with respect to Gerald Durrell's portrayal of his brother Larry, quotes and dialogue can be used not only to impart information but also to reveal something about the people speaking. And this can be done within relatively short pieces and about people who have been barely sketched out. Here's an excellent example from the December 2012 edition of *Lonely Planet Traveller*, in a 'round-up' feature about Queensland by Christa Larwood. In a 400–500-word piece about Noose Farmers' Market, Christa describes how the stall-holders have set themselves up well before dawn.

> By the time the sun is out and the main crowds arrive, the early risers are finished, settling down for a flat white coffee and a free-range egg and bacon roll. 'People love their food around here, so most of the very best stuff is gone early,' says one customer with several shopping bags at his feet. 'At times it's like the January sales, or the start of a horse race.' He grins widely. 'We are all very nice to each other, of course. But it's competitive.'

So, the reader learns that they will have to arrive at the market early if they want to find the top stuff – useful, practical information – but also gets a sense of what the un-named, undescribed person speaking is like. He's 'competitive'. It just adds an extra element to what could otherwise have been an unmemorable piece about food and travel.

A lot of the time, however, you may not be using quotes for

imparting (useful) information or revealing anything about the person being quoted – it can simply be to provide a change in the direction of the flow of the article and a change of pace – remember the 'accordion theory of time'? Your reasons for quoting can even be as superficial as the fact that quotes and dialogue break up the appearance of the printed text – this, on its own, communicates to the reader that they are not being asked to assimilate facts and figures or to imagine another beautiful view.

Quotes can, frequently, be humorous, or certainly lead to humour. Take this extract from a piece (which we previously looked at in Chapter 5) called 'House on the Hill', from *The Great Outdoors*.

Chris, warden of the Buttermere YHA, was kind enough to let me leave my car in the car park outside the hostel, which is quiet this time of year. As I did a few last minute bits of gear admin we chatted about where I was planning to go – a bothy I knew was in the rough vicinity of Haystacks.

'Careful,' he said, 'there's an evil Shetland pony up there.' I laughed, but he didn't seem to be joking. 'It doesn't take kindly to people on its territory. A couple of my friends were once chased by it. It has these dead, black eyes.' I already had a fairly considerable list of concerns – wind, rain, snow, hypothermia, not finding the bothy, finding it but discovering it was full of inebriated teenagers, finding it but discovering it was empty except for one silent man in the corner, sharpening a knife. Now I had to add to it the risk of being charged by a dangerously unhinged small horse.

I think this is a wonderfully controlled and understated piece of writing. In truth, the quote doesn't reveal anything useful to the reader (unless you are planning on visiting the bothy and have an aversion to territorial Shetland ponies), though it probably does say something about the warden, Chris. But it is certainly funny and curious, and the writer Carey Davies then uses it to discuss his 'real concerns' – ranging from the understandable to the slightly paranoid – and where the risks of running into a loose Shetland pony might come on that scale of things. (Probably not very high.)

It's really only an amusing interlude in the story, but such interludes are important in all travel writing. Newspaper and magazine readers are notorious in giving up on pieces they are reading, so if you want to keep them until the very end of your article – and ideally you do – then you must keep offering them something different to keep them intrigued. Imagine you have the following elements in your kit bag: description, information, quotes or dialogue and action – the key is to mix them up as much as possible so that there is never too much of one or another for too many consecutive paragraphs. Quotes and dialogue, in particular, are the best way of lightening the feel of a piece of writing.

I started this section on quotes and dialogue by looking at the way that Gerald Durrell used conversations remembered – or recreated – from some twenty years ago to affectionately lampoon members of his family, and I thought I would finish by looking briefly at a modern travel writer who also uses dialogue to great dramatic effect. Louis Theroux has made a name for himself by tapping into the eccentric beliefs of neo-Nazis, white supremacists and alien fantasists in the USA through his TV documentaries, so it was only a matter of time before he brought out a book on the same subject – *The Call Of The Weird: Travels in American Subcultures*.

His chapter on a UFO convention being held in the Nevada desert demonstrates both his ability to connect with people whom he nevertheless believes to be absurd (and who wouldn't?) and his ear for compelling dialogue. Here's a great example:

> At one table, hearing that I was from England, the talk turned to David Icke, the Coventry City goalkeeper who reinvented himself as a New Age prophet.
>
> 'Doesn't he believe there are twelve-foot lizard people running the planet?' I asked.
>
> 'He believes the reptilian people have an agenda here, that's correct,' said Darrell, a success coach from Las Vegas.
>
> 'But lizards?'
>
> 'Reptilians,' Darrell said.

'We're a prison planet,' said Jeanne, a grizzled-looking teacher from Colorado. 'Have you read his books? You should! He exposes the Queen of England. She's a reptile.'

There are two points to make here – first, that Theroux is getting people to speak to him because he seems to take them seriously. It would be easy for him to mock the convention delegates, but instead he asks straight questions that elicit 'straight' answers. Demonstrating empathy with the people you meet on your travels is an important skill: you might not always agree with what they tell you, you might not like their point of view, but you must – usually, anyway – treat them seriously. You are certainly more likely to get good material that way.

The second point is that the success of the dialogue is not just down to the left-field language such as 'twelve-foot lizard people' and 'prison planet', but also to some of the subtler nuances – 'He believes the reptilian people have an agenda, that's correct' is a good example. The success coach, Darrell, has tempered Theroux's more extreme interpretation of Icke's beliefs into something that almost sounds vaguely reasonable – the reptilian people aren't 'running the country', they merely have an 'agenda'. And at the same time, Darrell hasn't admonished Theroux for ribbing him, he's put him right but in a nice way. It's a beautifully civilized exchange with the give-and-take of kind, rational people – some of whom believe that aliens with scaly skin are living among us. It's true that most travel writers won't come across characters with such way-out beliefs in the normal course of their work, but it is nevertheless a lesson in how to give yourself every chance of finding them and of making full use of the material when you do.

USE OF DESCRIPTION AND METAPHOR

THE WAY YOU DESCRIBE what you see, hear, touch and smell will be one of the primary ways in which you communicate what you experience to your readers – it is one of the most vital tools of the travel writer. But it's not just a question of saying that this city was noisy, or those flowers were bright red or the rainforest was vast or the food delicious – your goal is to bring your experience far more to life than that, to give the readers verbal cues that feed off their senses, whether sight, hearing or smell. Remember: you are trying to entertain the readers, too, to give them a reading experience that they will not forget, so a bit of clever wordsmithery is always a bonus if you can summon up the inspiration.

For me, it is these moments of cleverness that are hardest to achieve; they often only happen after I have been sat in front of a computer for quite a while. For the first hour or so after I start a feature, I can often feel that my writing lacks panache and is dull and unsophisticated. Then – for no apparent reason – a nice little image will present itself to my mind and suddenly I feel that something has clicked into place. It's one of the reasons why it's always worth continuing to write, even if you feel that what you are writing is not very good: sooner or later, it will start to come right again, and sometimes it's just a question of working your way through a 'drab' patch. Of course, every person is different, but I have heard enough other writers say something along similar lines to think it an idea worth sharing.

When I first went travelling, after leaving school, to India and Nepal, it felt like every person I met had either read, was reading or intended to read *The Snow Leopard* by Peter Matthiessen. *The Snow Leopard* is the story of Matthiessen's trip, in the company of the noted field biologist George Schaller, to the Crystal Mountain of Nepal's north-west Himalaya, ostensibly because Schaller was interested in studying the *bharal* or blue sheep, but with the additional, fairly great incentive being that 'where bharal were numerous, there was bound to appear that rarest and most beautiful of the great cats, the snow leopard . . . the hope of glimpsing this near-mythic beast in the snow mountains was reason enough for the entire journey', Matthiessen notes in the prologue to the book.

The book is not just a classic quest in the sense of it being the search for something material but also because of the journey that takes place inside the writer's mind. He applies his Zen Buddhist faith to the dawning realization that the snow leopard will not reveal itself easily and he learns to cope with the disappointment. The writing is spare and taut, perfectly matching the mountain environment in which the book is set. I could have picked any number of examples, but here's one excerpt in which the author and George Schaller bivouac for the night:

> A sundown wind has died away to utter stillness, and a good thing, too, since the snowbanks all around are deep and dry, all set to drift. GS is a remorseless sleeper, but for me the night will be a long one. I think about the great black eagle that crossed the sky at twilight: this can only be the golden eagle, which I last saw in western mountain lands of North America. Perhaps this eagle is the one that passed over Snowfields Camp at just this same time of day. What can it be hunting, this heroic bird, in bitter white waste, at the edge of darkness?

Matthiessen uses the image of the golden eagle to represent both continuity and perseverance (in the face of a hostile world), subtly suggesting that these are qualities he, too, could use in his 'hunt' (which he is gradually beginning to realize may not be for the snow leopard, after all). Any aspiring travel writer who wants to learn how to write fine description could do worse than read this book.

Your first travel pieces are unlikely to be meditations on the nature of being, however grand your ambitions, but that doesn't mean you cannot aim to write beautiful and vivid descriptions of the places you visit. There are two qualities that I think every writer should aim for: clarity and freshness. It is very easy to think you are painting a marvellous picture of a city or landscape, when in fact the whole thing is a muddle and no clear image emerges. In terms of freshness, nothing wearies the reader more than comparisons they have heard a thousand times before – sea like glass, an otherworldly landscape and the twinkling lights of the stars are just three such descriptions I have read time and again.

Here's a passage that I find particularly evocative, clear and enjoyable, without – and I mean this in a good way – being in any sense stunningly original. The author, in this case the historian Bettany Hughes, writing in the June 2012 edition of *Lonely Planet Traveller*, is sticking to the main principles of travel writing, but doing it extremely well:

> The view from the boat is always best: this is how adventurers, heroes, pirates and princes have greeted Santorini for close on 7,000 years. The crescent-shaped island – the biggest in a cluster of volcanic remnants – sits in the Mediterranean like an oversized, submerged tiara. Santorini seems so ridiculously fairlytale-like, I remember on my virigin voyage here I had to blink twice to check that I hadn't nodded off on the chugging eight-hour ferry ride from mainland Greece. Titanic walls of rock jut up out of the ocean – a mille-feuille of colour, topped with postcard-perfect white homes: 'frosting on a devil's food cake', as one local baker proudly describes it. Donkeys and mules wind their way up what seems to be a sheer cliff face from the Old Port. They head in the direction of the chink of glasses emanating from a string of cocktail bars dotted 250 metres above the harbour – and all sheltering under an endless sky.

There's so much I like about this description of Santorini. First of all, the clarity – you know immediately from where the author is giving you the picture of the island, because she tells you in the first five words. Second, there is the nod to its rich history, with the reference to 'adventurers, heroes, pirates and princes'. Third, there is freshness, with the comparison to the 'oversized, submerged tiara', a beautiful and unexpected simile. Fourth, I love the way she maintains this theme by describing Santorini as 'fairytale-like', and once again there is great freshness in the more detailed mille-feuille metaphor. Finally, you get the image of the beasts of burden winding their way up the cliff face, heading in the direction of the 'chink of glasses' coming from the cocktail bars, so you get a feel for what Santorini sounds like, as well as looks like. The whole ensemble works perfectly, and that's even with what could be a clichéd conclusion ('and all sheltering under an endless sky'). I think the phrase is justified here because of the rich originality of the language that has come before.

It's worth just pausing for a moment to consider how a writer might come up with such novel comparisons as a tiara and mille-feuille. More usually, islands are described as 'jewels' or 'green oasis amid a sea of blue', but these would be lazy and clichéd descriptions because they don't tell the reader anything new. The reader already understands that the feature is about Santorini, and most will also know that Santorini is a sun-drenched island in the Mediterranean, an idea that immediately imparts certain images, such as 'jewel', for example. Coming up with fresh ways of looking at a place can be very hard, and if nothing comes to you naturally, then try and rid yourself of any preconceived ideas that you might have and look at the place anew. Sometimes, this might be after you have returned from the trip, so you can't literally go back and take another look – you might be able to look at photos, or you might just have to imagine or re-imagine it. I know that on many occasions I have this nagging sense of something reminding me of something else (without knowing exactly what it is), and I let it ferment inside my head until the image finally appears. In Borneo, I had this deeply unsettling feeling that the noses of the female proboscis monkeys brought to mind something from my child-hood, but I couldn't work out what it was – it was only when I got back to Britain, perhaps a month or so later, that it came to me: they reminded me of the Child Catcher from *Chitty Chitty Bang Bang*. It's no wonder, in retrospect, that I found it so unsettling.

Later in this chapter, I will look at two stages of one spe-cific piece I wrote – the original draft, written while suffering a severe bout of the flu, which was almost unprintable it was so poor; and the second draft, which was a massive improvement in a number of ways. It will show how coming back to a piece of writing can improve it considerably.

Here's another equally inviting description. It's by the writer Jeremy Seal, and it was published in a special travel supplement to *The Oldie* in January 2013:

In Cappadocia, a famously bonkers terrain of eroded volcanic tuff resembling everything from meringues to Emmental, from wigwams to – no getting round this – willies, I drew up by an improvised sign. It indicated the back-country village of Maziköy's 'underground city', one of numerous hand-dug human warrens scattered across this geological wonderland in Central Turkey. From a tatty booth, the wall covered with photos of former visitors to the site, a man called Yavuz emerged to take me on the tour. Torches in hand, we plunged down a dark tunnel to enter a multi-storey world in which all manner of domestic features – chimneys, shrines, stairs, sleeping chambers, holes designed to project voices, threshing floors and wine presses – had been hewn from the soft stone. There were even huge circular stones sat in grooved runnels which were once used for sealing off the entrances in the event of attack. It was to holes like this that Cappadocia's medieval population had once bolted when-ever the region was overrun, which was often, by raiders from the East; across the centuries I could almost hear the thundering hooves of Saracen or Mongol horsemen passing overhead.

The 'famously bonkers' phrase introduces an element of levity into the writing that is almost immediately matched by comparing the rock formations of Cappadocia with a diverse range of forms, including, of course, 'willies'. Because the writer has also drawn comparisons with more innocent subjects such as meringues he gets away with what could otherwise have been a puerile outburst, and it helps, too, that he apologizes in advance ('no getting round this').

Then from above-the-ground oddness, he plunges us under-ground into the 'human warrens' where the same rock has been used to carve out a domestic existence. He doesn't need to rely on great powers of description, but merely lists what he sees, and then he gives a final dramatic flourish by imagining the hooves of invading horsemen passing overhead. As with the first piece of writing by Bettany Hughes, what makes this passage work well – apart from the fresh images Jeremy Seal brings to the reader's mind – is the way that everything works towards creating an idea, and not just an image, in the reader's mind. In both cases, the writers are introducing the history of the places they are visiting through their descriptions, thus revealing something about the narrative structure of the article that the reader can expect. There is, in other words, a purpose to the writing that can be divined by the reader, and this helps to make someone want to read on.

RESEARCH

I ALWAYS TRY TO make it my mission to come up with a piece of research for any travel feature I write that an expert on the destination won't know about. I can't say I always succeed (indeed, it may be that I have never succeeded) but I believe that if I can produce something that surprises even an insider, then it is definitely going to surprise the average reader. Before I went on a trip to China's Qinling Mountains in 2008, where I was due to join a panda-tracking expedition, I did some research into the origins of the word 'panda'. My reading threw up some intriguing ideas, but none of them really satisfied, and clearly there was no consensus on the true etymology. While pondering this one night, something suddenly struck me: the Westerner credited with 'discovering' the panda was a Frenchmen called Père Armand David: take the 'P' from his title, the 'A' and 'N' from Armand and the 'D' and 'A' from David and you get, well, panda. Perhaps, I suggested, the word panda was really David's lasting joke on the rest of the world. Far-fetched? Probably. Ridiculous? Well, as I said, I haven't seen any other wholly satisfactory explanation for the derivation of the word. At the very least, an intriguing way to start a feature about panda-tracking? I thought so.

Now, you could say that, in this case, I may have gone a bit further than necessary in devising my own theory as to the origins of the word panda, but at least it allowed me to communicate some of the more orthodox theories in conventional fashion. While researching a piece about Shetland, I discovered that a naturalist from the islands had visited the Galápagos – just ten years after Charles Darwin – and this allowed me to have a bit of fun with the theme of 'The Galápagos of the northern hemisphere' that I was developing for this remote archipelago. It would probably be going too far to say that you can never do too much research for a travel article, because clearly you can never know everything about a destination, but the more you know the more likely it is that you will be able to place novel, interesting ideas in the minds of your readers. You should have this information at your fingertips, too: would Jeremy Seal have been able to recreate the image of the 'thundering hooves of Saracen or Mongol horsemen passing overhead' had he not had a deep and intimate understanding of Turkish history? Possibly not.

So, where do you do your research? What do you read? The most obvious place to start is the internet and, yes, I've even looked places up on Wikipedia – frequently, in fact. (A study by the peer-reviewed journal *Nature* in 2005 compared the accuracy of scientific entries on Wikipedia with those in *Encyclopedia Britannica*, and found the two sources were about as accurate as each other, so it's not necessarily laughable to use it as a source of information, though I cross-check any piece of information from Wikipedia with another source.) I also find out what are the classic books written about a destination's natural history.

In the case of Shetland, I came across a book called *A Naturalist's Shetland*, by J. Laughton Johnston while mooching around a museum in Lerwick, and instantly knew I should be reading it. When staying in lodges in 'wildlife' areas, there will often be well-stocked libraries that are always worth spending at least one evening in. While in Borneo, chasing after the 'Child Catcher' proboscis monkeys in 2007, I came across a huge book about the species by one of the world's leading experts, and I spent a good few hours diligently taking notes from it. Not only did it provide useful, reliable insights for my article, but it also shed new light on the proboscis monkeys I was seeing every day.

Doing research can work the other way, too – it can give you ideas for travel features. Reading a series of articles in *National Geographic* by the conservationist J. Michael Fay in which he describes his megatransect – a continuous, 3,200km hike across the Congo Basin towards a remote coastal part of Gabon

– inspired me to visit that country in search of lowland gorillas. As it turned out, there wasn't much more reading I could do after that, though I made sure – as I always try to do – that I had at least an elementary understanding of the country's history and its political system before visiting – if nothing else, it can give you something to talk about with local people.

ACCURACY

BEING ACCURATE IS, OF course, absolutely paramount, and it's not just a question of checking that you have spelled the name of the country, city, or person you've just spoken to correctly, though these things are certainly vital, too. If your piece touches on the history of a country or destination, can you be sure that you have understood that history correctly? If you've been told something by someone you met – even if they are an expert – can you be sure that what they've told you is correct? And, if you can't be sure, does that mean you can can't use that information? (No, not necessarily – as long as you attribute the information to them, you're fine.) This is particularly important if your source is obviously partial – to take an extreme example, if you were shown round Havana by Fidel Castro, would you take everything he said as the unvarnished truth? Well, probably not. But you would, I think, quote him, whatever he said.

So, part of the skill of travel writing is understanding when you are getting a partial, incomplete view. Either you make sure that you communicate this incomplete view to the readers or you find another source that confirms it. You'd also do well to recognize when you are dealing with a subject area on which your knowledge is a bit shaky. At *BBC Wildlife*, I get a lot of travel pitches from writers who do not normally write about wildlife as such – there's nothing intrinsically wrong with that, but it can lead to unnecessary errors. The word endemic – which, when talking about ecology, is applied to a species that is only found in one country or region – is often misused, while some writers get very excited about the concept of subspecies without truly understanding what a subspecies is. If you don't understand, or you're not sure, either get someone to explain it to you properly or don't write about it.

There are also some country and place names that are a trap for the unwary. I've seen respectable publications write about Equador (rather than Ecuador), for example. Other classic mistakes are Washington DC (it's Washington, DC) and calling the Isles of Scilly the Scillies.

Other aspects of accuracy are more subtle. In Chapter 2, we've already seen that in the UK we write traveller whereas Americans go for traveler. Some spelling is yet more nuanced: either mediaeval or medieval is correct, and the publication that you are writing for will have its own house style on a word such as this, which you are unlikely to be able to predict. Having said that, if you're writing a piece, say, for *BBC History* magazine, it wouldn't do any harm to find out (by reading a recent issue – it's bound to be mentioned somewhere) whether the editor there prefers World War II or Second World War. Small things matter.

DEVELOPING YOUR VOICE

Developing your own voice, both within a particular piece and in general as a writer, is important. It can add an extra layer of distinction to any feature. Readers will come to know what to expect from you and, if they like how you write, they might even start looking out for your work. This is less likely to happen if your voice is just one of hundreds or thousands out there that all sound the same.

The two main columnists on *BBC Wildlife* both have very distinctive voices: the nature writer Richard Mabey and the former Goodie and *Springwatch* presenter Bill Oddie. Neither is strictly speaking a travel writer (though Bill has done a lot of travel writing, both for *BBC Wildlife* and other magazines), but what's important is that most readers will know exactly what sort of writing to expect from both of them.

Richard Mabey is known for his thoughtful, often minutely observed and deeply personal reflections about the relationship between people, culture and nature. In early 2013, he published a book about the British weather titled *Turned Out Nice Again*, and here's an extract from a piece he wrote about the weather for *The Guardian*, in which he describes how he got caught in a rainstorm while walking in a wood in the Chilterns:

> The rain was ferocious, spattering off the golden leaves in silver jets. The whole wood began to change colour, the trunks slicking to slate grey, next year's beech-buds glistening like glazed fruit. I huddled under the nearest holly, and realised that I'd gone to ground right next to the remains of a dear departed, the tree I called the Praying Beech, on account of two branch stubs that had fused across it just like a pair of clasped hands. Four years earlier it had been split open by a lightning strike. Bees had nested in the hollow gash. Then it was toppled in a storm. Now this gargantuan supplicant, half as tall as our parish church, was prostrate on the ground. And it was liquefying in front of my eyes. The rain was hammering drills of water at the already rotting trunk, and flakes of bark, fungal ooze, barbecued dregs from the lightning-charred heartwood, began to drip on to the woodland floor like thick arboreal soup.

So how is this typical of Richard Mabey? Well, first of all, you know you'll always get plenty of beautiful imagery (the 'beech buds glistening like glazed fruit'), and while, as I said earlier, his writing is fiercely personal, it's always clear that he is less important than the things – birds, bees or birches – that he writes about. In this case, the 'Praying Beech' takes centre-stage and is virtually given a personality with that name. What you can also always expect is writing that throws up ideas, like bones, that the reader can gnaw on – here, Mabey surprises us by observing the literal disintegration of the giant tree. Any aspiring travel writer can learn a lot by reading Richard Mabey, and by considering in particular how his distinctive voice is ever-present.

Another way of developing your voice is through the language you use. Richard Mabey is a great example of this too – there aren't many writers who could describe a fallen beech tree as a 'gargantuan supplicant'. One of the best examples of a book given great distinction specifically by its language that I've read in recent years is called *Born to Run* by an American writer called Christopher McDougall, a former war correspondent for the Associated Press.

The book is about McDougall's quest to find the Tarahumara of Mexico, a group of people who live in almost impossible isolation in the deep-cut gorges of the country's Copper Canyons and who have been described as the world's greatest long-distance runners. As with Richard Mabey, I wouldn't describe McDougall as a travel writer, but *Born to Run* has many elements of travel writing, not least because it involves a quest – in this case for the Tarahumara – and because McDougall is at the heart of the story.

I was especially intrigued by McDougall's use of language, which turns American slang words into a deliberate aspect of his writing style. The effect is to create an anti-authoritarian, almost subversive atmosphere, mirroring the attitude of the unorthodox 'ultra-runners' that McDougall meets on his travels. I'm going to quote a few examples below, because they demonstrate how the writer sticks with his style throughout the book, and I'm going to italicize the words in question so you really get a feel for what I'm talking about:

'Hey! Uh, do you know Angel?' I stammered as I stepped between Caballo and his only way out. 'The teacher at the Tarahumara school? And Esidro in Huisichi? And, um, Luna, Miguel Luna . . .' I kept *shotgunning* names, hoping he'd hear one he recognized before body-slamming me against the wall and escaping into the hill behind the hotel.

By the time I *shanghaied* him in the hotel, he hadn't eaten since sunup and was nearly delirious with hunger.

From there, Fisher *moled* his way into lost worlds on five continents, sliding through war zones and murderous militias to pioneer descents in Bosnia, Ethiopia, China, Namibia, Bolivia and China [sic].

He made Rick and Kitty an offer – he'd roust some runners, if they'd *pony* up food for his entire village.

About two years earlier, she and Carl were running on a rainy day when Ann began grousing about the endless, slippery hill ahead. Carl got tired of hearing her *kvetch*, so he *blistered* her with the most obscene name he could think of.

But as they came down Mount Elbert on the single-track trail toward mile 70, Shaggy detected a little hitch in the beat. Martimano seemed to be *babying* one foot, placing it carefully rather than whipping it right around.

Until I looked it up, I'd no idea what the provenance of 'shanghaied' was (a Charlie Chaplin film called *Shanghaied*, apparently), but from the context, it was obvious what McDougall meant. The main thing, though, is that the choice of language gives the book a very distinctive feel, and while there were times when I began to find it a little contrived, overall, reading *Born to Run* was a memorable experience.

POLISHING YOUR STORY

As you will see in the interview with the travel writer Will Gray at the end of this chapter, not everyone polishes their writing in the same way. But, however you go about it, it's vital to polish – not just (or even mainly) to eliminate silly mistakes but to make sure it is the best-crafted piece of work you can possibly deliver to your editor.

My preferred method is as follows. Once I have outlined – either in a separate Word document or on a scrap of paper, or sometimes just in my head – the structure of the story, I simply get on with the writing. I may have my notebook at my desk, or sometimes I will go through the notes first, writing some of the key observations or quotes into another Word document, which I might even print out. It's almost like laying down the bricks of the story, and while – with luck – I may contrive some nice linguistic flourishes at this first stage, I try not to get too disheartened if the piece feels a bit flat at the end. My view is that you just have to keep on writing, and eventually something will click, but everybody is different. I have seen other writers suggest that you go for a walk (or something that will take your mind off the piece entirely), which absolutely doesn't work for me (my own experience is that it is only when I am writing *well* that I need to get up and walk round the room) or that you stop what you're doing and write about something else entirely, which I have never tried – it sounds a little masochistic to me.

I have seen it said that you should always aim to stop writing when you are in the middle of something good. The argument is that if you become 'blocked' and wrap up for the night, then you will return the next morning with the same blockage in your way, and that's a dispiriting way to start. But, as my girlfriend once said to me, the idea of 'writer's block' for a journalist or travel writer is unrealistic (like me, she does both) – we are mostly writing to tight deadlines and we can't stop working on a feature just because the 'muse' has deserted us. Sometimes, you just have to say, 'This will do,' even if you aren't happy with it, and then – if you have time – come back and polish it later.

Now let's turn to those two stages from the piece I wrote, which I hope will show how important the polishing stage is to your writing. The piece was about searching for Risso's dolphins while staying on Bardsey Island at the end of the Lleyn Peninsula in North Wales, and here is what I had by the time I'd finished the first draft:

> By surveying exactly the same stretch of sea, ideally for as long as possible every day for the six weeks the researchers are on Bardsey, it is hoped to build up, over time, a more accurate picture of what the Risso's dolphins are doing around Bardsey. Are they migrating and if so, where are they going? One theory is that Risso's dolphins are partial to octopus, and that octopus could be plentiful locally because of the horse mussel beds on which they feed to the north of the island. But, as is so often the case with cetaceans,

nobody really knows. Sightings appear to be most numerous in August and September, indicating some kind of migration.

It's when they do spot some fins, that things get interesting. The idea is to grab the island farmer, who then takes the team out in his 12-foot dory, in the hope that they can get close enough to take some photos. The dorsal fins can be used as ID markers, and sometimes matches can be made with animals from other parts of Europe or with ones taken in previous years. The week before I was there, Pine, Lucy and Vicky had an astonishing encounter with 10 Risso's dolphins and two common dolphins, with incredible acrobatic breaching behaviour that was a world away from the Rissos I saw in the Azores. 'I was yelling, 'No, don't jump, I just want to photograph your dorsal fins," Pine told me.

And here is what I changed in the second draft:

By surveying exactly the same stretch of sea, for as long as possible every day for the six weeks the researchers are on Bardsey, and on an annual basis, it is hoped to build up a more accurate picture of what the Risso's dolphins are doing around Bardsey. Are they migrating and if so, where are they going? According to Pine, one theory is that octopus are plentiful locally because of horse mussel beds to the north of the island, but as is so often the case with cetaceans, nobody really knows. Sightings appear to be most numerous in August and September, indicating some kind of migration.

A quick glance at online material before travelling to Barsdey implied I might as well be looking for sea dragons as these curious animals. 'One of the most enigmatic of cetaceans,' began ARKive, while the words 'relatively little is known' and 'poorly understood' completed the picture. Their preference for 'deep, shelf edge waters of 400–1,000m in depth' in reality means that Risso's dolphins are largely passing the world by unseen. Still, I like a challenge.

The thing is, after that rather underwhelming encounter

in the Azores, I felt like I had unfinished business with the 'great grey fish' – yes, that's what its scientific name rather unscientifically means. Most people, I reasoned, have never heard of Risso's dolphins, and certainly don't know that they're swimming up and down the west coast of Britain scoffing cephalopods.

And while Lucy took her turn on scanning duties, Pine powered up her laptop to show me some photos taken just a week earlier. After spotting a group out at sea one Sunday morning, Bardsey's tenant farmer had taken them all out in his 12-foot dory so that the team could get some close-up pictures of dorsal fins for identification purposes. As with many dolphins, fins are unique to each individual, and the idea is to build up a catalogue over a period of time. One Risso photographed off Bardsey in 2006 was spotted off Penzance three years later. It's not much, but it's a start.

But despite their reputation for coyness, this group of 10 Rissos (and two common dolphins) broke out of their comfort zone to do the cetacean equivalent of a can-can. Pine's images revealed spectacular breaching and leaping, sometimes three at a time, behaviour that was a world away from the Rissos I had seen in the Azores. 'I was yelling, 'No, don't jump, I just want to photograph your fins," Pine told me.

The most obvious difference between the two extracts is that the second draft is longer. The first paragraph has stayed largely the same, but in the first extract I've said very little about the elusiveness of Risso's dolphins, which was an important part of the story for me. I had gone to Bardsey because I knew that most people (and even many readers of the magazine) had never even heard of this species, but my first draft had failed to give any explanation as to why this was. The third paragraph was added to give greater significance to the sense of quest (my 'unfinished business' with the animal) and to drive home the point about their relative anonymity. I've also added some sentences that help knit the extract as a whole together: 'Still, I like a challenge' and then at the end of the next paragraph, most people 'don't know that [Risso's dolphins] are swimming up and down the west coast of Britain scoffing cephalopods.'

The second paragraph has also been changed considerably, because it relates to something that I didn't experience first-hand. Originally, I didn't make much of the team's encounter with a group of Risso's dolphins, because I hadn't been there but, because I felt it was important (and fun), I wanted to find a way of getting it into the story in a more visual and compelling way. In the end, I realized that I could use the device of the lead researcher, Pine, showing me her photos. In truth, this didn't happen at this point in the story; she showed them to me later that night, but I wanted to get this into the story at this juncture. The encounter with the dolphins has become more active, and I've given a tangible example of how photographing their fins can enhance our knowledge of them. Finally, I've added a little flourish – the dolphins doing the equivalent of a can-can, which was an image that came to me from looking at Pine's photos – this adds an element of levity to the writing.

In this chapter, we've looked at eight of the most important building blocks of travel writing: where you fit into the story, whether to use past or present tense, use of dialogue, use of description and metaphor, the importance of research and accuracy, developing your voice and, finally, polishing the story. Get all of these elements right, and you're heading in the right direction.

Q&A WITH WILL GRAY

WILL GRAY IS AN award-winning travel writer who writes regularly for magazines such as *Wanderlust*, for which he is a contributing editor, and the *Sunday Times Travel Magazine*. He's written several books on the theme of family travel for Footprint Publications and on what to do in England when it rains. He also co-edits the Kenyan Airways in-flight magazine *Msafiri*.

How did you get started as a writer?
After finishing my zoology degree in 1990, I took some time out and did voluntary work on Heron Island on the Great Barrier Reef counting little birds called silvereyes. I was rubbish at finding these things and I was hopeless at identifying them. The researcher I was working with said, 'Just go away and do something else.' So I did, and I spent several months taking notes and photos and doing illustrations – I had thought of a great idea for a book and, when I got back, I pitched it to various publishers and David & Charles took me up on it, and so I went all around the world looking at coral reefs and researching the book.

That was a good start . . .
That was my lucky break. It was a lovely coffee-table book, and fortunately it happened just after leaving university and before the bottom fell out of the market. But I did think that this is what I would like to do, and I wondered how I could carry on, and I used the book as a calling card to see what commissions I could get. I started very small – the first magazine I tried was *Trailfinder*, those magazines you see for free in those metal bins – and that was my first commission, and I was paid £75 for both the words and photos.

That wasn't very much!
No, but thanks to David & Charles, I got a meeting with Christine Walker [then editor of the *Sunday Times Travel Magazine*], and she said she'd have a look at something I wrote – luckily, that was accepted, too. And all this time, I did have a job – working for the RSPB as a public affairs officer.

So, you weren't just relying on your earnings from writing?
No, and that would be my first main tip: treat travel

writing like a hot bath – don't dive straight in. So while I was working for the RSPB, I was also trying to get pieces published. Then I got a part-time job with Coral Cay Conservation, running their volunteering programme. That was great: now I had more time to work on the freelance work but also had some reliable income. I'd always resented the more corporate elements of working for the RSPB – all those meetings – and I'd always known that I wanted to work for myself.

So, there was no Damascene moment when you suddenly went freelance?
No. I worked for the RSPB for a couple of years, and it just happened gradually. A few important things happened – I won some awards, and that certainly helped. Joining the British Guild of Travel Writers was important, too. I was making good contacts within the industry and I was beginning to feel part of the travel-writing world. Suddenly companies were prepared to give me trips and people were putting their trust in me.

OK, let's move on to writing itself. What's the goal of travel writing, in your view?
To me, it's very simple. From the very first piece I have ever done, my main criteria has always been that the writing must take people there and help people empathize with the place, both with the experiences I have had and the thoughts I have had about it. You need to create magical moments for them; if you can make them feel empathy for an Indonesian rainforest or whatever, then that's a bonus.

Do you have a particular way you write?
Yes, I am a bit weird. I create what I call a road map. I take very detailed notes when I am on location, normally with a pencil – that's so it can never run out. I've tried taking iPhones, iPads and digital tape recorders, but

I really can't be bothered with them. While I'm there, I pay a lot of attention to dialogue and lots of little descriptive things. Then before I start writing, I get a big piece of paper and I write down six to ten of the key points that I think should feature in the article. I pick a starting and finishing point, and make sure that the end relates to the beginning and finally pick a road map through the article. Only then do I start writing.

That seems quite sensible.
Yes, but most writers write a first draft and then polish and refine it until it sparkles. I do it completely differently – I grow an article. By the time I put a full stop at the end of the last sentence, that's it, it's done. I probably do this because I am a perfectionist, so every sentence has to be perfect. I can't move on from one sentence or one paragraph to another unless the last one was just right.

How do you pick your openings?
Sometimes it comes to me quite early on. On a trip to the Selous Game Reserve and Ruaha National Park in Tanzania, I was flying in a small Cessna plane when the pilot said, 'There you go, take the controls'. I knew almost immediately that I wanted to make that my opening.

Any other advice on openings?
A good beginning should pluck a reader from wherever they are reading the piece straight into the Indian jungle or onto a coral reef. Speech can be a good way of doing that – one very high-profile writer does that in almost every piece they write – but I am a bit reluctant to start with dialogue. It can feel a bit forced and unnatural and isolated. I think it does work if backed up with good characterization and a sense of place.

What are the big pitfalls to beware of in travel writing?
I think where a lot writers trip up is in not providing

sufficiently good stepping stones between the paragraphs. A great piece of travel writing is like a great piece of music – there are long and short phrases and nice links between different passages. There should be lots of variation in travel writing, too.

What advice do you have for writing description?
The most effective travel writers describe things with an economy of words. 'Madcap cackle' of the hornbill, for example. One I remember very well – and I admit to stealing – was by David Wickers, when he described New Zealand's North Island as having a 'crinklecut coast'. That's it, you don't need anything else. That economy of words is wonderful – a more inexperienced writer would have used more words and talked about all the lovely little inlets and bays but, when you have sufficient experience, you know when to stop.

What description have you written that you were pleased with?
There was a piece I wrote about a walking safari in India. We were walking through the forest, and there were these giant teak leaves lying on the ground. They snapped as we walked over them, it was just like walking over poppadoms, so that's what I wrote. Nothing else was needed.

It was apt because you were in India – that wouldn't have worked in South America.
No, if it had been South America, I would have had to come up with something else.

How do writers get better at writing description?
By reading lots of other writers and seeing how they use it in their pieces.

How do you avoid using clichés?
The cliché alert monitor is called my wife. I'm lucky

because she is an editor, too, so I totally respect what she says and if she says something doesn't work, or the whole piece is rubbish, then I listen to what she has to say. She always tells me off whenever she sees the word 'grin'. I use that word too often.

Is there one thing that's key to being a good travel writer?

It stems from writing about things that you are passionate about. You can always tell when somebody wasn't that interested in a place because they struggle to write about it. That's why I tend not to do city breaks – I'm not that interested in taking a city break and I think I'd find it difficult to write about. So you need to specialize. There are a lot of travel writers out there, so find out what you want to write about.

Any other tips?

Learn how to write proposals – look at how magazines and newspapers write their headlines and standfirsts [intros]. If you can get your head inside the editor's, then that helps enormously. Being an editor myself, I know how to do that. The headline and standfirst are the magazine selling the article to the reader, and what you've got to do is to sell the idea to the editor, so it's the same thing – if you can do that, the job's half done.

7. DON'T GO THERE: THE SEVEN DEADLY SINS OF TRAVEL WRITING

IN THE LAST TWO chapters, I've looked at all the ways in which you can strive to be a good writer, but I want to spend one chapter analyzing what you shouldn't do and why. There are a number of simple traps to fall into, and sometimes it is difficult to understand why you shouldn't do something until it has been clearly explained. In addition, by examining ways in which you shouldn't write, it will reinforce some of the positive messages about the way you *should*.

1. 'I ARRIVED AT THE AIRPORT': ELIMINATING POINTLESS INFORMATION

I wrote the passage below myself, but I have seen plenty of pieces that start along these lines over the years. You won't find it hard to work out for yourself what's wrong with it:

John and I were really excited to be heading off for New York, and packed the night before, making sure that we had our passports and airline tickets all ready for our departure the next day. The traffic during our taxi ride to the airport was terrible, and I was certain we'd be late, but in the end it was fine, and the check-in procedure was very smooth, and before we knew it, we were sitting in the VIP lounge (it was only £20 to do this, even though we were still travelling economy) and waiting for our flight to be called. I couldn't believe it: within just a few hours we'd be landing in The Big Apple!

As I said at the beginning of Chapter 5, most fans of travel writing or travel writers themselves would find it easy to agree on what constitutes bad writing, and this would clearly fall into that category. But why? I think it's worth examining what makes it so terrible, because there are lessons here even for someone who would never plumb the depths I have gone to here.

First of all, I've spent 120 words, and I haven't even got onto the plane, let alone landed at my destination. And second, it's really only a diary entry that lists a sequence of events – there's little attempt to provide any cohesive structure to the paragraph so that there is any purpose to the story being told. There's the ugly 'it was only £20 to do this . . .' in brackets, which breaks the flow (not that there is much flow), and finally – to cap it all! – the piece ends on a horrible cliché! More than anything, it totally ignores the 'accordion of time' concept we looked at in Chapter 6, failing to cut out the uninteresting, mundane details.

Clearly, this is an extreme example of 'including pointless information', and anyone with any aptitude for writing is unlikely to write something of this nature. But, at its best, travel writing is a concise literary or journalistic form, and you must select what details, incidents or quotes you include in your piece with great care. Always ask yourself why you are putting something in (not why you are leaving it out – that's fine) and how it contributes to the overall feel and angle of your article. Does it fit with the direction you are aiming for? If not, ask yourself whether it should be there.

Indeed, one of the great curses of the aspiring travel writer is waffle, and it's very easy to start waffling if you don't keep an eye on what you are doing. Take this example, which I also wrote:

Leaping out of the boat as the waves lapped on the shore of the beach, my feet crunched on the shingle. I helped the rest of the group pull the boat clear of the high-water mark, then

Dan retrieved an anchor from the rib's locker. 'Just in case,' he grinned. 'We don't want to get stranded here.' I took a moment to look around me: we were standing on a narrow, semi-circular isthmus that joined two islands together. There was a narrow, grass-covered ridge above the shingle beach rising to about ten or fifteen metres high. 'This is called a tombola,' Dan told us, 'because it was purely a matter of chance that it formed.' I'd been on a tombola before, I recalled to myself – the two islands of North and South Bruny, off the south-east coast of Tasmania, are joined by a much longer, narrow isthmus, and I felt a strange connection between the Shiant Isles of the Outer Hebrides and Australia's island state on the other side of the world. 'Come on,' laughed Dan, as we all stood there, 'let's explore.'

This isn't a terrible piece of writing – it's certainly not as bad as the airport story – but there's a lot of waffle here. The details about getting out of the boat aren't interesting and don't add anything, nor does the bit about getting the anchor out – that would only be needed if the boat had floated off and we'd been stranded, and that didn't happen. The phrase, 'I took a moment to look around me' is also unnecessary, and while the information about tombolas and Bruny Island are reasonably interesting, there is certainly no need to put in the line about the 'strange connection' – that's implicit and better left unsaid. The overall passage is nearly 200 words long, but it could be a lot shorter and punchier. Here's how:

Arriving at the beach, we all scrambled out and then helped pull the rib above the high-water mark. We were standing on steeply shelving shingle bank that rose to a narrow, grass-covered ridge and linked the two rocky humps of the Shiants. 'It's called a tombola,' Dan told us, 'because it was purely a matter of chance that it formed.' To my knowledge, I'd only been on a tombola once before – one that joined the two Bruny Islands off the south-east coast of Tasmania. Out in the bay, puffins, guillemots and razorbills were flying in all directions – in search of food for their chicks no doubt

– and cries of gulls rang through the air. 'Come on,' said Dan. 'Let's explore.'

This is much better. It's a third shorter – 120 words as opposed to 180 – and, by including the details about the seabirds, I've managed to say more and give some focus to the piece; clearly, the wildlife is one reason we're here, which wasn't obvious from my first attempt. I've still included the information about the tombola, but I've cut it back, and I've eliminated some of the details of the arrival at the beach, because they weren't interesting and didn't add anything to the story.

So, cutting out pointless information is much more than not including the taxi ride to the airport. Here's what Paul Theroux had to say about it in the interview published in *The Atlantic* (from which I quoted in Chapter 4) – while Theroux can be a little grumpy, he knows what he's talking about:

> The main shortcut is to leave out boring things. People write about getting sick, they write about tummy trouble, they write about having to wait for a bus. They write about waiting. They write three pages about how long it took them to get a visa. I'm not interested in the boring parts. Everyone has tummy trouble. Everyone waits in line. I don't want to hear about it.

2. THE CURSE OF THE CLICHÉ

IT'S ASTONISHING HOW EASY it is to fall into the trap of using clichés, but what, exactly, do we mean by 'cliché' and what's so wrong with using one, anyway? In writing, a cliché is a phrase or expression that has become so overused that it ceases to have the intended effect – usually, the use of a certain idiom is meant to bring language to life and help create a picture for the reader but, if it is a much-used word or set of words, it can have the opposite effect. But it can be more than that: take the expression, 'To avoid something like the plague' – many centuries ago, the plague was a genuine threat and worth avoiding, but these days you'd struggle to find any situation in which you'd be in a position to catch what was a once deadly disease. So we have a simile that has become meaningless not only because of overuse, but also because the issue it refers to is no longer current. No wonder it has ceased to have any power.

There are two types of cliché that you specifically need to be aware of. The first is using tired adjectives or comparisons when describing things – so, for example, why is it that cities are so often 'bustling', views are 'stupendous' and rainforests like 'cathedrals'? Does the wind really 'howl' and do the stars 'twinkle'? Does the sun always 'sink below the horizon' and do waves necessarily 'crash' onto the shore?

The first question to ask yourself, when you use any adjective or comparison, is whether it is accurate. What do we mean, for example, by 'stupendous'? According to the *Collins English Dictionary*, it means 'astounding, wonderful, huge etc.', and it derives from the Latin verb *stupere*, which translates as 'to be amazed', but elsewhere, I read something slightly different: that it comes from the gerund of *stupere* – *stupendus* – which means to be stunned. From this, I reach the conclusion that, to describe a view as 'stupendous', I'd have to be amazed by it, which isn't really saying an awful lot. What does it tell the reader to say that you have been 'amazed' by a view? Almost nothing at all. They want to know *why* you have been amazed by it. And amazement is a very broadbrush (cliché alert!) emotion – whenever I read that someone has been amazed by something they've seen or heard, my reaction is that they haven't tried very hard to analyze how they've felt. It doesn't communicate anything very substantial. And that's before we even to get to the fact that the word 'stupendous' is overused in any case.

If 'stupendous' is meaningless, what about 'howling winds' and 'crashing waves'? What's the problem there? Well, here I think the issue is subtly different – there is no doubt that one can, indeed, by 'amazed' by a view (though, as we've already found out, that's not telling the reader a lot), but do winds really 'howl'? I'd suggest that, for the most part, they do not. Take the dictionary definition, again – there's no harm in understanding the original and accurate definition of a word before you use it – '1. a long plaintive cry or wail characteristic of a wolf or hound. 2. a similar cry of pain or sorrow. 3. *Slang* a person or thing that is very funny.' It is rare, in my experience, for winds truly to make long plaintive cries characteristic of wolves or dogs, or to be hilariously funny, so why describe them like that? It is probably more accurate to describe strong (and cold) winds as 'biting', though even that is an overused phrase. So, what can you do? The answer is to try to delete these tired expressions from your mind and replace them with something fresher. If waves aren't 'crashing', what are they doing? Watch them again and again. Perhaps nothing will come to you at the time but, if the image sticks in your mind, maybe a more imaginative way of describing the scene will eventually form. And, if it doesn't, perhaps you shouldn't be writing about this in the first place.

The second main group of clichés to be avoided are those that are used as alternative ways of saying something. In travel writing, for example, a destination on someone's itinerary is often referred to as a 'port of call', while the 'acid test' of a good restaurant is whether it serves decent bread before your meal. Ask yourself: are these appropriate phrases in the context of your piece? And what do they really mean anyway? 'By the same token', you might observe someone 'busting a gut' to catch a bus. These clichés have the same problem as the first set we looked at: they don't tell the reader anything new or interesting. 'Port of call' is just a slightly pretentious word for destination, a word that tries to make it seem as though you're on an ocean cruise rather than a pub crawl. If someone is running really hard to catch a bus, and you want to write about it for your piece – it might add a touch of authenticity to your feature about using public transport to see the museums and art galleries of Berlin – then describe what you are seeing, not what you think you are seeing.

There's one other cliché trap to be avoided, and that's using them in an ironic way. Whenever I look back over travel articles I've written, I frequently think that I could have phrased something better or provided smoother links between paragraphs or ideas, but one particular sentence that still haunts me is something I wrote about watching a small group of lions in Kafue National Park in Zambia. It was six-thirty in the morning, and the alpha male of the pride was suddenly rather pathetically sick. 'So much for the dignity of the king of the beasts,' I wrote. Even though I wasn't trying to suggest that lions are 'the king of the beasts', this comes across as lazy, because you cannot ascribe notions of 'dignity' to animals such as lions that are not self-aware, and because I reached for a meaningless cliché that, even when it was coined, was not an accurate or helpful way to describe the species. (I was originally going to head this part of the chapter: 'Avoid clichés – like the plague!', but decided that it would once again give the impression that I couldn't be bothered to think of a better choice.)

It would take too long to list all the clichés that should be banned from any travel article, but here's a brief run-down of some of my all-time absolute stinkers:

'Feeling of awe': writers often feel moved to describe themselves as 'awed' when seeing a particular animal, but landscapes and buildings can do the same thing. Instead, think about how you *really* feel about whatever it is you're seeing.

'Rugged landscape': I was interested to see that the *Collins* dictionary definition of 'rugged' specifically says, '(of ground or terrain) Having a broken, rocky, and uneven surface', so you could argue that is accurate in certain circumstances. But I think the word is frequently used just to describe a wild place such as a moorland, which may not necessarily be rocky or uneven. The etymology is from the Norse word *rogg*, meaning 'shaggy tuft', and was originally used to describe animals as shaggy and careworn.

'Breathtaking views': natural landscapes, almost wherever they are in the world, have the power to induce the laziest writing, and this is one of the worst examples. Not only is it massively overused – I've probably used it myself in a moment of weakness, though I hope I deleted it before I filed the copy – but what does it mean? Was the person literally taking breaths while looking out from the mountain-top? One hopes so. Or is it that the person is having to take deeper, longer breaths in order to cope with the beauty of the scene before them? That was almost certainly the original idea behind the phrase, but it's also clearly nonsense, unless the person is at the top of Mount Everest. Either way, never, ever use it.

'Synonymous': as in 'The Serengeti is synonymous with wildlife' or 'Mexico is synonymous with violence'. Some people pedantically point out that 'synonymous' literally means 'having the same meaning', but that isn't my problem with this type of phrase – there is nothing wrong with adapting language in clever ways. Clearly, what the writer means in the second instance is that Mexico is such a dangerous place these days that the word communicates a feeling of violence, just as the word Serengeti immediately communicates the idea of wildlife. Again, I think the use of the word suggests laziness – if it's the case that everybody associates Mexico with violence, then why even bother to say it?

'My imagination ran riot': frequently used in moments of high excitement, danger or stress. Again, it's just a lazy way of describing your feelings. In fact, it doesn't actually say *what* you were feeling, and is often used to mean, for example, that a person was scared, which isn't really the correct use of the phrase.

'Iconic': applied to everything from the Sydney Opera House to the Taj Mahal, the New York skyline or almost anything that is well-known in some way or that people take to be representative of the place in it is found in. So, red deer are 'iconic' in the Scottish Highlands, for example. What's happened here is that many writers have taken this to sound intellectual and use it to make their work appear more intelligent, but through overuse, it's come to simply mean 'famous'.

'Take the plunge': travel writers are bound to have new experiences, so this is a much-favoured expression. Often, it can simply apply to a decision to go to country x or y or it can be taking part in a dangerous or exciting activity. It was probably quite a vivid use of language once, but isn't now.

3. SPREADING CONFUSION

ONE RELIABLE WAY TO induce someone to stop reading your article is to confuse them. They haven't sat down on the sofa with their magazine and a cup of tea in order to reread a particular sentence three times before understanding it. Absence of clarity can happen for a number of reasons, but here are some of the common things to watch out for:

– Muddling your homophones! Take this sentence:

In the distant passed, the cave I was standing in was home to an ancient race of people.

It's fairly obvious what the writer is saying here, but I have seen this mistake many times, and on occasions I have stumbled over the meaning. 'Passed' should, of course, have been spelled 'past'. Other obvious traps are 'bean' and 'been', 'lone' and 'loan', 'flee' and 'flea' and 'for' and 'four', but there are thousands more out there, and you can't avoid these pitfalls by simply doing a spellcheck. In many cases, making this mistake won't necessarily confuse the meaning, and it's highly likely that a decent travel editor will spot the mistake, but they are still best avoided.

– Poor punctuation and grammar. Take this sentence:

Having never been to Colombia before, I had to use all my powers of persuasion to convince my girlfriend that it was a safe place to travel.

What this actually means is that 'I' (the subject of the sentence) had never been to Colombia before ('Having never been to Colombia before' is an adjectival clause describing 'I', the subject of the sentence), but what I meant to say was that my girlfriend had never been to Colombia, and therefore needed convincing that it was safe. I see this sort of mistake surprisingly regularly and, if your grammar isn't one of your strong points, ask someone to read through your article before you submit it to eliminate these sorts of problems.

Poor punctuation often involves what I call 'punctuating by commas', and though this is easily remedied, it's irritating for an editor to have to deal with. Sentences such as the following are simply a nuisance, even if the problem can be rectified quite easily:

> I was travelling around Vancouver Island, I'd been there for three weeks, I was hoping to catch sight of a bear, or perhaps even a wolf, perhaps down on the beach looking for crabs.

Apart from the lazy 'listing' of the clauses, the big confusion here is who is looking for the crabs – the writer or the bears and/or the wolves?

– Going over the top. Originally, I was going to put this into a separate category of its own, but I realized that what bugs me about the use of overblown language and overly complex sentence structures is that they can become so convoluted that the reader no longer knows exactly what's going on. Take this sentence:

> The balloon soared over the lush green baize of the Amazon forest, and soon the chocolate-brown rivers resembled snakes writhing through the jungle, and the resonant sounds of the birds receded until there was nothing but the tumultuous roar of the gas burner and the heady feeling the we would continue to rise until we could see the whole, vast expanse of South America spread out below us like a banquet.

It's a silly example, but I have seen writing similar to this over the years. I think the reader will be so overwhelmed by images – 'lush green baize', 'chocolate brown rivers', 'writhing through the jungle', 'resonant sounds', 'tumultuous roar' and 'vast expanse of South America spread out below us like a banquet' – that they won't be able to take it all in. The key here is to use description and figures of speech sparingly. When you want to emphasize a particular aspect of what you have seen or heard, then go for it with a fresh and original figure of speech, not something that readers have heard 1,000 times before.

4. LECTURING: NOBODY WANTS TO BE PREACHED TO

WORKING ON A WILDLIFE magazine can be depressing at the best of times. There are so many stories out there of species going extinct, habitats being destroyed and trashed and environmental or climatic changes that threaten to affect entire ecosystems that it sometimes feels like we're being engulfed by a tidal wave of doom and gloom. Even when I have travelled to some of the world's most wildlife-rich parts of the world, I have invariably come across something that's endangering them – whether it's the spread of palm-oil plantations in South-east Asia that is bringing one of our closest relatives, the orangutan, to the brink of extinction, or the melting of sea ice in the Arctic that makes the long-term future of the polar bear doubtful.

But let's say you've managed to land a trip to Sabah, a state on the island of Borneo that belongs to Malaysia, and you've got a commission from a national newspaper. The chances are that you will see some of the palm-oil plantations that are wiping out natural habitats and you'll almost certainly hear from wildlife guides how that is affecting orangutans and other rare primates. You might consider using some of the quotes from your guide, if they're good and say something new or informative, but anyone reading the article is doing so because they want to understand more about a corner of the world they may not know much about. What you don't want to do is to start lecturing your readers about the way Western lifestyles (for example) are contributing to the loss of habitat. People aren't reading your article to be harangued. It's your job as a travel writer to bring the rainforest and the animals alive, not to tell readers what bad people they are for eating margarine or biscuits (both products that frequently contain palm oil).

Below is something I wrote – this is the type of hectoring copy that should definitely be avoided:

> *Homo catastrophia* hasn't quite destroyed everything in his path yet, but it seems like only a matter of time. Even in a natural wonder as vast and seemingly indestructible as the amazon, one can sense the awful fragility of the Earth's

precious living systems. But it's up to us – all of us – to stop this rapacious behaviour and give other living creatures a chance.

People aren't reading your article to be harangued. It's your job as a travel writer to bring the rainforest and the animals alive and, if necessary, to make readers aware of serious environmental issues, but not to make them feel bad for the impact they're having on the planet. This is just tedious and insulting to the readership. Of course, while this is probably the worst trap to fall into in terms of 'preachery', there are other, perhaps more subtle ones.

A good travel writer should become thoroughly immersed in the place they're in and the issues they're dealing with, but it's quite easy to do that and then consider yourself an expert on a particular subject. Step back a minute, however: it's unlikely you'd be an expert on a foreign destination even if you ended up living there for five or even twenty-five years, and the chances are that you'll be lucky to spend five days there. Can you really take in and understand all the sides of a complex issue in that time? Is it possible that you have spoken to all the people involved or with something to say about it? That doesn't mean to say that you shouldn't touch on the issues as you come across them, but you need to do so in a way that suggests that you are aware that you are only reporting a fraction of the opinions and that you cannot hope to fully reflect all sides of the argument or provide a complete and thorough analysis of the debate.

Another problem I occasionally see in travel writing is people feeling compelled to offer patronising or pointless advice. Here's an example I wrote myself, but again it reflects the sort of thing I have come across from time to time:

> My advice to anyone willing to take the plunge and go out on the town in Tallin? Just do it, you'll have a fantastic time. But remember that most people speak only faltering English, so give them a chance if they can't always make themselves understood. Don't drink too much, don't take all your money

or your camera with you and don't get into any unmarked taxis.

It's not your job to make sure tourists in Tallin don't get themselves into any sticky situations. If you felt it was important, you might find a way of introducing this into the piece by quoting someone you met. Something along these lines, for example:

My new friend, Villem, winked at me as he placed the two glasses of beer on the table. 'Hey, James, don't drink too much or you never know what might happen. There's plenty of people in this bar (and he swept his eyes conspiratorially around the crowded room) who will assume you've got lots of money on you. And never, ever get into an unmarked taxi.'

Of course, you can't just make this up but, if this is an issue of real concern, then presumably somebody will say it. And if you've only read it in a guidebook, then how do you know it's true?

The one caveat to this is that there clearly *is* a place for helpful information about dangerous parts of a city or tour operators with a reputation for risky practices in guidebooks. But that's guidebooks, and they serve a completely different purpose to general travel articles in newspapers and magazines or on the web.

I remember the day after arriving in Quito, the capital of Ecuador, for the first time. I was staying at the Gran Casino Hotel in the old part of the city and, after breakfast, I wandered outside. Way above me, I glimpsed the huge statue of the Virgin Mary on the hill known as El Panecillo. Without thinking, I ran up the winding steps that led to the summit on which the winged, 30m-tall figure stands, arriving with a pain in my lungs that I hadn't anticipated. I'd forgotten that Quito is nearly 10,000 feet above sea level, but I soon learned not to race around at altitude.

Unfortunately, that wasn't my biggest mistake. Arriving back at my hotel, I picked up my copy of the *South American Handbook*, the guidebook of choice for most travellers to South America in those days, to see what it had to say about this impressive if slightly eccentric landmark. I don't still possess the book, and I don't doubt that the advice has changed in the intervening years (this was back in 1988), but the words feel like they are etched into my memory. 'On no account', said the guidebook, 'walk up the steps from El Gran Casino to El Panecillo because you will almost certainly be mugged.' Whoops! I was only twenty-one, I'd been in South America less than twenty-four hours and I'd done the remarkably stupid thing of ignoring perfectly good advice in the guidebook that I'd probably spent £10 or £15 on. So, on second thoughts, say what you like about the dangers of a foreign destination – if my example is anything to go by, you'll probably be ignored anyway.

5. BEING SENTIMENTAL

I DISLIKE SENTIMENTALITY IN any form of writing, but it strikes me as especially tedious in travel writing, though that may simply be because I come across it more in wildlife writing than a travel editor specializing in, say, health and beauty or food does. There are reasons for this: people are more likely to have an emotional response to seeing wildlife or beautiful landscapes than they are to eating a meal or being pampered in a spa. That's fine: it just means that travel writers going on safari or trekking through a rainforest need to be on the alert for anything that's verging on sentimentality.

But what exactly do I mean by sentimentality? I was intrigued to see that there are two dictionary definitions – one is 'Prompted by feelings of tenderness, sadness or nostalgia', and there doesn't sound anything too bad with that. But the second definition specifically applies to works of literature, music or art, in which case sentimental is 'Dealing with feelings of tenderness, sadness, or nostalgia in an exaggerated and self-indulgent way'. Now that does sound like something to be avoided, and that's what I'm talking about.

Here's an example of some sentimental writing – as with all the examples in this chapter, I've written this myself, but I've seen plenty of writing like this over the years that falls into the same traps, though perhaps not always quite as obviously as this:

> Finally, the dolphins left us, and as they swam off in the direction of the setting sun, I said a silent 'thank you' for allowing me the privilege of experiencing that incredible moment of joy as they circled the boat, and I will always be grateful for the way they touched my heart and enriched my life forever.

So, what's wrong with this? Well, the first thing is that the use of so many words that imply 'gratitude' is over the top – even one word would be clichéd, but four – 'thank you', 'privilege' and 'grateful' – is far too many. Equally, there is the exaggerated sense of happiness – 'that incredible moment of joy', 'touched my heart' and 'enriched my life forever'. What's more, this is remarkably self-indulgent, because it implies that all that matters about the dolphin encounter is how the writer feels. While – as we have seen in earlier chapters – there is a place for revealing your emotions in travel writing, if this is all you do, it ceases to be of interest to your readers. While your personal, emotional or even psychological journey can be a vehicle for narrative intrigue, it is never (or rarely) going to be the whole story. Your job as a travel writer is to paint a picture of what you see, hear and experience, not to pour out your innermost personal feelings.

Even if we assume that, in this article, my emotions *are* the most important ingredient in the piece – well, writing like this isn't going to cut it because I'm choosing bland, overused words that actually say very little about my state of mind. Phrases such as 'touched my heart' and 'enriched my life' are not just clichés, they are also blunt and unrevealing. As a writer, I've got to work harder than that.

I'm sure that most people would never write anything like the example above, but there are more subtle forms of sentimentality that you need to be aware of. For example, it's very easy to write in simplistic and uncritical language about the people in a foreign country. I'm not saying that any writer should go out of their way to find fault with the people they meet on their travels, but it became a cliché quite some time ago to say what wonderful people country x or y is inhabited by, and therefore the phrase is meaningless. In any case, how can you generalize about a whole culture from the very few individuals that you have met? Is it not likely that you are bound to meet people who are persuaded of the advantages of being pleasant to tourists in their country? Don't you find many affable and friendly people in the country of your birth anyway?

While living in Ecuador in the 1990s, I attended a political meeting in a small, quite isolated region of the western cordillera of the Andes. It lasted for two days and, on the second morning, someone got up to revive the flagging energy of the delegates. 'The trouble with Ecuadorians,' he said at one point, 'is that we spend our lives believing we carry the weight of the world upon our shoulders. We've got to have more belief in ourselves.'

He had a point. I still recall attending a party – I use the term loosely – of a family who worked at the rainforest reserve that I had previously managed about three hours outside of Quito. They were poor *campesinos*, and the meal of fried chicken, rice, pasta and chips – Ecuadorians frequently seemed to regard the existence of green vegetables as simply a nuisance – wasn't much to crow about. However, I was nevertheless astonished when the hostess, a woman called Estella, stood up and apologized for the poverty of the food on offer (and probably what a miserable house they lived in). I remember interjecting to demur, claiming it all looked delicious, as though I were at some swanky dinner party in Ladbroke Grove, but when nobody else said anything, I shut up. The point about these stories is that they provide an alternative view of a foreign culture and it's a view that largely comes from the people themselves. And they are certainly not sentimental.

6. GETTING YOUR FACTS WRONG

THE FOLLOWING LINES WERE written by the revered former editor of *The Guardian*, C.P. Scott, in 1921 to celebrate the paper's 100th anniversary and his fiftieth as editor:

A newspaper is of necessity something of a monopoly, and its first duty is to shun the temptations of monopoly. Its primary office is the gathering of news. At the peril of its soul it must see that the supply is not tainted. Neither in what it gives, nor in what it does not give, nor in the mode of presentation must the unclouded face of truth suffer wrong. Comment is free, but facts are sacred.

The most famous quote herein is, 'Comment is free, but facts are sacred', but I thought it would be helpful to see this in context. Applying Scott's maxim to travel writing suggests that you can say what you like about the Taj Mahal – you can call it ugly and overhyped, if you really want – but don't get the date of when it was built, or why it was built, wrong.

Of course, getting your facts right goes well beyond making sure such basic historical details are correct. Have you spelled a person's name correctly? Just because they say that they're called 'Alex', don't assume that the name is written like that – I have a friend called Alix – so always ask how you spell someone's name if there's even a chance they'll make it into your story. In addition, even if they're called Alex in conversation, they may still prefer to be Alexander in an article. Vicki – as opposed to Vicky – is another pitfall (one I nearly made in a recent article), and there are so many variants of the name Jonathan (Jonathon, Jonothan, Jonothon etc.) that you cannot take anything for granted. Clark and Clarke, Smith and Smyth, Brown and Browne and even Jones and Jonze are all possible variants of the same surname. And that's just in Britain or other English-speaking countries.

Asking how you spell a person's name is one of the first things I was taught on my journalism course, and I now regard it as the most obvious thing to do (though, these days, with email and the internet, I am far more likely to know how a person's name is spelled before I even speak to them). Slightly less obviously, you can spell the name of a place right and still get it wrong. Ever heard of the Shetlands? They're the group of islands off the north coast of Scotland, right? Wrong – because while they are called the Shetland Islands or just plain Shetland, they are never the Shetlands. (It's one of the first things I was told on arriving there.)

Similarly, the Scilly Isles are never the Scillies. And if you think nobody could make such a crass error, you'd be wrong – it didn't take me long to find a story on the *Daily Mail*'s website about a 'well-being' survey, which told me 'those living in the Orkneys, the Shetlands and the Western Isles were the happiest of all'. My assumption has always been that 'the Orkneys' is similarly inaccurate, though I haven't checked this. If you ever want to write about the Orkney Islands, make sure you do.

Finally, on this subject, there are tricky little oddities that show the benefit of checking. Colombia the country is spelled correctly here, but the province of British Columbia, in Canada, has a 'u' instead of a second 'o'. It's Ecuador not Equador (as I hope you will remember from earlier in the book) and it's Dhaka if you're in Bangladesh but Dakar in Senegal.

This is the simplest part of getting your facts right – other things can be more complex. Can you be sure that a castle was built in the thirteenth century, just because your guide has told you so? Can you be sure that the wildflower they've pointed out to you is an orchid? They may be experts on local history but less sure about their natural history. You have to learn to assess what you can believe from what someone tells you and what you need to corroborate from other sources.

Having said that, in certain situations, it is acceptable to attribute a piece of information to someone, even if you yourself cannot guarantee its accuracy. While in North Cyprus a few years ago, I was shown some *poulia* by a restaurant owner – *poulia* (or *ambelpoulia*) is dead songbirds, regarded as a delicacy by Cypriots and some other Mediterranean cultures. I was told that the tiny, featherless beasts my host grabbed from the freezer were thrushes, but in reality they could have been any songbird and there was no way of corroborating this so, in the article, I attributed this information to the owner.

If, of course, I'd been told they were ostriches, I might have thought twice about repeating it, unless I'd decided to make a joke out of it, and this leads us into the next bear-trap to beware of – information that is completely false, but which has been repeated so often that it's easy to accept as true. My favourite example of this is the hippo: I have lost count of the number of times I have either read that the hippo is responsible for more human deaths than any other animal in Africa, been told by some well-meaning soul that this is the case or been asked if it is true. (The most recent example of this was the late Simon Hoggart repeating the claim as fact in his weekly Saturday column for *The Guardian* in August 2013.) But on one level, it is clearly nonsense: according to Unicef, the *Anopheles* mosquito kills an estimated 900,000 people in Africa every year through being the transmission vector of the malaria parasite – and I don't think anybody believes hippos are in that league.

But, let's leave aside, for the moment, the *Anopheles* mosquito, and assume by 'animal' someone means vertebrate. A few years ago, I was so determined to disprove the hippo hypothesis that I did some basic research. One of the first things I discovered was that poisonous snakes take a considerable toll on humans – up to 32,000 deaths a year – with two species – the saw-scaled viper and the puff adder – mostly to blame. Other research has shown that lions were responsible for 563 deaths in Tanzania between 1990 and 2005, so snakes clearly trump lions in the danger stakes. But what about hippos? How many deaths are attributable to them? Perhaps they could be given the 'most dangerous *mammal* in Africa' moniker? Well, probably not. When I contacted a scientist from the Hippo Specialist Subgroup at the World Conservation Union – the leading world body that deals with species conservation – I was surprised to find that, in fact, there are no statistics relating to human deaths caused by hippos whatsoever. While it is perfectly true that many Africans are rightly wary and even scared of hippos – never get between a hippo and water, I remember being told – that doesn't mean that, as a travel writer, you can turn them into mass killers.

Learning to smell a rat in a received piece of wisdom can be a question of simple common sense or developing your expertise. Take the oft-repeated truth that, 'You're never more than six feet from a rat in the UK'. Does that sound likely? Even if you assume that this is describing an urban situation, where rats might feasibly live in denser populations, you surely have to question the probability of such a claim. BBC Online clearly did, and asked Dr Dave Cowan of the Food and Environment Research Agency

(Fera) for his assessment. After numerous population estimates and urban area calculations, he came up with the more acceptable figure of, in cities, never being more than fifty metres, or 164 feet, from a rat. As the report concluded, '[This] doesn't have quite as much of a fear factor as 6ft away, but it's much more of a realistic estimate.'

Other examples in this line that could easily creep into your copy include the idea that the Inuit have fifty words for snow, the Chinese are building one coal-fired power station every day and marsupials are only found in Australia (this is demonstrably untrue – they're also found on the island of New Guinea and in the Americas).

The Inuit and snow story is interesting. I recently reread it in Bill Bryson's book about the English language, *Mother Tongue*, but had always assumed (and frequently read) that it was a myth. Double-checking it for this book, I found an article on the *Washington Post* website from January 2013 that said that it is, in fact, true – the Inuit dialect spoken in Canada's Nunavut province actually has at least fifty-three words for snow, while the Inupiaq dialect of Wales, Alaska, has some seventy terms for ice. Still, I would double-triple-quadruple check these facts were I ever to find myself writing about different words for snow in the Arctic.

7. MY LIFE AS A DOG: JUST BEING SILLY

WHILE I HAVE NEVER seen – as far as I can remember, anyway – any published travel article that takes on the persona of an animal, I have occasionally received pieces of writing, pitched as being suitable for *BBC Wildlife*, that do just that. Of course, you could argue that it's justified if you're writing fiction: there are plenty of famous works of literature, from *The Wind in the Willows* to *Watership Down*, that are written from the animal's point of view, though the Kenneth Grahame classic about Badger, Ratty, Mole and Toad is really using animals to describe people. But travel writing is too close to proper journalism – the 'gathering of news' as C.P. Scott put it – to allow you to take similar leaps of imagination.

'My life as a dog' is just one way in which travel writing can veer into the theatre of the absurd, and people who see the inanity of pretending to be a canine might still think it acceptable to ascribe human emotions to other living things, which is almost as ridiculous. How can anyone know if a beast is feeling angry, happy or sad? That's not to say that some species – elephants are good example, dolphins another – don't experience complex emotions that may be similar to those we feel; the point is that, unless we're Dr Dolittle, we cannot know what they are.

It's not just giving animals emotions that can sound silly. Over the years, I've read on several occasions that a lion (or tiger, bear or, in one especially dispiriting piece, a crocodile) was – quite literally – licking its lips in anticipation of a meal. 'Quite literally' is first and most importantly an overused cliché, but it also means 'precisely what is being described'. Too often, however, writers – er, quite literally – use the phrase to mean the opposite of this: 'The music was so loud that the ground was quite literally shaking'; 'People were quite literally racing everywhere at 100 miles an hour'. In these examples, the ground isn't shaking (the windows might be, I suppose) and people aren't travelling at 100 miles an hour. Generally speaking, avoid all use of this phrase, though I did once see an appropriate use by a writer describing a woman living on the famous Smokey Mountain of Manila in the Philippines: she was living quite literally on top of a dump. The phrase works here because we often say that someone lives in a dump, whether we're describing their house or their neighbourhood, but it isn't normally true.

Another area where writing can dissolve, from time to time, into silliness is dialogue. I've read imagined conversations in somebody's mind that just sound childish. I've written this example below myself:

The bridge was long and rickety and stretched over the torrential river below.
'Come on, let's go!'
'Oh, I don't know – is it safe?'

'It'll be fine – what are you worrying about?'
'Getting wet. Losing my life!'
'The bridge has been here for years.'
'That's what I'm worried about!!'

And so on. So, what *is* wrong with this? One thing to say is that it isn't a realistic description of the mental debate that takes place in someone's mind when faced with a dilemma of this nature. Thoughts tend to occur in a far more random manner and rarely – well, in my experience – take the form of an actual, internal debate. The other thing to ask is: what does it add to the story and what does it tell the reader? Do we care about the writer's concerns about a rickety bridge? Not that much – in such a situation, it might be valid to portray the flimsy nature of the bridge, even to briefly dwell on one's own fears and then watch and describe how local people use it without thinking twice. But by creating this imagined conversation inside my head, all I've done is trivialized things.

Note, too, another literary 'tic' that I would avoid – the use of exclamation marks to add emphasis to your text. The occasional 'screamer' is fine, particularly following an imperative (as in, 'Come on, let's go!') because it can suggest the tone and manner in which the words were said, though you can achieve the same effect with clever use of description. But mostly the use of exclamation marks just makes your copy sound as if it is shouting at the reader. They are best avoided – most editors will pluck them out on a first edit, so you're just making extra work for them.

To sum up, in no particular order, these are my 'Seven deadly sins of travel writing':

- Pointless information
- Clichés
- Being muddled and confusing
- Lecturing
- Being sentimental
- Getting your facts wrong
- Just being silly.

I think the important thing is to realize that, while you may consider it impossible that you would ever sink as low as some of the fictional examples I've come up with, we're all capable of verging towards some or all of them. If I had to pick out two, I'd say that the ones every writer has to work hardest to avoid are clichés and making factual errors, but as a writer you should know what your own weaknesses are.

Q&A WITH FRANCESCA SYZ

FRANCESCA SYZ IS THE travel editor of *Sainsbury's* magazine and also has a weekly column in the Saturday *Daily Telegraph*. After starting her publishing career on *Wallpaper* magazine, she quickly landed a position on *Condé Nast Traveller*, before leaving to become a freelance writer and editor.

Starting your travel writing career on *Condé Nast Traveller* sounds like a big break...
Well, I was a features assistant for five years, but it was quite frustrating, because there was no features editor so I couldn't be trained up in that job, and so I didn't make any real progress. My job was to come up with ideas and do any research that was thrown at me and some odd bits of writing.

Did you get any nice trips?
Eventually. I started moaning that I wanted to do more, and I got a few big pieces to do – I went to Fiji, for example, which was great. The thing about *Condé Nast Traveller* is that, if you are on staff, you are either one of three people who travel or you are a galley slave. But it started me off; it was a really good experience.

So, how has it worked out since you left?
I have been freelance now for six or seven years. I've

done a few jobs as maternity cover on *High Life* magazine and as travel editor on *Red*, and these made me feel less anxious. I have been really lucky not to be out of work, and it's helped that I've found quite a few regular gigs, such as the regular page on the *Telegraph*'s Saturday edition.

But your main 'gig' is *Sainsbury's* magazine?
Yes, I've been doing it for just over three years. We run four to eight pages of travel-related features and editorial a month. For obvious reasons, we are quite into 'foodie' stories, so we look to do 'foodie' city breaks and destinations pieces. Or we might do a piece where we send a writer to spend a few days with a well-known chef or rising star who is based in an interesting location.

Who reads the magazine?
The magazine is mostly aimed at professional women who have families and a disposable income, but don't have time to know where they want to go on holiday. They are more likely to go with a tour operator, so it's mostly tour-operator trips that we run in our pages. But we also do what I call 'canny travel' – we had one family go to the Seychelles but, instead of staying in luxury accommodation, they stayed in B&Bs and inns. We wanted to show that the Seychelles wasn't all ridiculously expensive and that it wasn't just for couples.

How do you get your trip ideas – do you approach companies for trips or do they come to you?
It's a mixture of both, but we find that when PRs send out invitations for a trip, they will go to lots of people who then all pitch the idea to us. Given that this story is now likely to be everywhere, are we going to commission that? Not really. *Sainsbury's* magazine tries to be quietly on-trend, so it doesn't want to be doing what everyone else is doing.

So, what do you do?

Well, we now say that if the company is running a group trip, we will never run a piece longer than a page. In an ideal world, I'd like to be going to PRs and suggesting ideas that we could do. For instance, it would be great to say to my editor, 'Burma looks interesting, what do you think?', and then send somebody on a trip. I don't work with tourist boards very much – trips they organize can sometimes be a bit dull because they have to tick boxes.

What sort of writers do you look for?

I'd like to say that we don't just pick 'foodie' writers, we pick good writers, but my editor has better foodie writer contacts than me, so she tends to suggest people.

Do you use new writers?

I am definitely up for using new writers but I need to see examples of their work. I do get a lot of pitches from people who have not picked up the magazine, and that's not very clever because they have no idea what we are looking for. Most weeks, I get about ten pitches but, at the most, I can get up to thirty.

How do you like people to send in ideas?

It's best to send your pitch in by email, but pick up the phone after that if I don't reply. One thing I always want people to be able to answer is: why now? Why run the piece now? It could be something newsy or it could be something that is happening in that destination at that time of year. I need to know: when would someone want to go there and what's the best time of year? When you're reading a piece, sometimes it's nice to imagine that people are doing exactly what is being described in the article.

What ideas don't you want?

Lots of people pitch round-ups, but I write all these in-house. We haven't got the budget to commission them out.

What do you look for in travel writing?
Writing should be intelligent, informative, colourful and accessible. The magazine has quite a chatty style. I also want writing to be really evocative and to transport someone there, while packing in as much practical information as possible. It could be something along the lines of, 'If you're like this, then you'll love this place'. In my experience, if you get the opening paragraph right, it sets it off and you can write a really great piece.

Do you give writers a very thorough brief?
The brief is really important. It has got to be tight, but I try really hard not to make it really annoying so that I write the piece for them. I try to make the brief a bit chatty, so it's like the style I'm looking for.

Do you ever 'spike' pieces – either because you don't like the writing or because the trip wasn't very good?
It happens. There have been times when someone's filed a piece, I've read through the first couple of paragraphs and it's seemed fine and I've left it. Then I come back to it later and find that it needs a lot of work, and I can't use it. One time, the writer filed her piece, but the trip had been terrible and I had to tell the tour operator I couldn't use it. They admitted that it was a new destination which they hadn't done before. So the writer didn't get her fee, but I did commission another piece from her, so she got another trip.

What sort of ideas are you not interested in?
One thing that always amazes me is when people come to me with a trip they've been offered that's described as 'The insider's guide to San Sebastian and Seville', for example and they're doing it all in three days. How's that going to work? How are you going to get an insider's guide to a city in a day or so? How is that going to be interesting to the reader?

What makes a good writer?
Having experience is so important. If a writer stays in a hotel that's really amazing and ticks all the boxes and then comes back and says, 'My god, there was champagne in the room', well, that's not enough. We need more than that. You have to get over things like that; you must not be wowed. You have to be able to notice how the place is run and other small details. But it's also true that sometimes seeing things with fresh eyes can be good too.

Do you advise writers to take lots of notes?
When I first started out, I had my notebook with me and I was writing in it all the time. Now I'll go to dinner, which may be an important part of the story, and just write down everything I can remember when I get back to my room. It's a bit like the dilemma of taking photos – if you spend your whole time with your eye glued to the view-finder, you'll miss out.

8. DO THE RIGHT THING: THE ETHICS OF TRAVEL WRITING

THE PROS AND CONS OF TOURISM

CHATTING WITH ANOTHER PARENT at the swimming pool one Saturday, halfway through writing this book, I was asked what I did for a living. While talking about my work for *BBC Wildlife* magazine, I also happened to mention this project and what it involved, and his eyes lit up with interest. 'What are you going to say about Sri Lanka?' he asked me keenly. 'I mean, the government there has been involved in appalling human rights abuses.'

The implication of what he said – the inference I took, anyway – was to question whether people should travel to Sri Lanka, given those human rights abuses. It is an important issue, certainly, but does it really have any bearing for a travel writer? The travel-writer's job is to observe and to report, not to judge – not morally, anyway. Is that really true? Let's examine the issue more closely.

The civil war between the majority Sinhalese government and the minority Tamil people in Sri Lanka lasted twenty-six years, and took the lives of hundreds of thousands of people. Both sides were accused of major abuses of human rights and, as recently as March 2013, a report by the London-based Sri Lanka Campaign for Peace & Justice accused the government of continuing to hold political prisoners without trial and torturing them – four years after the civil war had officially ended (in 2009). 'The war has now been over for nearly four years, yet prisoners are kept in abominable conditions and deprived of basic human rights', the report stated.

I agreed with the other parent that Sri Lanka was a complex issue, but I also had to admit to something fairly significant: I travelled there for the magazine in 2004 to write a special travel supplement solely about the country's wildlife and nature reserves. I said that I thought publishing the supplement had been justified because tourism to places such as Sri Lanka helps to protect wildlife. This has been demonstrated in any number of cases, and there are two main factors why: first, it gives wild animals a value, so that local people, who benefit by running hotels or working as guides, have a vested interest in protecting both them and the habitats that support them; and second, because the very presence of tourists in a national park prevents or at least inhibits poaching.

Indeed, there are tour operators who claim that tourism is virtually the only reason why tigers continue to cling on in India. The national parks system has become so corrupted, they argue, that the only thing that will deter poachers (who kill tigers to sell their bones into the traditional Chinese medicine trade, as well harvesting other 'by-products' such as pelts) is the presence of tourists in the park, which increases the possibility of getting caught.

Or take this example. Gorilla conservationists have told me that one of the main reasons that mountain gorillas have not just survived, but increased in numbers, in the past two decades or so is the millions of dollars that tourists bring to the countries where they are live (Rwanda and Uganda – mountain gorillas are also found in the Democratic Republic of Congo, but tourism there is of a much smaller scale), both through national park fees and the money they spend in hotels, camps and restaurants.

In both cases, you could argue that writing and raising awareness about these species is a positive thing. Wildlife tourism has come on in gigantic strides over the past couple of decades, and many conservation groups happily exploit its benefits to wider society – in 2011, RSPB Scotland published a report that said that the presence of white-tailed eagles on the island of Mull in the Inner Hebrides generated some £5m and supported the equivalent of 110 full-time jobs as a result of the tourists they attracted. Those travel writers who first highlighted the marvellous spectacle of watching Britain's largest bird of prey can feel they have contributed to what many would call 'sustainable tourism'. ('Sustainable' anything is a buzz concept among conservation and environmental groups these days and, while I certainly think that white-tailed eagle tourism anywhere is a good thing, I would personally hesitate to use the word 'sustainable' in any travel article – like the term 'ecotourism', it's so overused that it ceases to carry any weight. You are better off pointing out the ethical side of something in more subtle language.)

But it's not just wildlife and natural habitats that potentially gain from tourism. There is the argument that society as a whole in the place or country being visited benefits, both from the money and jobs it brings and from the exposure to different cultures. Hilary Bradt, the founder of the Bradt Travel Guides (who is interviewed at the end of Chapter 9) feels passionately that tourism is a force for good in many countries all over the world.

But there is, of course, another side to this argument – many sides, indeed. First of all, tourism frequently involves someone flying thousands of miles to sit on a beach or go shopping, spewing out tonnes of carbon emissions in the process. Then there's the issue of whether tourism is really an economic benefit: many hotels and large-scale tourism enterprises in developing countries are owned by foreign interests, meaning that much of the money comes in, only to leave again by the back door. Employees of those enterprises will be paid miserable salaries, leaving many to wonder whether they are truly better off. Some countries are stuffed with resorts that are like 'gated communities', which tourists have no need to leave, so they are barely exposed to local cultures. Developments can be damaging, so that the natural habitat is destroyed for the sake of a golf course or whatever. Finally – and this is where we come back to the example of Sri Lanka – another frequent concern is that tourism can help prop up abusive and repressive regimes. Clearly, therefore, travel writing has the potential to do the same.

THE ROLE OF THE TRAVEL WRITER

So, WHAT'S A TRAVEL writer to do? How do you decide what is ethical to write about and what isn't? How do you decide where to go and what trips to turn down? How much does it matter? There are a few things to say about this.

First of all, it's very easy to exaggerate the importance and influence of travel writing, either in a positive or negative way. One article about how the Dalmatian coast of Croatia is the new Costa Brava isn't going to persuade half the population of Birmingham to get on the next EasyJet flight to Dubrovnik, however brilliantly original the prose is, and however rich and textured the language. Equally, just because you as a travel writer find the Costa Brava isn't to your liking, that doesn't mean it's going to be suddenly abandoned by British tourists en masse. Travel writing is read for a variety of reasons and, for many people, it's pure entertainment.

The second thing is that, as a travel writer, you need to work out what you care about. If you're passionate about grass-roots projects, then you can probably justify writing about them in most countries in the world – even Sri Lanka or, say, Burma, a country frequently highlighted by campaigners as a place that tourists should steer clear of. As someone who writes almost entirely about conservation issues, I try to make sure that my travel articles are about or include conservation stories. Three of my most recent articles have been about: a project researching Risso's dolphins on the island of Bardsey off the coast of west Wales, conservation work to increase the survival rates of turtle hatchlings in the Turkish part of Cyprus, and the reintroduction of common cranes to the wetlands of the Somerset Levels. It helps that I find it more interesting to write about a place where there is something other than, 'Go there, see that,' to say, and I hope it's more interesting to read.

The third thing is that, wherever you go and whoever is taking you, you are still there ostensibly as a reporter, as a journalist, and you are there to report the truth. That sounds like a grand thing to say, but it is important to remember that you retain your independence from the government of that country even if it was the tourist board that paid for your plane ticket and is putting you up in its hotels.

So, work out what you want to specialize in, make sure you know as much about that subject as possible, and consider whether you are in a position to make a judgement about a particular project or trip that you are being offered. Many of my friends, and not a few of my work colleagues, mocked me when I travelled to China in 2008 to join one of the earliest 'panda-tracking' tours in the Qinling Mountains of Sichuan Province and then returned without having seen even the twitch of a panda's ears. What sort of wildlife trip is that, people wondered? It wasn't as if I saw much other wildlife – the only other mammals I saw were two large, goat-like animals called takins, three wild boar and one dead goral.

But it was a great trip, partly because (truism alert) Chinese culture, landscapes and habitats are so different to our own in Western Europe. But what made it special for me is that tracking is one way in which we in the West can help the Chinese protect pandas – the local people who earn money from this were once poachers. And by protecting pandas, you protect their habitat and the other wildlife that lives there. I believe that I have a sufficient understanding of this issue to write about it legitimately. To me, it matters that pandas and their habitat survive – the question is, what matters to you?

THE BURMA QUESTION

ARGUABLY, ONE OF THE biggest dilemmas for travel writers in the past two or three decades has been Burma – or Myanmar, as it was renamed by the military dictatorship. Just working out what to call the country has prompted numerous debates in our office, and no doubt in the offices of thousands of publications around the world. I don't think anyone has come up with a satisfactory answer to this problem: the country was known as Burma until 1989, when it was changed to the Republic of the Union of Myanmar by the military government because they considered 'Burma' to be colonial. However, because the regime lacked democratic legitimacy, some publications felt they should continue to call the country Burma. The country suffered many years of political and cultural isolation because of alleged human rights abuses by the government. With the release of Aung San Suu Kyi in 2010, Burma/Myanmar isn't quite the outcast it once was, but the issues it poses to travel writers are still relevant – even if it is no longer the pariah of the international community, there will always be countries that are.

Lonely Planet guidebook writer Adam Skolnick has visited Burma (which, on reflection, would be *my* choice) on a number of occasions, and in 2012 he had a piece published in *Outside* magazine about the so-called Free Burma Rangers, a sort of underground humanitarian and documentary outfit which has been operating in the country since 1997. It's what you would call a proper piece of journalism, albeit with a 'travel' aspect. But, when interviewed by another travel writer and journalist, Alice Driver, for a piece on the Matador Network website about writing travel pieces on Burma, he said, 'I personally have no problem with travelers experiencing the place. And I never have. It's magnificent and should be experienced.' And he carried on:

> When I first visited Burma in 2005 I was invited on a press trip by an adventure travel company, and I didn't ever question the invitation. I don't feel the same way that some of these people feel, that you shouldn't go to these places. It was spooky at times. We were followed at one point in the Shwedagon Pagoda. It was very much more of a distrustful time there, the internet was highly censored, secret police were everywhere, and there was still a passionate 'Don't Go There' attitude among informed progressives, because Aung San Suu Kyi was advocating a travel boycott. To me, that made it more interesting to be there.
>
> Sanctions are a debatable issue, and that's what that is, a travel sanction. I don't think sanctions work all the time. I don't see them working in Iran. I don't think they ever worked in Myanmar. That's not the reason these reforms happened.

The interviewer revealed that she had 'never received such flak for visiting a country' after she wrote about her trip to Burma, saying that other travellers had told her, 'I can't believe you support dictatorships.' She went on: 'I didn't manage to make them understand that volunteering at a school in Yangon, riding a bicycle through Bagan, and eating fish-head curry with locals created the kind of personal relationships I believed were part of both fomenting change and of human rights.'

I'm on the side of the travel writers, in this case, though I'm not sure whether a writer can really claim to be fostering human rights by talking to a few locals. That said, it probably doesn't do any harm.

THE *LONELY PLANET* AFFAIR

IT WOULD BE REMISS to write a whole chapter on the ethics of travel writing without referring to the *Lonely Planet* guidebook writer, Thomas Kohnstamm, who caused a media storm in 2008 when he published a book called *Do Travel Writers Go to Hell?* There were three main sides to the controversy: first, that he claimed to have written a guidebook about Colombia without having been there; second, that he made up, or plagiarized from other books, some sections of some titles; and third that he sold drugs to supplement his income while travelling and researching in South America. There was also a lurid story of him having sex with a waitress on a table in a restaurant he was reviewing. 'The table service is friendly', he wrote.

Most major media outlets in the UK covered the story at the time, and Kohnstamm was even interviewed on Radio 4's morning current affairs programme, *Today*. The whole issue of whether you could trust guidebooks was raised, and the internet was awash with other travel writers and bloggers complaining about his behaviour.

Some of it was undoubtedly sensationalized, whether deliberately by the writer in order to promote his book or not is unclear. But, for example, while it's true that he didn't go to Colombia for the book, all he was contracted to write was the introduction and the general information about the country's history, environment, food, drink and culture, which to a certain extent can be done from anywhere. In an interview with Matt Kepnes on the Nomadic Matt website (http://www.nomadicmatt.com), Kohnstamm said:

> Would my research have benefited from me visiting the country: yes. But the reality is that on many low-budget travel writing projects (i.e. countries like Colombia), publishers can only afford to send a couple of the writers into the field. Lonely Planet did not contract me to go to Colombia as there was not enough money in the budget for the book. I did the research based off of memory, notes, interviews with Colombians and research at the Colombian Consulate in San Francisco.

So, what lessons are there here for the aspiring travel writer? Personally, I think the Kohnstamm affair lifted the lid on something I have always partly suspected – that anyone can become a guidebook writer if they really want to, and that most are very badly paid. This doesn't mean that most guidebook writers aren't professional, merely that, given the way the industry works, a few rogue elements are bound to creep in. You could say that guidebooks continue to sell because the people who buy them find them useful – the information must therefore be accurate, and the books must have been thoroughly and properly researched. It's certainly true that, on the whole, guidebook writers are not like Thomas Kohnstamm.

And one final thought – while Kohnstamm effectively 'outed' himself, it's also the case that writers who make things up or plagiarize do get found out. In Britain, there was the case of Johann Hari, a columnist for *The Independent*, who had to admit that he passed off quotes that were either given to other journalists, or had originally been written in books, as things that had been said to him. Then there was the case of Jayson Blair, the *New York Times* reporter who, in 2003, was discovered to have made stories up on a regular basis. An article written by Jill Rosen for the *American Journalism Review* in 2003 explained how Blair had frequently taken reports from other newspapers and essentially rearranged them and handed them in to his own news desk with his byline. He even claimed to have visited the location he was writing about when he may not have been within 1,000 miles of it. According to Rosen's article, the only surprise about Blair's exposure was that it didn't happen sooner – plenty of people claimed to have seen it coming. Anyway, the point is that if you try taking short-cuts with the truth in the way Blair did, the chances are that you will be found out.

FINAL THOUGHTS

IN THIS CHAPTER, I have examined two of the fundamental ethical issues facing a travel writer: first, the extent to which they have a responsibility to make sure their writing fulfils a social or political 'good' in some way (and on the other side of the coin, to ensure that nothing they write has a negative impact) and, second, the responsibility they have to report what they hear and see (and not make things up). Earlier, in chapter three, I also looked at some of the ethical issues around accepting free trips.

There are other things to consider. I have already looked (in Chapter 4) at the responsibility a travel writer has to the people they meet and interview – in particular, what quotes they use and how they portray their sources, but it's worth delving into this again. One key thing to remember is that you have to make an assessment of the extent to which someone understands the media – how 'media savvy' they are. If they're the marketing manager of a massive hotel chain, you can assume that you can report what they say without asking permission to quote them. But if your guide tells you something indiscreet, you might think twice before using the quote in your piece. There are no absolute rights or wrongs on this, every case has to be taken on its merits. But you have to remember what your job is, and that is to bring the place you're writing about alive and make it an entertaining and informative read.

A friend of mine went on a rafting trip in Thailand a few years ago and amused me with his story about the briefing he and his fellow rafters received before they set out. 'Fun first, safety second,' one of the guides concluded. It's a great quote, and I would have been tempted to use it had I been writing a piece, though I certainly wouldn't have attributed it to a particular person. I have had specific instances where a guide has told me that poaching is rife in an area, but I haven't reported this because I have been unable to verify it. In that situation, you are operating as a journalist, rather than merely a writer, and I think as a result your responsibilities shift. As a writer, you can report what someone says if it tells the reader something about that person; as a journalist, you have to be satisfied that what they say is truthful.

Still, if you want my best advice on keeping your integrity as a travel writer, it would be this: don't become so caught up in your own self-importance that you lose touch with reality. I was astonished to read this blog on a well-known US website:

> I tend to be a favorite topic of conversation at parties and get-togethers. I'd like to think it's because of my sparkling personality but really, it's my job that lures the crowds. I'm a travel writer.
>
> It's true, I get to spend my days crafting prose that inspires people to spend their hard-earned dollars at various hotels and restaurants around the world – and, yes, I get paid for it. It is indeed a dream job for me, but that doesn't mean it's always dreamy.
>
> This summer has been packed with social events and the inevitable 'you're so lucky' comments, so I wanted to dispel a few myths about being a travel writer.

If you ever end up writing something like this, truly it's time to quit and spend some time in the woods.

Q&A WITH MARK WATSON

MARK WATSON IS THE executive director of Tourism Concern, the only charity in the UK that campaigns for ethical tourism. He has previously worked in the field of human rights.

What does Tourism Concern do?
We give out advice on how operators can have a positive impact on the destinations they work in and develop codes of conduct for them. We also lobby governments and authorities, but perhaps the most important thing we do is to give advice to tourists on how they can make better and more informed choices on where they go on holiday.

How do you do that?
We nudge people to think about the impacts of their holiday to the destinations they visit. Tourism is a major part of a lot of economies: for sixty-five out of the sixty-nine least-developed nations, tourism is the biggest source of their foreign income, so it brings huge benefits. It encourages local people to protect natural resources. And then there is the cultural exchange: we are social animals, and moving around the planet and meeting people is a very positive experience. It can be a force for good.

So what's the problem?
Unfortunately a lot of tourism does not do that, and lots of people are rushing around the planet not being very beneficial to the parts of the world they visit.

What do you think about travel writing?
If you look at the papers, travel journalism is always very positive about a destination, and one reason for this is

because companies or the destinations themselves have paid for their visit. Because you are already beholden to them, a bias creeps into the system. It is unlike most other areas of journalism.

Is that the only problem?

Well, there's a combination of factors. First, hotels and destination tourist boards are going to show travel writers the best things anyway, and they largely control what's on the itinerary. Second, if someone is funding your trip, you are going think twice about what you say if you want to do another one with them. And third, if you look at any travel writing, it's always in the glossiest part of the magazine or in a separate supplement of the newspaper. Travel editors don't want depressing travel stories in these sections.

Is all travel writing terrible, then?

No, that is not to say that all of it's bad, just that there is a big issue with it.

Should travel writers – and tourists – visit countries that have repressive regimes?

There's an interesting debate to be had here. Tourism Concern supported the boycott of Burma but, on the whole, I am not a big fan of boycotts. Those people who don't care will continue to go anyway, and those that do care won't – so you'll end up with fewer people who care going to the destination. The end result will be that the people who depend on tourism for their livelihood will suffer, so a boycott will not do them any favours.

So we should all go where we want?

I remember I went to a place where half the people in the city complained about living under a repressive regime and being under military occupation – and now Northern Ireland is quite peaceful. The point is, where do you draw the line? I don't think that you can say, 'You can't go here and you can't go there.'

Is there anything we should do, though?
The world is a complex place, and it's better to do good than harm. So if you do go to Burma and you put money into the hands of the junta by staying in a government-run hotel, that's not great. But if it goes into the hands of local people, that's a good thing. True, it's not always easy to know what will have a good impact, but there are some easy things that people can do to make these decisions. We have country by country guides – so, if you're going to Tanzania, here are three things [for example] you shouldn't do. If people can just change their behaviour a little, then they will not do as much harm.

What do you mean, change their behaviour?
Well, visit places that are better for the local community and local people. You will get a better holiday and a better experience as a result. And, from a travel writer's perspective, that's what editors are looking for anyway – they want unique and interesting places and great images. It is not very interesting to stay in, or write about, a three-star hotel in Cancun which is a concrete block and looks exactly the same as every other hotel in the resort. It's much nicer to say that you've stayed in a treehouse in Ecuador.

They tend to be more expensive, though.
Some people say that we only book holidays on price, but that's blatantly not true. If that were the case, we would all spend our holidays in a ditch. People will book the best holiday on the budget that they can afford. Many want a different experience, and that's something they will pay for. Yes, these community-run projects can be more expensive, but part of this is paying a decent wage to the people who work there. Most of us don't want to exploit other people.

Flying abroad involves a lot of carbon emissions – what do you say about that?

Everywhere we go, we have impacts. We have to work out whether, on balance, it's positive or negative. People say to me how can we publish an 'ethical' travel guide if you have to fly there. But if we stop flying tomorrow, it's the countries we visit that will suffer. If tourism disappeared in South America, for example, there would be much greater pressure to turn tropical rainforest into soya fields, and that would result in a corresponding increase in carbon emissions.

So, what's the answer?

If you are going to use up a big chunk of your personal carbon allowance going somewhere, you have to make sure you do some good when you get there. There are people who travel to countries such as Gambia who get off the plane and go to their resort and never leave – they never see any of the rest of the country. They barely know where they are. Ideally, people would go on longer holidays but less often. Picking towels off the floor and low-energy light bulbs aren't going to make a lot of difference.

Shouldn't we aim to fly less? Take the train instead?

Well, we're going down to Morocco to do a fundraising trip and, instead of flying, we're getting the train to Marrakesh. But one of our trustees said that we *should* be flying – by getting the train, we're spending three days getting there, three days that we could have had in Marrakesh, spending money and benefiting the local economy.

Are travel writers to blame when tourist places get ruined?

No, I don't think so. Imagine a small Greek island which has a ferry taking over 300 people a week. Then someone on the island says, let's build an airport and bring more than 10,000 a week – the reason for this sort of unsustainable development is not down to travel writers. The more that writers cast their nets about, the more it spreads the tourist load around.

Is there a problem with how writers reflect people?
Sometimes they want those people to be their image of what they expect them to be. It's about respect and understanding. It's clearly not right to go to see the Jarawa on the Andaman Islands, where police were taking bribes off tourists. But if this sort of poverty tourism is done well, and local people are benefiting, then it's OK, even though it is a bit odd for people to visit poor people as part of their holiday experience.

How can it be done well?
Well, imagine someone is going to Rio (for the World Cup, for example). Is it better that they spend some time in a *favela*, engaging with the local community and spending money with them, than if they had just lain on the beach for another day? The best ones take tourists walking round the *favela*. They get to meet local people and spend time in their bars. What locals don't want is coach-loads of people driving through the area and poking their cameras out of the window without getting out and without benefiting that community at all.

What advice would you give to aspiring travel writers?
A lot of travel writers tend to write only about things – waterfalls and beachfronts, for example, but a lot of the reasons we travel are to meet people. People are very important. Look at those places where they welcome tourists, these are good and interesting destinations. It is about meeting people. I do worry that, in this Facebook age, travel is becoming merely about pins on a map.

9. GOING HOME: STAYING IN THE TRAVEL-WRITING BUSINESS FOR GOOD

READING THIS BOOK – even if you have got this far – won't help you become a travel writer. Or, at least, it's not the only thing, or even the most important thing, that will help you become a travel writer. It might open a few doors or point you in the right direction of a few doors. It might give you some idea of how to open them, but you've got to push and you've got to push hard. There's a lot of competition out there, and – you know what? – it doesn't have to be that good to succeed.

That's one of the things about travel writing – and probably about writing in general – there are a lot of poor writers out there who have made millions or even gained critical acclaim. You will have your own ideas about who those people are. There are also a lot of very good travel writers, with whom you are in competition, who are only just keeping their heads above the water, and who find that they have to supplement their income with other, more commercial forms of writing or indeed other ways of making a living entirely. So don't expect to shoot the moon on your first deal.

As I've said before, travel writing shares something in common with straight reporting and something in common with the art of fiction. As a result, I think, it's peculiarly hard to say that this is the right way to do it and this is the wrong way. This makes coming up with a set of rules equally difficult, especially if you try to come up with some arbitrary number such as, say, ten. Clearly, there are not ten golden rules for travel writing, but

I've come up with a list of ten – well, let's call them command-ments – that offer a final insight into what you need to do to make yourself successful. Or just get a few articles published.

1. You're only as good as your next pitch

JUST BECAUSE YOU'VE HAD something published, even if it's a double-page spread in a major national broadsheet or one of the big-shot travel magazines, it doesn't mean that the travel editors of all the other publications are going to be beating a path to your door and thrusting tickets to Honolulu into your hands, crying, 'Spend a month there, have some fun, write what you want.' Even the editor who has published your piece, and given you your 'big break' isn't going to call. They might even forget to tell you when your piece is being published, and they may not care if they never hear your name again. It's *even* possible that they might be less willing to publish your second piece, because they know what you're like now – reliable, yes, technically sound, yes, even funny at times. But that's just it – previously, you were a bit of a mystery to them, and that might have per-suaded them to take a chance. Now you're just like everybody else – but with fewer contacts.

What this first published piece has shown you (and a few other people, but mostly you) is that you can succeed in this game. But now you've simply got to apply the lessons you learned from getting that article accepted to another – many other – situations. It's almost like you have go back to square one again. When I first started as a junior reporter, I remember a fellow novice telling me (as if he were the most experienced person in the world), 'You're only as good as your last story.' But in the fiercely competitive world of travel writing, it's even worse than that: you're only as good as your next pitch.

2. You don't have to love travelling

ONE OF THE THINGS I often see stated as fact is that the fun-damental thing you need to be a travel writer is to love travelling. Well, I'm not so sure. Undoubtedly, some (and some very successful) travel writers love travelling, but I don't think it's an absolute prerequisite. I was struck by a column by the renowned travel writer and guidebook publisher Hilary Bradt (interviewed at the end of this chapter) in the May 2013 issue of *Wanderlust* in which she discussed her love/hate relationship with travelling: 'I don't want to go. I don't want to go to Poland tomorrow. I want to stay in my nice cosy house. I don't want that long journey from Devon to Luton, an airport hotel and the five o'clock wake-up call.'

I don't recall ever feeling quite like this – but then, I've never been to Poland. However, I do know that arriving at an airport can make my stomach muscles tighten slightly, and not in a good way, that the sheer boredom of 'airport life' has, on occasions, made me feel that I'm wasting my life away and there have been times on long-haul flights when I have wished to be anywhere but 40,000 feet up in the sky.

I'm sure every travel writer has these moments. What's important is that you retain a love of exploring, which I think is a very different thing to travelling. Exploring doesn't have to mean hacking your way through dense tropical rainforest, it simply means trying to discover something new about a city or savannah. For me, the great excitement about travel is getting up in the morning (perhaps having arrived late the night before) and simply nosing around before breakfast.

I remember my first time in Africa, waking up at a bushcamp in Kafue National Park in Zambia at about six in the morning. The campfire was alight, but breakfast wasn't ready, so I just wandered to the edge of the camp and peered out at the vast expanse, wondering. A great distance away, possibly half a mile or more, two shapes (and they *were* little more than shapes) swaggered slowly across the plain: lions, my first wild ones. It was one of those moments in my life that I will always remember. That's travel.

3. Great ideas will be rejected

LIONEL SHRIVER'S EXTRAORDINARY NOVEL *We Need to Talk About Kevin* was rejected by both her agent and thirty publishers.

Shriver spent eight months trying to find another agent, before sending her manuscript (presumably in some desperation) to an editor at a small English publishing house called Serpent's Tail. The editor read it over the weekend and gave her an offer on Monday morning.

Of course, there are dozens of famous stories of novels that were rejected again and again that went on to become massively successful bestsellers (J.K. Rowling's *Harry Potter* books spring to mind). Such examples are not only found in the publishing world. The Beatles were, even more notoriously, rejected by Decca after one of their executives concluded that 'guitar bands were on their way out'.

The point is that people get decisions wrong and they can't always see when there's a great idea in front of them. That's why you not only have to have thick skin and self-belief (that's easy to say, of course), but more importantly, why you must send your idea to another editor if it's rejected by the first. And then another. And another. And another. Occasionally – and I do mean occasionally – you may even find that someone will give you a bit of feedback that helps you to fine-tune your pitch. But what you don't want to do – however good your idea – is to start calling up editors and haranguing them for not giving you the commission. That's the surest way to find yourself unofficially 'blackballed'. Accept their decision with good grace; if possible, ask them why; and then move onto to the next editor on your list.

4. You don't *have* to take lots of notes

FOR MY FIRST EVER press trip for *BBC Wildlife*, I was fortunate to go to Tasmania. There were two other journalists, and the woman from the PR company that organized it. Young(-ish) and keen as I was, I fastidiously scribbled endless notes about what I was seeing and hearing (I probably didn't realize that I ought to be recording smells as well), and I returned with a copiously filled notebook. I didn't see the chap from the *Observer*, Euan Ferguson, even lift a biro or pencil once during those two weeks but, when we got home, he published a beautifully written piece of some 2,000 words that was streets ahead of anything I managed. Somehow, he'd been able to pick out the details that mattered and filter out those that didn't and produce an article of pure unadulterated elation. Here's how it began:

> You get a lot of thinking done on a three-hour walk along a beach, especially if it happens to be empty and absurdly beautiful and soft as talcum and every cloud in the sky is off annoying the idiots who choose to live up in mainland Australia. Random thoughts: some big, some small.
>
> Thoughts such as: isn't this wonderful. Or: I wonder if this wave's going to reach my shorts. Or: maybe this one, then. Or: whee, yes! Or: I wonder if countries get the beaches they deserve (answer: probably. Think Austria, or Rwanda). And: how many oysters I can eat tonight – 30? 40? And: if only the buggers could see me now, the grim work buggers, who would seethe at my happiness. And: Tasmania is the most perfect country on God's earth. And, finally, the big one: why don't I just move here? It's been a week of unalloyed joy – why not keep it going?

What I love about this opening is that it perfectly captures the mood of everyone who was there. Indeed, reading the piece at the time, it felt like he'd reflected feelings in me that I had scarcely recognized myself. And while he might have made a note of the softness of the sand on the beach and the fact that there wasn't a cloud in the sky later that evening, my best guess is that he didn't. Euan simply managed to pinpoint both poignantly and humorously what it was he felt about Tasmania. The reader is transported there, because anyone can imagine watching the waves and wondering how far up your body they are going to reach and we've all thought about moving to a place while on holiday there.

I'm not saying don't take notes – indeed, take as many as you feel are necessary, but remember that the more you do clutter up your notebook, the harder it could be to access the details that really count. There's no doubt that much of the writing that I am most proud of has come, not from taking something out of a notebook, but from what was inside my head.

5. Being a writer opens doors

WHILE TRAVELLING IN SOUTH America in 1993, I became intrigued – perhaps obsessed – by a search for the continent's endemic ursid, the Andean or spectacled bear, a rare and elusive beast (or so I was told). In the ancient Inca city of Cuzco, I was given the name of a lecturer at the university, a young Peruvian called Tino Aucca. I gave Tino a ring, and in faltering Spanish, explained that I was a journalist from Britain and I wanted to go looking for bears – well, who wouldn't? Tino's response was instant. 'Vamos,' he said. 'Let's go.'

And so we did (though it would take about six weeks to organize the two-week-long expedition). It was a memorable trip into a little-known, untravelled part of the Peruvian highlands, and it formed the heart of the first big travel piece I ever wrote. It didn't make me a fortune, but it did make me realize that this was how I wanted to earn a living.

Of course, Tino was a lovely man, and he might have taken me on a bear hunt even if I'd said I was an actuary or a toilet cleaner, but it does seem to me that saying you're a journalist or a writer often persuades people to drop whatever they're doing and help you out. (I've certainly never been pelted with rotten eggs, despite the popular idea that journalists are benthic bottom-feeders who share the professional seabed with estate agents.)

So, exploit your status, even if you've only ever had a short weekend break in Cheltenham published in the *Biddington Bugle*.

6. Think small, think local

WHILE YOU MAY HAVE grand plans to retrace Shackleton's momentous journey across South Georgia or to swim the entire length of the Amazon – the wrong way round – from mouth to source, most people will need to start their travel-writing career with more modest aims. And one key thing to remember is that you don't have to travel to the remotest corner of Kyrgyzstan to get something published.

As I have previously mentioned, one of the things I notice most as travel editor of *BBC Wildlife* is that, while I get pitched ideas for stories about tiger-watching in India or the wildebeest migration in the Masai Mara all – or at least a lot – of the time, I rarely, if ever, receive any good ideas about places in our backyard. What's wrong with France, for example, or other countries in Europe? Or even, frankly, travel ideas about Britain?

It is a great shame, because I think that there is a great demand for travel pieces set closer to home, especially at a time when money is tight and fewer people can afford the thousands of pounds required for organized wildlife trips like African safaris. So, do some research, find a great wildlife phenomenon that nobody else has ever heard of – or another travel story that is equally underexposed – and then pitch like hell (without forgetting to take account of golden rule 3 – great ideas will be rejected).

7. You're never too old (but you can be too young)

EVERY YEAR, THE *BBC Wildlife* travel-writing competition tries to unearth a great new talent, and every year it does throw up some amazing writers. Some have gone on to become highly successful – Mike Unwin, for example, won the competition in 2000, and is now regularly published in national newspapers and travel magazines.

In 2013, the winning entry was especially memorable – a beautifully written and perfectly conceived and structured piece about a schoolteacher who takes his class to a music festival in Newfoundland, and – for one day only – to watch humpback whales feeding on the so-called capelin run. Though I hadn't thought about the winner's age, I was mildly surprised to discover, when I rang him, that he was retired. But I shouldn't have been: rereading the entry, it had a richness, both in the way it was structured and in the language he used, that I think a younger person would have been unable to match.

While it is unfair to make generalizations, a lot of the entries from younger people do possess a slight callowness – a lack of a broader cultural understanding, perhaps, I'm not quite sure – that can make them unsatisfying. (That may say something about me, of course.) There's no doubt, too, that I am a better writer now than I was in my twenties or indeed my thirties, and

my accumulation of experience, perspective and indeed knowledge have all helped to add depth to my writing.

8. Short words and simple sentences work just fine

I NOTICE SOMETIMES THAT when somebody is clearly trying very
hard with their writing, the sentences start to elongate and multi-
syllable fancy words such as 'excoriating' and 'pantechnicon'
start appearing, like a runner straining to win a race lengthening
their stride, often counter-productively, in their efforts. They
layer every sentence with more and more meaning – adjectives,
adverbs and sub-clauses are peppered around like pellets out of
a shotgun.

One very popular newspaper columnist, whose main job is
as the chief sports correspondent of *The Times,* is Simon Barnes.
He also does nature-writing and wildlife-travel features for the
paper, and has written a series of popular and well-received
books that are mostly about his relationship with nature. Simon
does the opposite of what I have described above: when he's
really trying, his sentences shorten to staccato, and his writing
takes on an almost childlike quality. When he's written for *BBC
Wildlife* in the past, his pieces have provoked a lot of reaction,
which I always think is a good sign. Here's a couple of examples
of his writing from his book, *A Bad Birdwatcher's Companion . . .
or a personal introduction to Britain's 50 most obvious birds.* Writing
about greenfinches, he says:

> They are handsome birds – plump-looking and chunky,
> with a large beak and a noticeably forked tail. The drawback
> is that they don't look terribly green. Only when you catch
> them in strong sunlight do you say, 'Ah yes, they really are
> rather green, those finches.'

And here's what he's got to say about sparrowhawks:

> Sorry, but you're on your own here. The sparrowhawk is the
> bird that no one can show you. There! What? Sparrowhawk!
> Where is it? Gone. If you see a bird appear and disappear in

an instant: well, it might have been a sparrowhawk.

You get the picture. His travel writing, for the most part, is slightly more sophisticated than this, but not greatly so, and personally I think the sheer brevity and wit of 'There! What? Sparrowhawk. Where is it? Gone' is hard to beat, portraying as it does an exchange between two people (and the elusive nature of sparrowhawks) in just seven words.

So, try not to panic if you feel your writing isn't quite hitting the mark, and definitely don't resort to longer words or more complex sentences in a mistaken attempt to add sophistication to your writing.

9. Travel doesn't necessarily broaden the mind

WHEN I WAS DOWN our local pub a few months ago with some friends to do the weekly quiz, I was delighted to see that the hand-out sheet asked us to name the capital cities of twenty mostly obscure countries around the world. I've travelled a lot, I know my capital cities, I knew I'd be good at it. Actually, it's not even quite that. It's more that I've spent a lot of time looking at maps and thinking about where I'd like to go, so I know my capital cities. Madagascar – Antananarivo; Honduras – Tegucigalpa; Kyrgyzstan – Bishkek: bring it on! (And I haven't been to any of these countries.) But the sad truth is that such knowledge, while earning me a few brownie points for my contribution to our victory that night, is essentially pointless. Anyone can look up such information on their smartphone these days if they need to (except when they're at the pub quiz).

But has travel broadened my mind? Has it made me a better, more rounded person who has a greater understanding of different cultures and people? Possibly, but I'm not convinced. There are all sorts of ways in which I could have stretched my world view, and probably a far simpler and more carbon-friendly way would have been to go and volunteer at my local homeless shelter. A friend of mine became addicted to crack in the mid-1990s, and I used to hear stories of his trips to crack dens in Streatham. I remember thinking at the time that he was seeing the world just as surely as I had in Ecuador or Peru (not that I'm advocating crack addiction for broadening your horizons!). All I'm saying is: don't ever think that, in order to become a fully rounded person or to understand global issues properly, you have to travel. In many ways, travel writing has to be one of the most self-indulgent careers on the planet.

10. Go the extra mile

I HIT ON THIS idea as a kind of personal philosophy – which, let's face it, can apply to anything, not just travel writing – when working in Bolivia on a study project of Andean bears. Andean bears are shy animals, and we rarely came close to them, but if you got around the rugged (oh, yes, it really was rugged) landscape of the Apolobamba Mountains enough, then you'd chance upon some of their scats eventually, and those were just as important to the woman running the project.

After four months or so of working on the project, I liked to think that I had a 'nose' for finding the scats, a sixth sense that told me, 'There's some over there, just past the crest of that hill'. However tired I was, I'd always go that extra little bit further, just to make sure – normally, of course, I was wrong and there was nothing, but I was right a sufficient number of times to make me think, first, that I did indeed have a personal bear-poop detection system, and secondly, that 'Going the extra mile' was worth it.

In reality, this is just another way of saying any number of clichés that we are all familiar with, such as 'Writing is ninety per cent perspiration and ten per cent inspiration' or 'You make your own luck' or, indeed, in the words of the golfer Gary Player, 'The harder I practise, the luckier I get'. But for a travel writer, I believe that 'Going the extra mile' has a particular resonance, because just over that hill or down that street is something that may give you some really great material for your piece. Talk properly to the person in reception every morning, and you never know what insights you might get; stay up round the campfire with your safari guide, and you might get a really funny quote. It can even apply to polishing your prose: 'go the extra mile' there, and it can make all the difference.

Q&A WITH HILARY BRADT

HILARY BRADT FOUNDED BRADT Travel Guides with her former husband George Bradt in 1973 and ran the company for four decades before stepping down from full-time involvement (she is still on the board and involved in publishing decisions). She still travels and writes, and has recently published two books – both for Bradt – on long-distance horse rides she took through the west of Ireland.

How did you start travelling?
I was working as an occupational therapist in the early 1970s, but I was travelling more and more and taking bigger gaps in between jobs. I had an awful CV and I was painfully honest when people asked why I'd left my last job – I wanted to travel, I'd always say. I used to work for a year and then save up enough money to travel for some time. In those days, I was always able to find a job when I got back, so it wasn't a problem.

And when did you start writing?
In the 1970s, people did a lot of self-publishing. There was no pressure to produce beautiful books like there is today – anything would do. My husband at the time [George Bradt] was American, and he was a much more entrepreneurial character, certainly than people I knew in Britain. Anyway, we decided to publish a walking guide to Peru and Bolivia – we had no business plan, no business idea and no business sense. We just went with what we knew. It was handwritten and then sent to George's mother to re-type, who got rid of a lot of the mistakes.

How did you sell it and did you make any money?
We had 2,000 copies printed and sold each one for $1.95. We made a profit of something like $2,000 and we

thought that was fantastic. We sold it both locally and by mail order, mostly in South Africa (where we were living at the time) and America. After we got back to England, we peddled it there, too. But the fact that we were thrilled to make $2,000 tells you everything. Lonely Planet started at around the same time, and they made a very sensible decision to publish an overland guide for travellers to Asia [which was far more commercial].

So, what changed? How did you start to make money?
In 1977, George hitchhiked to Frankfurt for the book fair, and he met a guy there who told him how he sold enough books to fund all his travelling – that was what we were going to do, George said. In any case, we lived off very little, never had a house and sponged off other people, so we didn't need much money.

What were your other early books, then?
After that first book, which was called *Backpacking in Peru and Bolivia*, we did backpacking guides for Colombia, Ecuador and Venezuela, then Chile and Argentina, then Central America, North America and Canada and finally Africa. We were constantly travelling and were writing the books by hand on the road. We did the maps, too, and I did the illustrations, and wherever we were at the time, we'd find a local printer.

What particular trips do you remember from that time?
In 1978, we crossed the Darién Gap, which was truly adventurous. I was mugged in Panama City and my notebook was in my bag. But luckily, with the sort of guidebooks we were writing, most of it was in my head anyway. There was not that much hard information, though I do remember going, 'Ugh! There goes the note-book.' We rarely got ill either – we both had hepatitis once, but that was it.

Did you think you could make a living from it?

I suppose so – it was never going to be easy until we published more books, and gradually we realized that we could not do it all ourselves, so we started commissioning people. I also remember one time in San Salvador when we were buying maps for hiking. George came out carrying 100 maps, and I remember being furious. But he said we'd sell them when we got home and he was right. After that, we used to buy hundreds of topographical maps and sell them back home for a huge mark-up, and that underpinned our publishing business.

But you didn't just run the business, did you?

No, George and I started tour leading in the late 1970s and, though we split up soon after this, I carried on. By this time, I was writing two or three books a year and tour leading, mostly in Peru. This was perfect, because it got me back to the places I was writing about. For me, at this stage, tour leading was an integral part of being a writer and publisher. And, by this stage, even before email, lots of people wrote to me with information about places for the guidebooks that I could use. That really helped.

How did you progress the business?

Even after George and I broke up, I was determined to make a success of it because I love a challenge. All through the 1980s, I had one employee (and she still works for us) and then, in the 1990s, I employed Tricia Hayne, my first proper editor. I think around this time it became a proper business, up until then it hadn't been run very professionally. I even got a sales manager.

How has the business changed?

With Amazon and huge discounts in the USA, it's much harder to make money than it was before. If we can't sell 5,000 copies of a guidebook in a couple of years, it won't be profitable. The exception is something really exclusive, like a guide to the Congo or Angola – you can sell these books for a higher price, so that offsets the fact that they won't sell in huge quantities.

So, what's the secret, do you think?
You have to take risks. For example, we commissioned a book on Iraq in the late 1990s [after the first Gulf War, but before the US invasion in 2003]. I was very taken by the woman who proposed it, because she was very anti-sanctions and wanted to see them lifted. I really wanted to do the book because it was a cause I believed in and, between us, we found an author who could write it. The manuscript was delivered in July 2001, and it was all ready to go when 9/11 happened.

Oh no! What happened next?
Well, Frankfurt Book Fair was coming up in October, and we'd already had the posters printed. We'd always thought it was a book that would do well internationally, but we assumed that we couldn't now publish it. But when we were at the book fair, international distributors came by, one by one, saw the posters and said 'We could sell a few of those'. And as it turned out, we sold the first 3,000 copies to the Pentagon, and it was our biggest seller that year. It was hugely ironic – it did well because of something that happened that I disagreed with and marched against.

No one could have predicted that a book on Iraq would sell so well.
No, and that's the thing about business plans and predicting the future – you don't know what's going to sell, so if there's something you believe in, you should just go on and do it. A lot of book-buying is impulse-buying anyway. There was a chap who bought a Bradt guide every year to read conspicuously on the beach in Spain or wherever he was going on holiday that year – he

bought the one to North Korea, for example, just to find out more about the country. He'd ring Debbie once a year and ask what we had just published, and she'd talk him through what we had. A lot of people who have no intention of going to the countries read our books.

How is the internet changing things for you?
You have to remember that the internet is not edited. It has a lot of misinformation and a lot of bad writing. Yes, we are looking at ebooks and other products, but I think with our sort of books, you need them in print: you are not going to hold a hand-held device in the middle of a street in Angola because you will be surrounded by hundreds of kids and it might be stolen. We don't do city guides anyway, which are more suited to that sort of thing.

Looking back, would you have done anything differently?
No, I don't think so. Before publishing that first book, I remember approaching a publisher and asking him if he would publish our book. He said that there was no market for it, which was true, but we went ahead and just did it ourselves – and now we are doing a lot better than our competitors. If we had had a business plan, we would have done mainstream country guides and we would have been swallowed up by now. But because we do niche guides, the business is still out there and nobody has bought us.

10. ESSENTIAL KIT: USEFUL TRAVEL-WRITING ORGANIZATIONS AND WEBSITES

WRITERS' RESOURCES

British Guild of Travel Writers
www.bgtw.org; secretariat@bgtw.org; 020 8144 8713

Membership is open to travel writers, photographers, editors or broadcasters working in any medium. An applicant must have published at least twelve full-length travel articles a year for the past three years or written a guidebook or another travel-related book. Benefits of membership include monthly meetings in London where you can meet other guild members and other people within the travel industry. Your name, contact details and areas of travel writing that you specialize in will also be listed in the annual BGTW handbook, which is sent free to all travel editors in the UK.

International Travel Writers Alliance
www.internationaltravelwritersalliance.com; contact director general Ashley Gibbins, Ashley@ITWAlliance.com; 0776 419 8286

Provides a press card and opportunities for press trips.

Matador Network
http://matadornetwork.com

Describing itself as 'The largest independent travel publisher online, now reaching over 2 million unique monthly visitors', Matador is a US-based media company specializing in travel writing and journalism. The website is literally crammed with features offering travel-writing advice, from a piece helping 'writers transcend the way they normally see a place' to 'Does your writing suck: Plight writing and travel "porn"' (this is an American site). Well worth a visit, but don't take it too seriously. Matador does pay for articles, but a risible amount: normally $20–25 for full-length features.

Outdoor Writers & Photographers Guild
www.owpg.org.uk; contact membership secretary Dennis Kelsall, memsec@owpg.org.uk; 01257 793062

Members of this group must be 'actively and professionally involved in outdoor activities in any outdoor setting'. Provides opportunities for networking and mutual support. Members offer advice on issues such as tax, copyright law or rights of way free of charge.

Press4travel
www.press4travel.com; info@press4travel.com; 0845 6038310

An online service that attempts to bring those who work in the travel industry together with those who write or broadcast about it. As a travel writer, this could be a potential source of free trips or accommodation, or at least put you in touch with some of the people you'll need to know.

ResponseSource
www.responsesource.com; 020 8681 7733

ResponseSource is an online service that puts journalists in touch with the people who handle the PR for a wide range of products, including hotels and other parts of the tourist industry. Got a story commission, perhaps, but need some free accommodation? Try ResponseSource.

Tourism Concern

www.tourismconcern.org.uk; info@tourismconcern.org.uk; 020 7666 3095

Tourism Concern campaigns for 'better tourism' – essentially, tourism that doesn't exploit or degrade local people and that doesn't trash the environment.

Travel Culture Magazine

www.travelculturemag.com; info@travelculturemag.com

Travel Culture Magazine is an online resource that describes itself 'as a medium to share knowledge and educate the globe on responsible travel'. It seeks contributions from writers on eco-tourism, sustainable tourism and responsible travel, as well as personal stories about actual travel experiences, but does not pay for contributions – all it offers is to run a 100-word biography of the writer, a photo and a link to the person's Twitter account.

Travelwriters UK

www.travelwriters.co.uk

Including authors, journalists, photographers, broadcasters and editors, Travelwriters UK describes itself as 'a professional travel journalists' association'. It can host a personal webpage, or you can search for travel writers with particular specialisms. There are only 100 members, so it's not huge and the website is limited.

Writers & Artists

www.writersandartists.co.uk; writersandartists@bloomsbury.com; 020 7631 5985

Every year, Bloomsubury publishes the *Writers' & Artists' Yearbook*, which contains a massive 4,500 media contacts in its directory, as well as articles giving advice about how to get published and other useful information. Writers & Artists also runs a special mentoring service for people who want advice on their book idea or their first draft or who want a line-by-line edit of the finished product.

TRAVEL-WRITING COURSES AND TUITION

Bath Spa University

www.bathspa.ac.uk; admissions@bathspa.ac.uk; 01225 875875

The university has recently started an MA in 'Travel and Nature Writing' under the aegis of its School of Humanities and Cultural Industries. The course director is Dr Paul Evans, who writes regularly for *The Guardian*'s Country Diary section. Tuition fees, for a one-year course, are £6,330 (in 2013) – that's a lot, when you consider that nature writers are much less in demand and even more poorly paid than travel writers.

Travellers' Tales

www.travellerstales.org; info@travellerstales.org

Set up in 2004 by travel writer Jonathan Lorie (interviewed at the end of Chapter 5), Travellers' Tales runs a whole host of travel-writing and photography courses ranging from one day in length to week-long residential programmes abroad.

Travel Writing Workshop

www.travelwritingworkshop.co.uk; travelwshop@gmail.com

Freelance travel writer Peter Carty offers a choice of a one-day workshop or four evening classes, always in Central London. He's been running his classes since 1999, and has travel features published regularly in national newspapers and magazines such as *Condé Nast Traveller*.

TRAVEL MAGAZINES

Condé Nast Traveller

www.cntraveller.com; cntraveller@condenast.co.uk; 020 7499 9080

A travel magazine that only does luxury, daahling. When I contacted the magazine to find out whether it ever commissioned inexperienced, unpublished or unfamiliar travel writers, I was told, essentially, no. *Condé Nast Traveller* also won't accept copy resulting from a group press trip. It receives about fifty unsolicited articles a week and publishes 'perhaps two or three a year'. So, don't hold your breath.

Lonely Planet Traveller
www.lonelyplanet.com/magazine; 020 7150 5000

Launched by BBC Worldwide when it owned Lonely Planet, *Lonely Planet Traveller* steers a line between the luxury travel of *Condé Nast Traveller* and the more down-to-earth nomadism of *Wanderlust*.

National Geographic Traveller
http://natgeotraveller.co.uk; editorial@natgeotraveller.co.uk; 020 7253 9906

The UK-published magazine is *Traveller*, the US version *Traveler*, so try not to get them confused. *Traveller* is published under licence by Absolute Publishing in London. There are only eight issues a year, so opportunities for new writers are limited. It mostly deals with adventurous and outdoorsy travel. The magazine requests that all pitches and ideas are sent in by email. Writers' guidelines can be found at: http://natgeotraveller.co.uk/about_us/

The *Sunday Times Travel Magazine*
http://thesundaytimestravel.subscribeonline.co.uk; travelmag@sundaytimes.co.uk; 020 7782 7200

Now, of course, this is hidden behind a paywall, so you either have to buy the magazine, flick through a copy while waiting for your train or cough up to get behind that paywall. Like *Condé Nast Traveller*, it mostly deals in luxury travel.

Wanderlust
www.wanderlust.co.uk; info@wanderlust.co.uk; 01753 620426

Describing itself as 'The leading magazine for adventurous and authentic travel', *Wanderlust* was launched by publisher and editor-in-chief Lyn Hughes and the late Paul Morrison in 1993 after they planned it out on the back of a sick bag on a flight to Ecuador. It doesn't do luxury resorts, activity holidays, wacky races across continents, family travel or articles on destinations blacklisted by the Foreign Office. Writers' guidelines can be found at: www.wanderlust.co.uk/aboutus/writers.

Wild Travel
www.wildlifeextra.com/go/world/wild-travel/#cr; editorial@wildtravelmag.com; 01242 211080

The only magazine in the UK solely dedicated to wildlife travel and tourism, *Wild Travel* offers reasonable opportunities for freelance writers. Its rates – £500 for both the text and any photos you can supply – aren't great, but it runs well-written features by some of the best wildlife travel writers in the business.

TRAVEL-GUIDEBOOK PUBLISHERS

AA Publishing
http://shop.theaa.com/content/aa-publishing; 01256 491524

Claiming to be the UK's biggest travel publisher (and the tenth-biggest worldwide), AA Publishing produces guidebooks to many destinations around the world, as well as walking and cycling guidebooks.

Bradt Travel Guides
www.bradtguides.com; info@bradtguides.com; 01753 893444

Set up by tour guide and travel writer Hilary Bradt (interviewed at the end of Chapter 9), Bradt Travel Guides is renowned for publishing guidebooks about the places no one else bothers with – Iraq, Haiti and North Korea are three notable examples. It has also recently started a strand of UK guidebooks called 'Slow Guides' (Slow Cotswolds, Slow Devon and so on), and the company welcomes new book ideas.

Cadogan Guides
www.newhollandpublishers.co.uk/cadogan-guides.asp; enquiries@nhpub.co.uk; 020 7953 7665

Popular with American travellers, apparently. According to IndependentTraveller.com, 'All Cadogan authors are natives of, or have lived in, the countries they write about'.

Crimson Publishing
www.crimsonpublishing.co.uk; info@crimsonpublishing.co.uk; 020 3627 1865

Crimson publishes *Pathfinder* walking guides and a number of travel guides, including one series called *Live & Work in* and another called *The Best of Britain*. The company says that it welcomes 'speculative' applications – you should send a CV and covering letter to: applications@crimsonpublishing.co.uk

Eyewitness Guides
www.dk.co.uk; 020 7010 3000

Published by Dorling Kindersley. Opportunities for writing are unclear, but it certainly employs a vast team of editors in its London office.

Fodor's Travel Guides
www.fodors.com; editors@fodors.com; 001 212 782 9000

Its city guides tend to be the most popular. 'Whenever possible, Fodor's hires writers who are local experts living in the destination they're writing about instead of "parachuting" writers into a country or region for a short time', it says on its website. Writers are paid a one-off fee, and sign a contract stating that their work is original – any writers found to have plagiarized content are dismissed.

Footprint Travel Guides
www.footprinttravelguides.com; contactus@footprintbooks.com; 01225 469141

Its *South American Handbook*, first published in 1924, is claimed to be the longest-running travel guidebook in the English language. Aimed at independent travellers with a yen for getting off the beaten track, the guidebooks now cover the globe. Footprint says that it has about fifty authors, and dozens of contributors, on its books, but there's no indication that it is looking for more.

Frommer's
www.frommers.com; 001 212 332 3332

Job opportunities exist at its parent company, John Wiley, in New Jersey. Frommer's tends to choose writers who live in the region they are writing about or who have a 'long-term familiarity with a city or region'. If you want to write for Frommer's, you have to say why you consider yourself an expert on a location.

Insight Guides
www.insightguides.com; 020 7403 0284

Insight Guides (and Berlitz travel guidebooks) are published by Apa Publications. Together, the two imprints publish 400 guidebooks covering 200 destinations. The company says that it is always looking to recruit new writers, especially those that live, or frequently travel to, a destination. 'One of our key selling points is that we use authors who know the place intimately rather than people who fly in and out', it says.

Let's Go
www.letsgo.com; recruiting@letsgo.com; 001 617 495 9649

Claiming to be the leader in student travel, Let's Go says that all its guides are written 'for students by students'. Based in Cambridge, Massachussets, USA.

Lonely Planet
www.lonelyplanet.com; 020 8433 1333 (in London), 001 510 250 6400 (in the USA)

With offices in the UK, Australia, the USA and India, Lonely Planet has grown from being a few people photocopying and stapling guides on overlanding across Asia to a truly multi-national organization. Opportunities to write for Lonely Planet are few (in 2012, according to its website, it recruited eight writers from 500 applicants).

Rough Guides
www.roughguides.com; editor@roughguides.com; 020 7010 3000

Rough Guides is always on the look-out for new writers, particularly 'curious travellers capable of digging out the most arcane information', it says on its website. 'An obsessive eye for detail is also a great bonus.' It also welcomes new book proposals. Email: write@roughguides.com.

TRAVEL-WRITING COMPETITIONS

I can't guarantee that any of these competitions will take place from year to year, but I have picked the ones that appear to have a decent longevity.

Bradt *Independent on Sunday* Travel-Writing Competition
www.bradtguides.com/travelwriting

An annual award that includes the prize of a paid-for holiday and a commission from *The Independent on Sunday*. It's open to both published and unpublished writers. Unpublished writers also win a two-day course with Travellers' Tales.

Guardian Travel-Writing Competition
www.guardian.co.uk/travel/travelwritingcompetition

The 2012 *Guardian* competition had seven separate categories, ranging from one in which you had to write about a place or campsite you stayed in to another where you were asked to describe a holiday that went disastrously wrong.

National Geographic Traveller Magazine
http://natgeotraveller.co.uk/competitions/80513

National Geographic Traveller ran a competition in 2013, asking for just 300 words on 'your most inspirational travel experience'. The prize was a trip to Svalbard.

The Telegraph's Just Back Competition
www.telegraph.co.uk/travel/travel-writing-competition

The *Telegraph* runs a travel-writing competition called 'Just back', which is run on a weekly basis with a prize of £200.

inTravel Magazine
www.intravelmag.com/in-print/travel-writer-contest

Small prizes can be won from *inTravel* magazine's regular travel-writing contest.

The British Guild of Travel Writers (BGTW) Travel-Writing Competition
http://www.bgtw.org/awards/10.html

The BGTW ran a competition for unpublished writers in 2012 (the results were published in 2013). First prize was a travel-writing holiday offered by Travellers' Tales.

Writers' Worldwide Prize
www.writersworldwideprize.com

This is a new competition which only started up in 2012. It asked writers to 'tell us about your journey' in up to 5,000 words. The prize was £1,000, with an entry fee of £5.

TNT Blogging competition
www.tntmagazine.com

TNT magazine runs an annual travel-blogging competition. Prizes have included a six-week visit to South Africa and a trip to Oktoberfest in Munich.

Great Hotels Travel Writing
http://www.ghotw.com/travelCompetition/

Great Hotels runs a competition where the winner is picked by the readers. The last prize offered was a five-night trip to a hotel in Istanbul.

World Nomads Travel-Writing Scholarship
http://journals.worldnomads.com/scholarships/story/97633/China/Travel-Writing-Scholarship-2013-Beijing-China

World Nomads has been running a travel-writing scholarship since 2009. The prize in 2013 included a writing assignment in China with Rough Guides.

INDEX